New Immigrants, New Land

NEW WORLD DIASPORAS

UNIVERSITY PRESS OF FLORIDA

Florida A&M University, Tallahassee
Florida Atlantic University, Boca Raton
Florida Gulf Coast University, Ft. Myers
Florida International University, Miami
Florida State University, Tallahassee
New College of Florida, Sarasota
University of Central Florida, Orlando
University of Florida, Gainesville
University of North Florida, Jacksonville
University of South Florida, Tampa
University of West Florida, Pensacola

New Immigrants, New Land

A Study of Brazilians in Massachusetts

ANA CRISTINA BRAGA MARTES

Translated by Beth Ransdell Vinkler

Foreword by Maxine L. Margolis

University Press of Florida
Gainesville/Tallahassee/Tampa/Boca Raton
Pensacola/Orlando/Miami/Jacksonville/Ft. Myers/Sarasota

All photographs taken by Ronaldo Porto Macedo Jr.
Printed in the United States of America. This book is printed on Glatfelter Natures Book, a paper certified under the standards of the Forestry Stewardship Council (FSC). It is a recycled stock that contains 30 percent post-consumer waste and is acid-free.

16 15 14 13 12 11 6 5 4 3 2 1

LIBRARY OF CONGRESS CATALOGING-IN-PUBLICATION DATA
Martes, Ana Cristina Braga.
[Brasileiros nos Estados Unidos. English]
New immigrants, new land : a study of Brazilians in Massachusetts / Ana Cristina Braga Martes ; translated by Beth Ransdell Vinkler ; foreword by Maxine L. Margolis.
p. cm.—(New World diasporas)
Updated ed. of: Brasileiros nos Estados Unidos. São Paulo, SP : Paz e Terra, 2000.
Includes bibliographical references and index.
ISBN 978-0-8130-3528-4 (acid-free paper)
1. Brazilian Americans—Massachusetts. 2. Immigrants—Massachusetts. 3. Massachusetts—Emigration and immigration. 4. Brazil—Emigration and immigration. 5. Brazilian Americans—Massachusetts—Social conditions. 6. Brazilian Americans—Massachusetts—Economic conditions. I. Vinkler, Beth Ransdell. II. Title.
F75.B68M37 2010
304.809744—dc22
2010024270

The University Press of Florida is the scholarly publishing agency for the State University System of Florida, comprising Florida A&M University, Florida Atlantic University, Florida Gulf Coast University, Florida International University, Florida State University, New College of Florida, University of Central Florida, University of Florida, University of North Florida, University of South Florida, and University of West Florida.

University Press of Florida
15 Northwest 15th Street
Gainesville, FL 32611-2079
http://www.upf.com

This book is dedicated to Ronaldo Porto Macedo Jr.
and Francisco Martes Porto Macedo with love.

Contents

Tables

Foreword

More than a decade has passed since the news that "one million Brazilians are living abroad" made headlines in Brazil. In *New Immigrants, New Land* Ana Cristina Braga Martes, Professor of Sociology at the Getúlio Vargas Foundation in São Paulo, provides us with an engaging picture and incisive analysis of one group of those emigrants: Brazilians living in Massachusetts, primarily the city of Boston and its surrounding communities.

What is most welcome about this work is that it is based on more than a decade of field research, making it a rare longitudinal study of an immigrant community in the United States. Such a study allows Martes to chart trends that might not be apparent in a shorter time frame. For example, when she began her research a majority of Brazilian immigrants hailed from the state of Minas Gerais, while a decade later the immigrants she encountered in Massachusetts came from nearly all parts of Brazil; emigration became a truly national phenomenon. Because the research was carried out over a number of years she was able to chart changes in the diversity of immigrants in terms of background, motivations for emigration, and ethnic identity.

Using the framework of the new economic sociology, Martes sets the stage for analyzing this new immigrant stream, seeking to reconstruct the reasoning that motivates emigrants' decisions to cross international borders. She finds the discourse that legitimizes emigration—for those who emigrate as well as for their families, friends, and compatriots—is one that views emigration, especially for the young, as a low-risk personal investment opportunity, a "What have I got to lose?" option.

Immigrants have explicit goals for coming to the United States. Economics motivates the majority. An overarching factor that prompts many immigrants to seek their fortunes abroad is the loss of social mobility in Brazil, particularly for the middle class. They come to the United States to get higher-paying jobs or to save money for specific purposes; they are what social scientists call "target earners."

Emigration is not only an economic process, but a social process as well. Variables such as foreign investment, familiarity with American lifestyles through globalization of the mass media, and, most importantly, personal social networks all come into play when analyzing specific population movements. Social networks in both the country of origin and the country of destination help reduce the economic and psychological costs of international migration. Moreover, since the expenses of emigration are generally within reach, Brazilian immigrants have a chance to experience a foreign country, and if things do not work out, they can always return home.

Despite the importance of social networks to the immigrant experience, Martes faults social scientists who take solidarity among immigrants of the same national group as a given and not as an object of research. Simply stated, solidarity should not be taken for granted; rather, the internal dynamics and forms of solidarity, in this case among Brazilians, should be considered objects of investigation and not automatic attributes of ethnicity.

One striking insight is that while Brazilian immigrants in Boston are almost uniformly employed in low-prestige jobs such as housecleaning and some are undocumented, many nevertheless see their experiences in a positive light. The benefits granted to immigrants by the state of Massachusetts facilitate their adaptation to life in the United States as well as their favorable opinion of this country. Martes analyzes the ways in which Brazilians experience certain aspects of American society, especially those that involve notions of rights and citizenship. As they evaluate American society, many Brazilians reassess the ways in which the same notions are practiced back home in Brazil.

Yet despite their admiration for some features of American life, Boston's Brazilians express discomfort with the label "immigrant." This uneasiness is related to the larger issue of ethnic identity and their strong desire to distinguish themselves from other immigrant groups, specifically Hispanics.

A major theme running through Martes' study is the role that religion plays in the lives of these immigrants. She does a splendid job of analyzing the divergent appeals of Catholicism and evangelical Protestantism and the central position of churches in immigrant life—not just social life but economic life as well. The discourse of the evangelical churches is particularly comforting to immigrants. By encouraging hard work and lauding prosperity and social mobility, evangelical Protestantism is decidedly attuned to their own aspirations. It is within this religious ambience that Martes locates the social solidarity she finds lacking in the immigrant community at large.

Martes has presented us with an excellent study. Her insightful analysis of issues surrounding emigration from Brazil and the nature of Boston's Brazilian community are accessible to the nonspecialist. This is due in no small part to the clarity of the writing and the avoidance of the academic jargon and postmodern constructions that have come to characterize so much of contemporary scholarly discourse on immigration.

Maxine L. Margolis

Preface

Brazil tends to be identified stereotypically with *carnaval* and soccer, with the sun, beaches, and happiness. In a similar way, Brazilians tend to be characterized as a people of easy sociability, instantaneous smiles, and friendly relationships. In this country, cordiality, a word whose etymology refers to the heart (*cordio*), founded the spirit of the nation and is a part of Brazil's roots, according to Sergio Buarque de Holanda. This is a kind of myth, just like the myth of "racial democracy" to which anthropologist Gilberto Freyre refers. But myths do not arise out of nothing. They are representations that Brazilians make a point of reaffirming; they are a matter of a kind of image that Brazilians choose for themselves.

These representations are the object of constant anxiety and questioning among Brazilians who have left the country. Such representations were not initially identified as a principal focus of this study, but they permeate the whole book due to their far-reaching nature that was found in the process of the field research. This is because they are part of day-to-day discussions and conversations: they are at bar tables, in social encounters, and in the workplace. They are used to explain the multiple aspects that becoming a Brazilian immigrant involves.

This book has as one of its objectives the presentation of an analytical account of the insertion of Brazilians into the new society and the internal social dynamics of the group. It brings an attempt to understand how the representations of Brazil and Brazilian identities are remade, negotiated, or reinforced in specific contexts such as churches, the workplace, or NGOs. However, the book also rejects two ideas: that of treating Brazilians as a homogeneous group or a unique and uniform community, and the idea of victimizing them. If there is a uniform tendency it is that, at least for the first generation, Brazilians want to be recognized above all as a national group, avoiding the U.S. framework of race and ethnicity.

While the stereotypes are easily propagated, day-to-day social relationships as well as internal conflicts and competition remain almost invisible to the eyes of the nonspecialist. One of the purposes of this book is to show the process of insertion being constructed alongside the representations of their own condition: being Brazilian and being an immigrant. This is the particular challenge that I accepted by retracing the course of this migratory process from its beginnings in the 1980s up to today.

Penetrating the universe of Brazilian immigrants—accompanying their departure—means, in reality, delving more deeply into Brazil. If in the beginning of the 1980s that country was going through a long period of social and economic instability, currently, that is, thirty years later, the "B" of the acronym BRIC stands for Brazil (BRIC refers to the combined economies of Brazil, Russia, India, and China, which some speculate will be wealthier than most current major economic powers by 2050). Under these circumstances, the question raised is: Are we looking at the last migratory cycle? I believe that the answer demands caution and the recognition that economic factors alone do not propel this movement.

It is my hope that this point will be duly evident in this book. The inflation that rose to 25 percent per month in Brazil by the end of the 1980s became stable in the mid-1990s, and thus it has remained until today. The exchange rate, which is the first and most important variable considered in making the decision to emigrate, has been stable for almost eight years. The parity between the U.S. dollar and the Brazilian *real* lasted from the mid- to the late 1990s. None of these factors resulted in a decline in Brazilian emigration. Not even the terrible events of September 11, 2001, and the deportation of hundreds of Brazilians that has occurred since then were sufficient to cause Brazilians to stop leaving Brazil. More profound and not merely tangential contradictions help to explain the continuity of these flows. They have to do with the lack of opportunities for the Brazilian middle class, especially the lower middle class, whose members do not have access to higher education and professions with satisfactory incomes and who further do not have access to credit or lack sufficient savings to begin their own businesses. However, those in this same social segment do have access to means of communication and transportation, access to international networks, and especially information about patterns of consumption that they ardently desire to enjoy and that they think are available to them in the United States. From a strictly economic point of view, changes like access to credit and to quality education would be the key variables to reversing this process. The current economic-financial crisis in the United States is, clearly, a factor that undermines return as much as it discourages emigration. Without some certainty of finding better paying work, the vast majority of Brazilians would not emigrate. However, although U.S. economic conditions have been much more favorable, the conditions available in Brazil to the lower middle class can be even worse, and in the decision to emigrate, the cost-benefit relationship always takes both sides into account.

I conclude by emphasizing the invitation to all those who are interested in Brazil and in Brazilians, in migratory and ethnic-racial studies, in Latino studies, and in the approach of economic sociology to read this book. I hope that the pleasure of reading it will be comparable to the pleasure that it gave me to write it.

Acknowledgments

This book is the result of fifteen years of research and could not have been written without the support of a number of people and institutions. My particular thanks go to Judith Tendler for her support, dedication, and affection and to Ruth Cardoso (in memoriam), with whom I had the pleasure of enjoying an intellectually stimulating and at the same time pleasant relationship for more than twenty years.

On all of these paths, I have had the good fortune of the acquaintance of Maxine L. Margolis—the pioneer of the study of Brazilian emigration—who, always solicitous and generous, read various drafts of this study and gave many suggestions. This book project would not have been carried forward without Maxine's support. She has, over the course of these two decades, become a good friend. I thank her as well as Jerald T. Milanich, Curator of Archaeology, Florida Museum of Natural History in Gainesville, Florida, for their dedication to and support for the publication of this book in the United States.

In Boston, I received support, goodwill, and encouragement from the Brazilians who reside there, who invited me into their homes, and who granted me part of their time to answer my questions and to tell me about their lives. In addition to my interviewees, whose names I promised not to reveal, I am especially grateful to Jamila Xible, Ana Vera Wynne, Graciane Silva, Heloísa Souza, Ana Paula Fioravanti, Elza Holtz, Julia Story, Sisters Judith Clement and Maria Alice, Father Roque, Alderi Matos, and Paulo Taveira. I also want to thank Fausto da Rocha of the Brazilian Immigrant Center and Horácio from the Cape Cod Brazilian Immigrant Center (Centro do Imigrante Brasileiro de Cape Cod). More recently, my thanks go to Father Pedro, Sister Elizete, and to all who work as volunteers at the Good Samaritan Center (Centro Bom Samaritano).

I am extremely grateful to all of the professors and researchers from the United States with whom I was able to discuss this work, especially Susan

Eckstein, Bish Sanyal, Diane Davis, Paul Osterman, Marcelo Suárez-Orozco, Yasmin Soysal, and Elizabeth Leeds. My thanks also go to Peter Berger and Brigitta Berger, Peggy Levitt, Clemence Jouet-Pastre, and Jose Mazzotti. My very special and affectionate recognition goes to Marilyn Halter.

I thank my interlocutors on different occasions: Eduardo Rios Neto, José Alberto Magno de Carvalho, Maria Rosário Sales, Mary Castro, Bela Bianco, Flávio Pierucci, Beatriz Carlini Cotrim, Sylvia DeBiaggi, Maria Cecília Mariz, Heloísa Pontes, and Bernard Appy. I could not fail to mention my particular thanks to Sérgio Micelli, Gilberto Velho, Boris Fausto, Neide Patarra, and Roberto Cardoso de Oliveira (in memoriam). I am grateful to Teresa Sales for helping me define the topic of my doctoral thesis that gave rise to this book, for my first contacts in Boston, and for discussing with me the paths taken.

The accomplishment of the field research and the analysis of the material collected were conducted in various phases throughout the years and relied on the help of Mauricio Serafim, Carla Fernandes, Cristina Lopes, Wilson Flanders, Hilary Burger, Aline dos Santos, Bruno Frossard, Danielle Pessoa, Thaisa Ierei, Maria Paula Bertran, Tania Christopoulos, Fernando Oshima, Leonardo Barone, Daniela Mansour, and Daniel Valente. Without them, this work would not have been possible. I appreciate Mauricio's assistance and that of Luciana U. Coentro, and Maria Clara S. Carneiro in making final revisions. I also relied on the participation, support, and work of Rene Decol, Weber Soares, and Dimitri Fazito. In addition to valuing their friendship and role as interlocutors, I relied on their professional assistance during different phases of this study and received from them critical opinions and influence.

I thank Pamela Ex, Sandra Faria, Maria Helena Lima, Giannina Ricci, and Célia Sakurai for their assistance, encouragement, and friendship. Over the past ten years I have had the pleasure of enjoying a debate about the most varied aspects of Brazilian emigration with Gláucia Assis, Adriana Capuano, Gustavo Lins Ribeiro, and especially Soraya Fleischer.

I thank Fernando Henrique Cardoso and the Brazilian Ministry of Foreign Relations, especially the Consular Assistance Corps, and Ambassadors Afonso Massot, Lúcio Amorim, Renato Faria, Afonso Carbonar, Márcia Loureiro, and Maurício Costa, for ensuring the availability of data, information, and interviews.

I am grateful to the Fulbright Commission and the Coordenação de Aperfeiçoamento de Pessoal de Nível Superior (CAPES), for their support during the period in which I completed my doctoral studies at MIT. I owe much to the Getulio Vargas Foundation and to the São Paulo School of Business Administration for support received and especially to the Getulio Vargas Research Foundation (GV-Pesquisa), which financed part of this study, in the persons of Fábio Mariotto and Peter Spink.

I must also acknowledge the effort, competence, and professionalism of John Byram and of Beth Ransdell Vinkler of Benedictine University in Lisle, Illinois, who made this work available in English. I make a point of recording here my satisfaction with and recognition of Beth's work in translating the manuscript.

To my husband, Ronaldo Porto Macedo Jr., and my son, Francisco Martes Porto Macedo, who were with me during this long journey, I give my thanks, and I dedicate this work to them.

Introduction

A young university student residing in Copacabana (Rio de Janeiro) goes to Boston with the objective of learning English and "getting to know another culture." There, she will have to "get a little money" because her family does not have the means to support her. A recently retired widow from Criciúma (in the Brazilian state of Santa Catarina) moves permanently to Marlborough, Massachusetts, to help her daughter, who already has a green card. Because this widow values her independence, she plans to keep working part time and to care for her grandson during the rest of the day. A man leaves a small farm in Mantena (in the Brazilian state of Minas Gerais) and goes to live in East Boston, leaving his wife and his father, a cowhand, waiting for him in Brazil. A young father from the Baixada Fluminense region (in the Brazilian state of Rio de Janeiro) who completed his degree at a small, private college of business administration in the Rio de Janeiro Metropolitan Area and worked as a banker is terrified by the growing unemployment in this sector. Profoundly dissatisfied with his salary and without any prospect of getting a better place in the labor market, he decides to "try another life" by immigrating to Boston, where his brother has been living for eight years.

These four Brazilians may take the same plane to the United States and, once in Boston, find themselves working in the same restaurant washing dishes, serving tables, or preparing food. If it were not for the distance between the towns in which they have now chosen to live, they could even take the same subway line to work each day. However, since becoming immigrants and beginning to interpret what this means, each one would report his or her new circumstances as an immigrant in ways that would certainly reveal differences among them.

Clearly, these four cases are not random or isolated; neither do they exemplify the extremes. They succinctly illustrate characteristics that demarcate the different profiles of the Brazilian population in Massachusetts.

The demographic data gathered in this study are analyzed in Chapter 2 of this book, where I present a general characterization of the migratory movement. Incorporating the diversity that the data reveal is fundamental to the understanding of the different motivations for emigration, the identities established, or the divisions constructed among Brazilian immigrants. After all, are the young woman from Copacabana, the dedicated grandmother from Santa Catarina, the small farmer from Minas Gerais, and the banker from Baixada Fluminense all immigrants in the same way? I do not think so. The social, demographic, and economic variables highlight perceptions and representations, imposing differences in the generic meaning of the term "Brazilian immigrant."

Brazilian immigration to the United States has unique characteristics that are as relevant empirically as they are theoretically. The first of these is the central position that churches occupy not only in social and community life but also in the economic life of Brazilian immigrants. Although Brazil is traditionally a Catholic country, the significant presence of evangelicals among immigrants is notable, as is the evangelicals' ethos that is frankly favorable to the creation of social capital and entrepreneurialism among Brazilian immigrants. The second characteristic has to do with an invariably favorable opinion of the United States and of Americans that differs from the predominant pattern among Latino groups, which tends to be one critical of and reactive to the context that receives them. This positive attitude is directed toward Brazilian immigrants' American employers but does not extend with the same intensity to their own co-nationals or to the Latinos who both collaborate and compete with them—especially for jobs. The third characteristic is related to the rapid growth of ethnic entrepreneurialism, which—at least until the 1990s—was believed to be a strategy for social mobility that was typical of Asians and Europeans but not of immigrants of Latin American origin. The fourth is the practice of job selling (Chapter 4 of this book has a detailed explanation of this practice) among both men and women who do housecleaning. This practice, along with other features of the community dynamic, led me to question the place of solidarity, or the lack thereof, within the group given that solidarity is repeatedly stressed in the literature about ethnic communities. A fifth characteristic has to do with ethnic-racial belonging. Although they are constantly identified as Hispanic or Latino and nonwhite, Brazilians make a point of stating their national origin and of rejecting both of these labels that tend to be assigned to them. Finally, after more than fifteen years of migratory flow, transnational links are being formed, albeit very slowly, with the critical support of Brazilian governmental agencies, which are a kind of third element in the promotion of the connection between the two (or several) poles of the flow.

In this study I intend to use the approach of economic sociology to understand Brazilian emigration, the characteristics of which I presented briefly in the preceding paragraphs.[1] The value of this approach lies particularly in its ability to explain the main features that international migrations have acquired from the second half of the twentieth century on and, at the same time, to challenge traditional theoretical models, especially those based on the premise that migration is a phenomenon of an economic nature and moves from poor countries to rich ones. The presumption of unidirectional flows suggests a series of counter-examples, one of which involves Brazilian immigration to Paraguay. Since the 1970s, 500,000 Brazilians have left the country with the highest gross domestic product (GDP) in Latin America and have made their destination this country with the third-lowest GDP in the region.

Conceiving international migrations as a phenomenon that is not merely economic means revealing the enormous range of motivations that guide the migrants from a young age and that culminate with their departure: the political forces that drag them from one country to another and the social structure that sustains flows of population over the course of years. In the Brazilian case, these dimensions seem to correspond to their most outstanding and visible characteristics: they are lower-middle-class immigrants who are attracted by the dream of consumption and the lifestyle in the United States and who see little possibility of fulfilling their expectations in Brazil; or, worse yet, they see themselves facing an imminent risk of poverty or decline in their familial social mobility.[2] A considerable proportion emigrate thanks to the diffusion, especially in the place of origin, of social networks composed of strong ties (family ties or bonds of friendship) but also of weak ties (acquaintances or friends of friends), and they almost always take advantage of the indispensable role of "professionalized" intermediary agents. Without a doubt, strong market forces solidify the emigration industry more and more each day. It is a network of speculators with many tentacles that is capable of situating people who are barely literate in their native language (much less in

English) who have never left their small hometowns but who, thanks to the ability to finance the services of the intermediary agent, will be able to make a long and risky trip to the other side of the hemisphere.[3]

Brazilian immigration to Massachusetts began to become visible during the 1980s when Brazilians started to join the millions of others who likewise bet on immigration to the United States as a means of changing important aspects of their lives. However, in contrast to the immigrants who up to the mid-twentieth century filled boats headed from Europe and Asia to the New World, immigrants today are able to land in America after only a few hours of flight, and their letters no longer take months to arrive in the small towns from which they departed. As soon as they land, it is possible to make a telephone call to someone in the immigrant's native land, just as it is possible to get daily news about the country on a computer or a television set.

Once it began, immigration to the United States rapidly expanded to include many points of origin throughout all of Brazil. If during the 1980s the Brazilians in Boston could be immediately identified as almost invariably from the city of Governador Valadares in the state of Minas Gerais, by the mid-1990s there were few Brazilian states that were not represented in this flow. This same tendency held in the year 2000. It would not be an exaggeration to suppose that, except in the poorest regions of Brazil, anyone has never heard the topic discussed or does not have an acquaintance, friend, or relative who in the past fifteen years has gone to "live in another country."

The phrase is in quotes because it is unlikely that someone will say that the person emigrated. I do not mean that he or she is possibly unfamiliar with the term, which is technical and not very popular, but rather I am referring to the notion of what this migratory process is becoming and how it is represented or simply imagined. Truthfully, several notions are involved in this process. Just as it is rarely said that "so-and-so emigrated," it is equally rare to hear that "so-and-so went to work in another country." What people say is that "he (or she) is living in another country." I believe that in this lies special meaning because, just as family members and friends in Brazil rarely define those who leave as emigrants, Brazilians in Massachusetts also show some reluctance and much ambivalence about putting themselves into the immigrant category. Why is this so?

There is not one easy answer. However, among the possible approaches that may be taken is a recurrent theme: the identity/identities of the

Brazilian immigrants. Here I set out merely a few of the points relevant to this topic, the rest of which runs through each of the chapters of this book. One of the results that this study reveals is the very difficulty of speaking of "the" Brazilian immigrant. The Brazilian population of Massachusetts is diverse, and the reasons Brazilians are relocating there are also varied. I consider the motivation for emigration, whether it is individual or family, to be a fundamental variable in the definition of the profiles of this population. Returning to the point: identities that are equally divided correspond to this demographically and socioeconomically diverse population.

The theme of identity runs through each chapter of this book not because it was defined in advance as an object of study but because it comes out in every aspect of analysis regarding the Brazilians residing in Massachusetts, whether that aspect is religious groups, community organizations, interethnic relations, the labor market, or any other. For each of my interviewees, Brazil constantly reappears as a great obsession. Alongside the critical desire to "make money in America," the Brazilians continually express in the most varied ways and in different contexts what Brazil is, what it is like to live in Brazil, and what it means to be Brazilian. Similarly, they constantly seek to decipher what the United States is, what it means to be an immigrant in this country, and what the American people are like. This is why one objective of this study is to investigate the construction of the identity/identities of the Brazilian immigrant in different contexts, especially in the workplace, in church, in associative practices, and in how they interact and experience the country that they have chosen as their destination.

Who are the Brazilians who immigrate to Massachusetts? How do they interrelate? How do they see each other? How do their social and demographic differences affect the forms of sociability of the group as a whole? One of the things that most surprised me in the beginning of the study was the manner in which the Brazilians referred to each other. In the course of the interviews and the field observations, complaints about the lack of solidarity, excessive greed, and low community participation came to demarcate a discursive field replete with ambiguities because, in the midst of the complaints, a great love for Brazil and for the people of that country was vehemently reiterated. From the very first accounts it became clear that there was a kind of tension between promoting economic interests (earning money) and acting with solidarity (helping others) within the community itself.

In the face of this discovery, I began to take the theme of solidarity (or its absence) as one of the principal research foci. This approach struck me as stimulating to the point that I came to contrast my data with the recent literature from the United States. One of the characteristics most emphasized by that literature is the predominance of relationships of solidarity within immigrant groups. The immigrant is presented as "the solidary man" in relation to his national group. An example of this can be found in an enlightening passage written by the sociologist Alejandro Portes (1995: 256), one of the principal researchers on the subject and a specialist on Latino immigrants:

> Since the nineteenth century, immigrant groups in the United States have been recognized by the solidarity that exists among their members and by their success in promoting their businesses. This model is maintained today with a basis in similar forces. Given the devaluation of their abilities and of their education in the labor market of the destination country, and in the face of constant discrimination by the natives, the immigrants have few resources, except that of aggregating to obtain moral support and economic survival.

This is an enlightening statement because it clearly illustrates how the literature from the United States tends to overvalue solidarity within U.S. immigrant communities. Studies that risk taking other directions are few and recent.[4] One example is Maxine L. Margolis' study *Little Brazil* (1994), in which she identifies the absence of community organizations and manifestations of solidarity among the Brazilians in New York. Precisely because solidarity is accepted as an a priori fact, studies oriented toward investigating relationships of competition, conflict, or exploitation within groups are rare; these relationships, however, also tend to occur in the same networks that promote forms of solidarity.

The data obtained early on in this study already began to contrast with the romantic vision of immigrants and the almost idyllic perspective of their communities. Consequently, I came to attribute greater importance to the investigation of the manifestation and forms of solidarity, which I judged to be indispensable even in defining their limits and configuration.

Thus, solidarity in this study is considered an object of investigation and not a presupposition.

"Do you know that here Brazilians even sell jobs?" This question, frequently directed at me by the interviewees, was generally expressed in an indignant tone. I quickly learned that job selling was common among those Brazilians who do housecleaning. However, the vast majority judge that people are selling something that ought to be given away for the simple purpose of helping whoever needs help.[5] This opinion was even shared by those who sell jobs. It is precisely in the world of work, which is discussed in Chapter 4 of this book, and especially in the area of job selling that this ambiguity appears most explicitly.

Furthermore, the world of work involves valuing a set of occupations that are devoid of prestige in Brazil but in which Brazilians in Massachusetts engage. To move from being a teacher, an accountant, a small farmer, a student, or a homemaker to become a dishwasher, a lawn-care worker, a nanny, a food preparer, a busboy, or a housecleaner causes a loss in occupational status. However, other compensation accompanies these moves. The increase in remuneration is an important condition, but it is not sufficient to explain the fact that middle-class Brazilians accept engaging in such occupations. Work relationships that are considered more formal, professional, and respectful, as well as the nature of the work itself, especially in the area of housecleaning, are equally important to understanding the acceptance of the change in occupational status. Despite the contrast between the occupations in the two countries, the data from this study reveal that Brazilian immigrants, just like other undocumented immigrants who live in the United States, have access to occupations that are limited to the informal labor market in the United States. It is interesting, however, that even while still in Brazil, a significant proportion of Brazilians who emigrated were already involved in activities linked to the informal economy. In Chapter 4 I also analyze small businesses. My particular interest was in understanding how it would be possible for a Brazilian immigrant to open a small business in Massachusetts given very adverse conditions with regard to the absence of startup capital, as well as problems with legal status, a low level of proficiency in English, and little knowledge of the operation of local institutions. To my surprise, however, when asking about the difficulties, the business owners interviewed tended toward a kind of inversion. They emphasized the advantages that the United States offers to entrepreneurs like themselves.

How do Brazilians manage to get jobs in Massachusetts? What type of help can they expect? How and where do they seek to socialize? Churches are the institutions that offer the greatest support to Brazilians. However, the ways in which that support is institutionally organized results in significant differences. Chapter 3 presents the principal differences between the religious work undertaken by evangelicals and that conducted by Catholics. But whatever denomination they may be, members perceive and value their churches as institutions that promote safe spaces for experiences of reciprocity and solidarity among Brazilian immigrants. In other words, Brazilians seek churches because they want to socialize, and they recognize the social control mechanisms established in churches as safe because they have the promotion of socialization in mind.

Although solidarity may be a constitutive part of the identities and the religious practices of the Catholic Church as well as the Protestant churches studied in this book, the evangelical pastors tend to view job selling as more natural, whereas this practice is more frequently identified by priests and nuns as the expression of a lack of solidarity. However, the Brazilians who work in the area of housecleaning sell jobs whether they are Catholic or evangelical, and they all complain equally about the lack of solidarity among Brazilians and declare that they are, at a minimum, made uncomfortable by the existence of this strange trade.

How do Brazilian immigrants relate to one another? How do they see one another? How do they evaluate their migratory experiences, and how do they perceive U.S. society? These are the principal questions I raise in Chapter 5, in which I explore the perceptions that Brazilians develop about American society. In addressing these questions, I was particularly interested in understanding why my interviewees generally had a positive opinion of the United States even though they might be in the uncomfortable circumstance of being undocumented aliens and employed in unskilled occupations that are devoid of prestige and considered poorly remunerated. Understanding their perceptions above all required considering the ways in which Brazilians experience certain aspects of American society, especially those that involve notions of rights and citizenship. In a complementary way, I was able to perceive that these experiences make sense because when they evaluate American society, Brazilians reevaluate the ways in which they experienced the same notions in Brazil.

What are the future perspectives facing the migratory movement of Brazilians en route to Massachusetts? What are immigrants' possibilities of returning to Brazil or remaining in the United States? How do second-generation Brazilians evaluate their circumstances and the circumstances of their parents, and what types of connection do they maintain with their country of origin? These are the questions addressed at the end of this study. However, the Conclusion does not merely involve a synthesis of the principal results presented in each of the chapters; rather, it raises some considerations regarding the future possibilities of Brazilian emigration, an emigration that does not seem to be a temporary phenomenon.

In the United States, a Brazilian would readily be identified as black (or not white) or as Hispanic by the local population. However, as we will see, when they are called on to classify themselves, Brazilian immigrants tend to reject both categories. The research presented in Chapter 6 was conducted in 2002, when I spent three months at Boston University as a visiting researcher. During those months, I collected data about various aspects of Brazilian civic culture in an attempt to explore further questions about solidarity and the social dimension of respect and citizenship, questions arising from the research conducted for this book. These latter data will be the object of analysis in a future study.

Methodological Procedures

This book presents a condensation of fifteen years of research about Brazilian immigration to Massachusetts. I began to study this social process in 1994 when I was a visiting scholar at MIT, a position I held until 1996. During the subsequent years, I continued following the developments and gathering new material and data about many other important aspects of Brazilian emigration. I returned to the field in Massachusetts five more times. I conducted an extensive survey of Brazilian businesses in Massachusetts in 2001 and in 2003; I again immersed myself in the field for three uninterrupted months in 2002 when I was a visiting researcher at Boston University, and I carried out a new sociodemographic survey in 2005. Following developments in the immigrant community and administering another survey almost ten years later allowed me to conduct a longitudinal analysis of Brazilian immigration to Massachusetts.[6]

When selecting which procedures and instruments I would use, I sought to combine various research techniques and sources. The quantitative data, collected through direct sources, made possible the construction of a broader picture within which the phenomenon of Brazilian emigration is situated. That picture demarcates the socioeconomic variables that underlie this movement, without which it is not possible to understand why emigration from Brazil began to occur in the 1980s and why a large proportion of Brazilians specifically seek out the state of Massachusetts.

The combination of macro and micro structural elements present in the phenomenon of Brazilian emigration allows one to relate the social structure that underlies the practices to the discourse of the subjects involved in the process. It would not be possible to establish this relationship without combining quantitative and qualitative data. The principal quantitative data from primary sources were collected via a survey consisting of 300 questionnaires. The survey permitted a definition of the profile of the Brazilian immigrant and thus avoided idealizations and generalizations about "the typical Brazilian."

Surveys

Two surveys were conducted, one in 1996 and the other in 2005. Both were conducted among a random sample of 300 Brazilian immigrants.[7] In both cases the instrument and the research procedures were the same. The interviewees were selected in Brazilian commercial establishments in Cambridge, Somerville, Marlborough, Framingham, Allston-Brighton, and East Boston based on the presupposition that the biggest concentration of Brazilians in Massachusetts is found in these communities.[8] The data collected in the survey permit a basic socioeconomic and demographic profile of Brazilian immigrants residing in Massachusetts to be drawn. It is important to emphasize that it is an approximate profile. It was not possible to obtain a random sample of this population since many Brazilian immigrants are undocumented, and the number of Brazilian residents, as well as their places of residence, are unknown.

Interviews with Brazilian Immigrants

The interviews with Brazilian immigrants contain accounts of the story of immigration and the story of life in Brazil and in the United States. Each of them was open-ended and was conducted individually, having an average duration of an hour and a half. Preference was given to conducting the interview in the interviewee's place of residence. Forty of these interviews were conducted from 1994 to 1996, and twenty-one were conducted from 2000 to 2005.

Life stories have proven to be a useful instrument in migratory studies. This technique is being adopted by researchers of various orientations and employed to analyze objects of study that are also diverse. Among the researchers who have used this method with success, Virginia Yans MacLaughlin (1990), Gareth Jones (1983), and Josselson and Lieblich (1995) stand out. According to MacLaughlin, quantitative analysis, like factual information, comes from a set of information about the organization and behavior of a social group. However, it takes on new meaning when analyzed through individual narratives in light of the interviewees' perspectives. More than empirical information about the past, life stories can transmit a set of meanings that the actors attribute to present actions (MacLaughlin 1990). Complementarily, the narratives as a form of interpretation of experiences must be recodified and recontextualized by the interviewer based on the broader cultural context in which the interviewee is situated. "Personal narratives are particularly rich because they permit individual actions, as well as the effects and constraints produced by the contexts in which the individual courses of action occur, to be understood" (Jones 1983: 27).

Gathering information through qualitative data such as narratives and life stories requires special care in the choice of interviewees, for it is necessary to obtain a sample that is as representative as possible of the population about which one wishes to speak. In the selection of interviewees, the sampling technique known as "snowballing" was used (Cornelius 1982). As disadvantages may result from this technique, including the impossibility of generalizing the results obtained and, principally, the risk that the interviewees selected will belong to the same networks, I attempted to diversify as much as possible the profiles of the interviewees as well as increasing the number of initial points of contact. Thus, the interviewees were selected from a variety of religious or service organizations to which Brazilians have access in Massachusetts, such as the Massachusetts Alliance of Portuguese Speakers, Rio Maria Committee, Brazilian Immigrant Center, the Catholic church (Brazilian Apostolate), the Assembly of God church (Brazilian), the Baptist church (Brazilian), and the Presbyterian church (Brazilian and American). Brazilians who did not belong to any of these agencies or institutions also were contacted in their workplaces and interviewed.

There is one additional observation that is no less important. In conducting this research, my attention was drawn to the fact that no matter how much I may have attempted to vary the initial points of contact in forming the network of interviewees, the results collected through the survey revealed the existence of a demographic and socioeconomic diversity in this population even greater than that which the snowballing technique managed to encompass. This is particularly important because with the people indicated through the networks alone (and despite their being representative of a vast majority), I was not able to incorporate Brazilians of rural origins or those who had lower levels of education. Through the survey alone I was able to verify that among Brazilian immigrants a small number of people barely know how to write their names and were rural workers in Brazil.

Interviews with Qualified Informants

The interviews with qualified informants, that is, professionals and community and religious leaders who work with Brazilian immigrants in Massachusetts, helped to draw a profile of Brazilian immigrants and their principal problems and difficulties and to understand the operation of the Brazilian communities, their relationships with other groups of immigrants and non-immigrants, and their religious lives. These interviews did not follow a fixed format since the information varied according to the activities performed by these informants and their incorporation in religious networks, social networks, and so on.

Control Interviews

When I visited workplaces and the Brazilians' cities of residence, I sought to obtain basic information through informal conversations that I later noted in a field notebook. The questions asked involved place of origin, personal reasons for migration, occupation in Brazil and in the United States, family's place of residence, and plans for and date of return to Brazil. These interviews were important so I could verify that the data I was collecting in the interviews were representative.

Participant Observation

Over the fifteen years of my study, I continued to follow and observe the communities I first researched in 1994. To complement the interviews, I sought to observe, accompany, and participate in a series of activities promoted by Brazilians in Massachusetts. My observation and participation extended to various meetings of Brazilian community organizations as well as to wedding receptions, birthday parties, masses and religious services, Brazilian workplaces and businesses, public gatherings, and the Brazilian consulate in Boston.

Through this series of activities, I obtained data and information that I could not glean from qualitative interviews or through the quantitative survey alone. Complementarily, the observation of the practices and operations of the community and religious organizations provided a broader basis of reference for the expressive discourse of the interviews and helped to discern what "is said" from what "is done." In other words, the interviews, combined with participant observation and the survey, made it possible to relate discourse to collective practices and to incorporate socioeconomic variables into the analysis of the representations.

Complementary Research

In 2002 and 2003, a survey was conducted of Brazilian firms in the cities of Somerville, Cambridge, East Boston, and Allston. Concomitantly, 100 questionnaires about the sociodemographic characteristics of the business owners and firms were completed. With regard to the business owners, the information stressed included age, date of arrival in the United States, level of education, place of origin in Brazil, marital status and number of children, reasons for emigration, religion, community participation, reason for opening the business, and legal status of the owner. With regard to the firms, the following data were collected: location, size, number and national origin of employees, date of establishment, amount of startup capital necessary to open the business and how it was raised, profile of the clientele, identification of suppliers, whether or not there were partners and their national origins, and the existence of any plans to expand the business. In the second phase, in-depth interviews were conducted with the owners and representatives of organizations that sought to support Brazilian business owners in Boston. Finally, the Brazilian consul in

Boston was interviewed in order to analyze the type and extent of support the Brazilian government offered to small business owners.

Field Research in Brazil

When I returned to Brazil in 1997, I visited the city of Governador Valadares in the state of Minas Gerais. I conducted interviews and got to know the neighborhoods and locales where emigrants congregated.

In 2004 I conducted research that simultaneously included Governador Valadares and Boston, Massachusetts, with the objectives of identifying the sociodemographic profile of Brazilians who send remittances and of estimating the frequency of remittances, as well as their value and purpose. Through the field research in Governador Valadares I sought to verify the existence of nongovernmental organizations (NGOs) in the city that were the beneficiaries of remittances; once these organizations were identified, I analyzed the ways the money was sent and used, and I investigated the impact the remittances had on the immigrants' families in Governador Valadares.[9] In-depth interviews were conducted in May and June 2004 with three families there that received remittances from the United States. Twenty-four questionnaires were submitted to representatives of NGOs in Governador Valadares.

In 2005 research was conducted in the city of Poços de Caldas in Minas Gerais. We chose that city because we were surprised by news published in the Brazilian press that illegal agents of Brazilian emigration were "migrating" there. The agents, who had previously been in Governador Valadares, had begun to be pursued by the Federal Police. Therefore, they decided to "invest" in Poços. If this was a "promising city," it was certainly due to the large number of emigrants there. This news left the researchers a bit perplexed because the importance of Poços de Caldas had not yet been verified in academic work. In total, nineteen returned Brazilian emigrants were interviewed in Poços, and the snowball method was used to select the interviewees. Those who were selected were interviewed based on a semistructured questionnaire with a focus on the apprenticeship provided by the migratory experience and the difficulties they faced in finding employment and developing the skills they brought back to Brazil. The interviews were recorded and lasted about an hour. In addition to the nineteen interviewees, to lay the groundwork, unstructured interviews or simply conversations were conducted with people whom the team found downtown: merchants and retail workers, a journalist who broadcast a program about emigration on a local radio station, a manager from the Bank of Brazil, and some waiters.

In contrast to these two cities in which emigration is an important and daily topic among residents was the São Paulo Metropolitan Area, from which a substantial number of emigrants depart: there the topic of emigration is barely perceptible except in the media. In the past fifteen years of research, I have been able to conduct several interviews with returned emigrants, people who were planning to emigrate, and family members of emigrants, albeit not in the form of a structured investigation. I have discovered that the migratory network in this large metropolitan area is sparse except to Japan. Networks are more structured in the cities surrounding São Paulo, especially in the so-called bedroom communities (for example, Embu and Taboão da Serra) and in industrial cities (for example, São Bernardo and Diadema).

Carrying out field research in both the places of destination and of origin made it possible to obtain a more far-reaching picture of emigration and of immigration, as well as of the migration of return. We were able to measure some aspects of the impact of emigration on the places of origin and to follow, from a transnational perspective, the processes of Brazilians' incorporation into life in Massachusetts.

1

Economic Sociology and Brazilian Immigration

New economic sociology has become a promising path for migratory studies since the 1990s. This approach has proven capable of incorporating the networks, individual motivations, and social orientations that underlie migratory flows and the immigrants' means of incorporation into the host society, means that are not limited to those resulting from the simple equation of labor supply and demand. It is clear that the sociological perspective already was present in the work of various unorthodox sociologists and economists such as, for example, the remarkable book *Birds of Passage* by Michael Piore (1979). However, publications like Saskia Sassen's *The Mobility of Labor and Capital* (1988) and Alejandro Portes' *Economic Sociology of Migration* (1995) represented a more definitive step toward the fusion of economic sociology with the classic sociology of migration. That fusion contributed to the renovation of migratory studies by questioning former interpretations and giving continuity to a debate based on new evidence and arguments.

In fact, one of the most consistent academic debates about immigration in the 1990s was the one that resulted from a kind of confrontation between neoclassical economic theory and the "others"—or rather, between them and neoclassical theory since, at least in this area of the social sciences, the neoclassical theorists find themselves isolated and, to use a phrase that is perhaps too informal for a book, out of date. Although few researchers would defend its premises, the neoclassical model still shows some vitality because many attack it. That is, the "others" define themselves precisely by adopting this theory as their main opposition. And therein, I believe, lies its power.[1]

The relevance of this debate arises in the way it calls into question important sociological and economic theoretical and methodological premises and currently occupies a prominent place in academic discussions in the United States.[2]

The neoclassical approach to migratory studies—push/pull theory—when explaining the emergence of migratory movements stresses the economic inequalities between nations, inequalities that are capable of producing significant differences between the salary incentives offered in the various countries and regions that will constitute the poles of the migratory circuits.[3] On one side, the greater volume of job opportunities and better remuneration available in wealthy countries (destination countries) are considered the principal "pull" factors. On the other side, the "push" factors appear to be related primarily to conditions of poverty, unemployment, and low salaries found in the poorer countries (the countries of origin). Since economic expansion in industrialized countries increases the demand for workers to numbers larger than are available, poor countries begin to supply industrialized countries with some of their workforce that, given the socioeconomic conditions, cannot be absorbed domestically. It is not coincidental that this is also called the "equilibrium model" because it attributes to the migratory processes the positive function of favoring the reconciliation of supply and demand with regard to employment in the immigrants' destination countries as well as in their countries of origin.

If from a macro point of view the socioeconomic variable "inequality between nations" is considered the principal factor in unleashing migratory movements, from a micro point of view, the displacement of populations is interpreted as the result of individual choices. This is the model's most important methodological premise: the individual who decides to emigrate is motivated by a utilitarian calculation based on the cost-benefit relationship of his or her personal advantages. The comparative advantages of this calculation are primarily of an economic nature—the salary differential, which constitutes a serious vulnerability in the model (Thomas 1973).

As Portes observes, the fact that the flows of emigration tend to occur in the poorest areas and move toward the wealthiest areas—and not vice versa—has not been contested. The predominant tendency of emigrants to leave in search of better salaries and opportunities has not been contested, either, but what has been contested is that this approach ignores factors of any nature other than strictly economic. Yet these other factors, of a social and cultural nature, are indispensable to understanding the origin and persistence of contemporary migratory movements. Consequently, the criticism falls on two basic points of the neoclassical argument: on the macro analytical level, the emphasis on the variable of income (especially the salary differential); and on the micro analytical level, the supposition that the immigrant is an "economic man" par excellence (Portes 1995).

Push/pull theory began to be severely criticized by authors who, from the 1980s on, have sought to approach the topic from a sociological perspective. Classified as "institutionalists" (Michael Piore) and "historical structuralists" (Saskia Sassen, Alejandro Portes), these authors have emphasized the role of socioeconomic structures in migratory movements, perceiving migration as a distinctly social phenomenon.

Over the past twenty years, the sociological approach has introduced and made available a new agenda of emerging research topics: How do social networks transmit information and break the rigid boundaries of the orthodox model of the labor market (Sassen 1995)? How do the "socially expected durations" (Robert Merton's SEDs) affect economic adjustment and ethnic identity itself (Roberts 1995)? How do patterns of solidarity result in advantages for ethnic entrepreneurialism (Granovetter 1995)? What is the nature of the relationship between social capital and cultural capital (Kelly 1995)? How do the generational question and the context that receives them affect the new immigrants' assimilation process (Portes 1995)? Alejandro Portes provides a precise and clear summary of the recent contributions of economic sociology to migratory studies vis-à-vis the previous explanatory models: the salary differential does not suffice to explain the displacement of populations; the immigrants' adaptation process does not necessarily culminate in assimilation, as the critical factor for adaptation is the second and not the first generation of immigrants. Beyond the possibilities of remaining or returning, immigrants begin to construct transnational and binational communities (Portes 1995).

Even if the 1990s can be taken as the moment of the integration of new economic sociology and migratory studies and although this integration resulted in a more comprehensive area of knowledge, we must go back to the 1950s and the pioneering work of Talcott Parsons and Neil Smelser in *Economy and Society* (1984) to find the roots of this approach. In their book the authors present key propositions of economic sociology: economic actions are social actions and socially situated; economic institutions are social constructs. These points challenge the presumptions of neoclassical economic theory, according to which economic action should be conceived as merely individual and noncontextualized and that economic institutions are taken for granted and not socially constructed. In fact, from its beginnings, the (old) economic sociology planted a series of questions regarding the basic presumptions of mainstream (neoclassical) economics,[4] especially regarding the epistemological presumption of "economic man," who is invariably guided by instrumental rationality, acts egotistically to maximize his advantages, and has unrestricted access to abundant information for decision making.

Methodological individualism is the instrument adopted by this model, which is constructed abstractly and deductively and whose epistemology is established on an atomistic base. Consequently, "economic man" does not find himself embedded in networks or institutions, and he is not contextualized socially, culturally, or politically. For economic sociology, rationality guides only one of the modalities of action, and even if the individual is taken as the basic unit of analysis, his or her action is necessarily influenced by others, even when it is rationally guided. For Max Weber, understanding human action means questioning the motives that guide individual behavior. However, Weber contends (1968), the meaning of individual action as the sociologist understands it always takes others into account, and rational instrumental orientation is only one possibility among "pure" types of action—three others being those guided by values (ethical, aesthetic, religious, and so on), by tradition (and habit), or even by affection.

Thus, one of the fundamental points of economic sociology in general—and particularly relevant to the sociology of migration—concerns incentives for and restrictions on action, especially those that originate in the social structure and in the structure of meanings and that are not merely economic restrictions and incentives arising from situations marked by a scarcity of resources or options (Smelser and Swedberg 1994). This allows the questioning of hypotheses such as that poverty, unemployment, and/or low salaries are necessary and sufficient causal factors to unleash migrations and that population displacement is a positive mechanism that is freely regulated by market forces, especially by the labor market.

The premise that action should be understood based on the social structure that underlies it, a premise that marks the very birth of sociology in the nineteenth century, acquires new impetus and challenges in the work of Mark Granovetter in the second half of the twentieth century (1973, 1974, 1985). Initially centered on analysis of the labor market (more specifically on access to employment positions), Granovetter's research contributed to the development of the analysis of social networks and the incorporation of social relationships in understanding the meaning of individual action and access to information about available jobs. In the 1990s the social networks that underlay the population flows came to occupy a central position in the research and open new pathways for migratory studies.[5]

The work of Douglas Massey et al. (1987) and Charles Tilly (1990) recovered the social dimension of the individual decision to emigrate by attributing that "decision" to the social networks (friendship, family, neighborhood) that constitute a social field capable of interconnecting the destination country and the country of origin, thus enabling the displacement of populations. Tilly stresses the role of minimizing the risks of emigration and the costs of return that social networks play in decisions about emigration: "The higher the risk and the cost of return, the more intense the trust in previously established connections" (84). The author further proposes that migrations be thought of as "community structures" because they are "not reducible to individual characteristics and intentions" (98).

In my opinion, it is worthwhile to propose the hypothesis that migratory networks can be conceived of as "community structures." Conceiving of immigrant groups or social structures that constitute the migratory processes as communitarian leads us back to an old discussion about so-called modern, complex, or industrial societies on one hand and so-called primitive, simple, or agrarian societies on the other. Community structures would obviously be linked to the second type. Recall that community structures stand in opposition to hierarchical relationships and complex and diversified (nontraditional) roles. Community structures are further constituted by reciprocal relationships and solidarity as opposed to noncollective, selective, and selfish interests. The notion of community mitigates or even eliminates rationally instrumentalized individual and objective economic interests. However, would these characteristics already exist in the social dynamic of emigrant populations in the country of origin, and/or would they be developed in the very dynamic that constitutes migratory movements and their supporting institutions? Would there be "less communitarian" groups as a function of the specific characteristics of each movement? In this latter case, would the migration structure of the first generation of "target earners," for example, be less guided by community connections and interests than that of political refugees?

Studying networks as social structures is not incompatible with the notion of an immigrant as an economic agent, that is, as someone who acts by calculating cost-benefit and by maximizing advantages. The fundamental thing is that sociocultural variables come to be incorporated in this case. It is these variables taken together that permit the distinction between the groups and communities involved in the migratory processes (Truzzi 2008).

Massey is one of the sociologists who, while upholding the network approach, did not abandon the discussion of the cost-benefit calculation of the actors involved (Massey et al. 1993). In their assessment, the expectation of monetary return is the main motivational factor in contemporary flows, so that emigration can become an investment in human capital as well.[6] In this case, emigrating can be conceived of as a choice, which evidently does not mean that it is an action free from any type of social and political constraint. Consideration of the social structures that affect individual action is, as previously mentioned, a fundamental premise of the sociological approach, especially as developed theoretically in Max Weber's comprehensive sociology.

Where spontaneous migratory flows are concerned, the themes of rationality and decision making deserve greater diligence in sociological research and analysis. This would be, in my opinion, a new and promising path if the methodological instruments, theories, and hypotheses accumulated by economic sociology were used. Once again, Brazilian emigration can serve as an example. Its spontaneous nature and the lack of interference by the state make evident the importance of understanding emigration as a choice, regardless of whether it is encouraged by collective or individual units. This does not mean conceiving of emigration as a response to economic demands that are limited to the labor market (Harris and Todaro 1980, Borjas 1990) or making use of the deductive and mathematical models of economic theory; rather, it means seeking to reconstitute on an empirical level the reasoning processes that support, motivate, and legitimize the decision of emigrants who spontaneously cross national borders.

Rationality and Propensity for Risk

One of the basic topics of the social sciences is that of the rationality of actors. However, there is still much left to be studied and discussed about actions and motivations that configure intermediate spaces on the continuum formed by "economic man" on one end and "community and solidarity" ("solidary men") on the opposite end.

Individual reasons (socially oriented) for emigrating, justifications based on calculations that consider the cost-benefit relationship when making the decision, and the process of the social legitimization of the decision to immigrate based on the representation of immigration as an investment are only a few examples of the research questions that economic sociology would open for researchers to investigate. In total, this approach makes it possible to preserve and understand the volitional and optional components that spontaneous migratory flows have presented in a more marked way since the turn of the twentieth century as well as to reconstitute the limits of economic and rational elements on the social and political representation of that process.

The importance of these dimensions in studies of contemporary international migrations is evidenced by the Brazilian case presented here. Is emigrating a decision whose principal motivation is economic? For the majority of Brazilians, certainly it is. It remains to be discovered if the motivation is only (or predominantly) economic and if it is individual. Saying that it is economic implies asserting not only that one emigrates in search of an economic benefit (money, work, savings) but also that this is a rationally directed decision. It is rationally directed in the sense that it is, in the majority of cases, planned and that when people emigrate they utilize the best possible resources to which they have access to achieve their objectives. In the interviews gathered over fifteen years of research, it can be observed that the difficulties and risks were calculated in advance, but only in part. That is, to make sense of the decision to emigrate, a complicated cost-benefit relationship is established between economic variables centered around work (remuneration and working hours), savings (remuneration for the work minus living expenses), and the exchange rate (the greater the devaluation of the *real* and the greater the value of the dollar, the more one can save in less time). The rationality of the arguments in this type of "game of compensation" (what one loses and gains by either staying in Brazil or emigrating) is mainly, but not exclusively, based on remuneration for work. The question, however, is whether a decision to emigrate based on remuneration can artificially minimize other costs, especially those of an affective nature, and risks that arise from the situation of fragility that the condition of being displaced inevitably makes possible (Martes 2000a). The complement to this "fragmented calculation" is self-deception.

In this book, we will see that the discourse that legitimizes emigration, for those who emigrate as well as for their families, compatriots, fellow believers, or any other groups to which they have significant ties, is a discourse that identifies emigration as a kind of investment. Like any investment, it involves seeking out information and resources, exposure to risk, and planning.

Risk and adventure are two characteristics that immigrants like to attribute to themselves: breaking with a routine, accepting new challenges, and "changing everything in life." It is not coincidental that some studies point out the similarities between the typical entrepreneur and the typical emigrant. According to Waldinger (1986), the profile of the immigrant worker tends to be more inclined to risk taking than that of those who did not leave their native lands even though they also had the opportunity to emigrate. The inclination to take risks would reinforce in a special way the thesis that emigration is a highly selective process. Motivation and satisfaction with the remuneration received for work are two other characteristics that studies highlight. Some studies conclude that immigrants prove to be more motivated than natives to do work that is poorly remunerated. Since the studies compare the salaries and incomes available in the destination country and the country of origin, they show that immigrants tend to be more satisfied with the smaller profits generated by small businesses (Light et al. 1995).

Despite the reductionism that results from typologies, considering the affinities that exist between the typical immigrant and the typical entrepreneur can be useful. It is interesting to observe that among the classic studies of entrepreneurs, that of Joseph Schumpeter (1934) emphasizes several characteristics, including psychological traits, of this particular type of capitalist. An inclination to take risks (a prerequisite for innovative action), an adventurous nature, the desire to do something unusual ("a leap into the dark"), allowing oneself to be guided by passion, and so on are characteristics of the capitalist pioneer and lead us back to what, at least metaphorically, is stressed and idealized about immigrants. The history of American business is replete with examples of immigrants with a profile similar to that of the Brazilian immigrant.

The entrepreneur's principal motivation, according to Schumpeter, is not that of economic man. Although the entrepreneur directs his actions rationally, by taking on the high price of fleeing from traditional behaviors and patterns, he obviously is not seeking the most economic action by maximizing advantages and reducing risks. His motivation is not necessarily hedonistic, either, because what he seeks is not just the satisfaction of individual needs. The meaning behind his actions should rather be sought in the "dream and desire of founding a private kingdom" (the modern equivalent of medieval nobility), the "desire for conquest," "the impulse to struggle," "proving himself superior to others," and "the joy of creating and making things" (Schumpeter 1934: 65). Therefore, profit in and of itself is not the final objective; rather, it is the consequence of the actions guided by the innovations that he introduces. This seems to be a useful, although imprecise, description of some characteristic features of the self-idealized image of the emigrant as well. In the case presented here, emigration is configured as a low-risk choice of a temporary nature that has the value of an investment.

Migrations and Globalization

Recent authors have introduced two new dimensions to the studies of international migrations that are designed on a macro level: the attraction developed by countries that are capable of producing global cultural patterns and the insertion of the units that constitute the migratory poles into the global system of transnational production. The new approaches seek to respond to the challenge of incorporating the transformations that the phenomenon began to present in the 1960s. This was when the displacement of populations arose in a specific phase of the expansion of capital that differed from the phase that had resulted in the arrival of thousands of foreigners to the American continent up to the middle of the twentieth century. It is precisely this new context that sociologist Saskia Sassen considers in order to redefine the characteristics and meaning of the most recent migratory processes.[7] Sassen seeks to answer how the current configuration of spaces of transnational production affords the conditions necessary for the mobility of the workforce.

When framed in this way, the migratory question comes to be presented through a different lens than that of push/pull theory, which, supported by the free-market hypothesis, was intended to explain the mobility of workers but not the mobility of capital. For Sassen, it is necessary to explain the movement of both in a relational way. The premise of the free market should be abandoned in favor of study of the role of state regulation in the process of the mobilization of capital and work. The internationalization of markets also means, in this context, the internationalization of the loci of production. In the sphere of transnational production, not only workers circulate, but rather, above all, capital, merchandise, services, and information do.

The production and diffusion of "global cultural patterns"—lifestyle and consumption—identified by Sassen as factors of attraction, reaffirm that immigration cannot be reduced to a phenomenon of a strictly economic nature nor interpreted as an "objective reality" independent of the cultural institutions and social relationships that surround it (Sayad 1998, Baker et al. 2005). In the Brazilian case, the expansion of U.S. sociocultural patterns to Brazil precedes the recent period of internationalization of production and the productive restructuring initiated in the 1970s.

But the growing fascination that the United States began to exercise over untold numbers of Brazilians from the 1940s on constitutes one of the critical factors of attraction. It can be said that emigration represents the closure of a circle, the end of a successful "game of seduction," to use an expression coined by historian Antonio Tota (2000), a game that began in the last century.

The threat of the conquest of the tropics by Nazis and Fascists marked the opening of the circle with a strategically planned action for the diffusion of the U.S. lifestyle in the Southern Hemisphere through the so-called Good Neighbor Policy, or Panamericanism. That strategy proved more effective and astute than any sort of military intervention. In this game, Americans began to praise Brazilian coffee and music, particularly through the promotion in Hollywood of Brazilian film star, singer, and entertainer Carmen Miranda (1909–1955), and Brazilians began to turn their backs on Europe and came to admire U.S. industrial progress, cinema, lifestyle, and patterns of consumption.

Worried about the future of his enterprises in Latin America, Nelson Rockefeller led the beginning of this long process because he believed that the success of his businesses depended not only on the sale of products but also on the assimilation of liberal democratic values, which were used as an ideological platform to confront the nearly 1 million German immigrants in Brazil. The Office of the Coordinator of Inter-American Affairs (OCIAA) under Rockefeller's leadership operated, according to Tota, as a "true ideology factory." It included a cinema division that got Walt Disney as well as Carmen Miranda to join the "cause of liberty in the Americas." Its function was to promote the production of films and newsreels about the United States and "the other Americas" to combat the films produced by the Axis powers and to transmit a likable image of "the States." The OCIAA brought Walt Disney and his characters into the war effort and helped to produce Carmen Miranda's first film, which at that time was able to pull 20th Century Fox out of the financial difficulties it was experiencing.

Even Orson Welles took part in the game. The renowned director of *Citizen Kane*, when called on by the cinema division, disembarked in Rio de Janeiro in 1942 as an ambassador of Panamericanism. Along with the visits to Brazil of Hollywood stars, Brazilians made their presence felt, albeit more modestly, in the United States. During the war, Ari Barroso became as popular in the United States as in his native land after his piece "Brazilian Watercolor" was sung in Walt Disney's film *Hello, Friends*. Cultural exchanges of students and researchers and the dissemination of English schools (an effort of the Cultural Center of Brazilian and the United States) flourished during the dictatorship of Getúlio Vargas. That is, paradoxically during the political regime most identified with totalitarianism, U.S. influence was disseminated throughout the country. Since then, U.S. media and consumption patterns have appeared in immigrants' accounts as sociocultural forces capable of attracting hundreds of thousands of Brazilians to the United States.

The Insertion of the Migratory Poles in the Global System of Transnational Production

Sassen asserts (1985) that the composition of international foreign investments began to undergo alterations in the late 1960s, at the same time that a new migratory wave to the United States emerged. These alterations were felt in the destination countries and in the immigrants' countries of origin, therefore affecting the organization of production at the two extremes of the movement. The rise in the level of direct international investment in the immigrants' countries of origin caused an acceleration of the development of domestic agricultural production and of industrial manufactured goods and services, notably those for export. Industrial plants are transferred to those places, and the processes of industrial subcontracting multiply. Export zones are given as typical examples of these changes. At the other end, certain American cities emerge as administrative centers of the global economic system, New York being the most salient example. Beginning in 1981, the United States again became the country to which the largest volume—almost half—of all international investment was directed.

Taken in isolation, none of these factors explains the emergence of contemporary international migratory movements, according to Sassen. However, together they establish the connection between the internationalization of capital and the mobility of the workforce: they redefine the forms of organization of production and occupations, and they disorder domestic labor markets, thus providing the United States with low-skilled, low-paid, and disciplined labor. On the other side, the reorganization of the productive structure in countries recently incorporated into transnational spaces accelerates the growth of the informal economy, subcontracting procedures, and outsourcing of production.

The transnationalization of production and the reorientation of the investment flows that occurred from the 1960s on explain why the migratory waves grew at the moment that the United States began to experience high rates of unemployment and the immigrants' countries of origin, notably in Asia, began to exhibit higher rates of economic growth. The immigrants who arrived in the United States from Mexico, Central America, and the so-called Asian Tigers (Hong Kong, South Korea, Singapore, and Taiwan) left the very cities where foreign investment had a great impact on the traditional industrial sector, causing transformations in the structure of employment, an increase in labor-intensive work, and higher levels of unemployment. The variables related to poverty, overpopulation, and economic stagnation that neoclassical theory employs to explain the origin of international population movements cannot, in isolation, explain the current flows. Poverty, stagnation, and overpopulation in these countries should be associated with the way they are incorporated into transnational spaces.

For Sassen, direct foreign investment should not be taken as the only cause of or seen in isolation to explain contemporary population displacements. What the author highlights is that investment flows tend to

Table 1.1. Inflows of Foreign Direct Investment (Average Annual Inflows in Millions of Dollars)

	1982–1984	1985–1987	1988–1990	1991–1992	1993–1994
All countries	54,620	92,820	190,180	164,769	218,494
Developing countries	20,310	18,081	30,780	47,757	77,387
Asia	4,891	7,655	16,804	26,125	53,298
All Latin America	6,417	7,606	8,896	16,464	19,077
Brazil	2,023	964	1,379	1,276	1,151

Source: World Investment Report 1995, Dunning and Hamdani (1997: 129).

promote the conditions for emigration to the extent that: they provoke disorder in the traditional productive structure, increasing the number of available workers; they increase the level of female industrial labor and at the same time generate an adverse impact on employment opportunities for male workers; and they promote and tighten economic, social, and political links between the immigrants' destination countries and the countries where the capital originates. The expansion of U.S. military exercises and diplomatic activities in the immigrants' countries of origin, along with the image of the United States as a "country of immigrants" (and therefore of opportunities), favor immigration to the extent that the United States begins to exercise greater ideological control and influence in transnational spaces.

These are, in general terms, the characteristics of contemporary international migratory movements. To what extent, though, can the explanatory model Sassen presents be applied to the Brazilian case? Sassen's interpretations enable understanding because the United States began to receive a significant number of international immigrants beginning in the 1960s and 1970s. However, I do not believe that such explanations can be extended to the Brazilian emigration that burgeoned in the second half of the 1980s. Besides other factors,[8] one can note that from 1985 to 1994 the foreign investment directed toward Brazil decreased, as Table 1.1 shows, in contrast to what Sassen finds in the Asian and Caribbean countries that she analyzes.

Table 1.1 clearly shows the implausibility of establishing any sort of relationship between the entry of international investment into the country and the rise in Brazilian emigration. Although productive restructuring in Brazil caused by the entry of a new flow of international capital did not affect the beginning of the migratory process, there is reason to believe that the restructuring process in progress in Brazil in the 1990s contributed toward maintaining the migratory movement. One of the fundamental factors in the Brazilian case that is not as important in Sassen's model is the growth of the informal economy in Brazil, as the present study will demonstrate.

The Labor Market

In addition to analysis of the processes of the internationalization of production, the labor market has merited detailed treatment in recent sociological literature as an intervening factor in the broad articulation between migration and global economic change. Two basic premises of the economic sociology of immigration are related to the labor market that is open to immigrants: the labor market is self-regulated, and the labor market is closed and embedded in the "community" (Sassen 1995, Portes 1995). Portes notes that "The immigrant community places distinct obligations on its members and has distinct mechanisms for their enforcement" (113).

In fact, self-regulation of the labor market also can be verified by the present study. The question is: Which are the regulatory institutions and agents? The "community," when referring to the self-regulation of this market, seems to be an overly broad concept that does not allow for the identification of the actors who struggle to define and institutionalize norms, forms of action, and power. Because Brazilians are spread out territorially as much in their country of destination as in their country of origin and because Brazil is a diverse nation of continental proportions, the attempts at self-regulation of the labor market in the United States began in the churches, which are indeed closed communities capable of putting into place mechanisms of social control and reciprocity. It is not the community formed by Brazilian immigrants but rather Brazilian churches in the United States that seek to institute norms to prevent exploitation of the workforce.

Despite the closed nature of the market, it is internally competitive and socially constructed and represented. These are not market niches that are free from competition, based on solidarity, on gifts, or on future expectations of reciprocity. Among Brazilian immigrants in this segment of the market one observes inter- and intra-group competition as well as competition with Hispanic immigrants but not U.S.-born workers. Although the market is delineated into segments or niches, internal mobility is supported by a social process of revalorization of the work, and satisfaction with remuneration and income level is seen. To understand this process, one first must consider the comparative perspective that has been permanently adopted by Brazilians, for these are first-generation immigrants. This study shows that the labor market, like other markets, is socially constructed through the standardization of behavior and the institution of norms (Steiner 1999).

Studies of the ethnic economy find that the labor market is not that closed, or else what is called the immigrant economy would not exist (Light et al. 1999). In contrast to the ethnic economy, access to which is limited to only one ethnic group, the immigrant economy occurs when co-nationals begin to employ immigrants of another national origin. By connecting different ethnicities, this arrangement diversifies the social networks with which they are connected, thus permitting wider access to other sources of work; the traditional literature about networks—these authors say—considers only the effect of the expansion of jobs through the ethnic economy. Yet this is not the only means of organization in the immigrant economy or the way in which migratory networks increase the demand for employment at different points (Light et al. 1999). I think it is useful to take two dimensions that are implicit here a bit further and deeper: although closed off into segments, the labor market is connected to the local institutional system; and because the market is closed, the presence and role of intermediaries between the niches and the surrounding society should be researched, particularly the role of some institutions as "brokers" to suppress eventual "structural holes" in immigrant networks.

The work of housecleaning, as will be presented in Chapter 4, is transformed into merchandise that is bought and sold among the immigrants themselves. Housecleaning is a market that is clearly formed and sustained by social structures (friendship, family, church, city of origin), and it is self-regulated. The buying and selling of jobs was transformed little by little into a socially reiterated standard of behavior for which the restrictions and attempts at regulation by religious organizations were initially significant, especially in the 1990s, with regard to whether this "market" should exist and the institution of a fair price. If the market could be defined as a simple price mechanism and cost-benefit calculation, the idea of a fair price would not make any sense at all. For Polanyi (1944), a fair price reaffirms the value in social connections, which also seems valid in this case. However, what should be emphasized is that the commercialization of job positions calls into question the extent of what is defined as ethnic solidarity in the labor market. It will be necessary to research what else could exist between reciprocity and the market.

Ethnic Groups and Solidarity

Despite the contributions of the sociology of international migrations, I believe that it contains an intrinsic perspective of solidarity in analyses of the internal relationships of immigrant national groups. On this point the case of Brazilian emigration analyzed here can be revealing because it permits the questioning of that perspective or at least allows it to be considered in another way. In other words, the sociological approach tends to take solidarity among immigrants of the same national group as a given and not as an object of research, and I believe that this stems from a conceptual stance that in my opinion merits reconsideration.

In the literature from the United States, very diverse immigrant groups are defined as "ethnic groups." The literature speaks of "communities," "ethnic communities," "ethnic identities," and "ethnic solidarity," no matter what the group in question may be: Spanish or Catalan, Peruvian or Puerto Rican, African American, Jewish, or Greek. I believe that, in fact, no matter what concept one adopts of ethnicity, the two principal characteristics of ethnic groups are solidarity and cultural identity (Weber 1982, Glazer and Moynihan 1975, Bell 1975). I understand that the emphasis placed in the literature on the solidarity of immigrant groups stems above all (but not only) from the view that such groups are ethnic groups and therefore have the same attributes.

But considering immigrant groups as ethnic communities leads to a specific notion of solidarity: the solidarity born from identity, solidarity among equals. This is a solidarity close to what Émile Durkheim defines as "mechanical solidarity" (1984) precisely because it emerges from communities with very little differentiation in contrast to modern industrialized societies. Taking such a notion of solidarity as a reference mitigates relationships based on power, conflict, and competition in favor of positive relationships of reciprocity within the groups. Thus ethnic solidarity, or the internal solidarity of an immigrant group, becomes incorporated as a presupposition and is not seen as a question that should be investigated empirically. Analogously, solidarity does not arise as a mechanical response given by the social structure. Forms of reciprocity and solidarity are also socially constructed.

Few authors have dedicated themselves to studying the limits of solidarity or the forms of competition and conflict between and within immigrant groups. Margolis (1994), Mahler (1995), Menjivar (2000), and Pessar (1995) are a few exceptions. This last author presents an interesting critique of the traditional and moral notion of home according to which the immigrants' homes are considered as organized only around principles of reciprocity, consensus, and altruism. Pessar shows that although occasionally they are guided by norms of solidarity, within them can also be seen power hierarchies defined by gender and generation.

If on one hand solidarity does not exhaust the set of social relationships predominant between and within ethnic groups, on the other hand attributes of ethnicity have become the object of manipulation for strictly economic purposes. Hallmark Cards Inc., for example, has been very successful in developing lines of greeting cards that reflect ethnic values and make use of ethnic cultural references. This endeavor by Hallmark has been as successful as the "go ethnic" marketing plan for the Barbie doll (Halter 1995). Halter finds that transforming culture into merchandise has always been one of the characteristics of capitalism, an inevitable result of a market society. In its new "politically correct" version, the Barbie doll comes with Latino, African American, and Native American outfits and has physical characteristics seen as typical of these groups, a strategy that, the author notes, doubled the sales of the doll in only one year. Halter shows that the valorization of ethnicity, far from being a manifestation of cultural authenticity or a means to promote the inclusion of minorities, constitutes a kind of marriage between marketing and culture that helps to construct another American myth—that of cultural diversity.

If ethnicity cannot be considered synonymous with solidarity, it is also worthwhile to understand the diverse cultural meanings the latter has. Notions of solidarity that in the United States seem very connected to community participation and forms of association acquire other connotations in Brazil. In general, solidarity in Brazil has a highly religious, and especially Catholic, connotation. Practicing solidarity means "helping whoever needs help" simply because that person is going through a period of hardship. In that situation, helping is a duty coming from an obligation to God. The other, after receiving help, should immediately and humbly recognize that he or she was helped and compensate whoever helped him or her in some way. In the American case, solidarity relates to civic culture; in the Brazilian case, it is linked to religious practices or those guided by religious values or doctrine.[9] Thus, there is a specific meaning in the Brazilians' complaint about the lack of solidarity because they are complaining, above all, about the lack of reciprocity: "I helped, and I received nothing in return."

Means of Incorporation

Finally, there are two premises regarding the means of incorporation that I believe are worth highlighting:

1) Government policies, public acceptance, and ethnic communities are as important as the immigrants' human capital in determining their means of incorporation. Intermediaries and ethnic enclaves facilitate transactions when there is confidence in the community's ability to supervise (Portes and Rumbaut 1990). More specifically, positive qualities of the social relationships within the immigrant community compensate for the low level of education of the migrant laborers.
2) The context that receives poor and working-class migrants favors the fragmentation of social ties.

In general, the literature interprets the receiving society as being invariably hostile to the immigrant workers, and the means of incorporation makes inclusion difficult and tends to keep the immigrants in poverty. But could there be peculiarities in local institutions that are modeled on the complex U.S. federal institutional system?

In the case presented here, the adoption of public policies that value or are guided by multiculturalism by the public institutions of Boston and the benefits granted by the state of Massachusetts facilitate incorporation, and thus they favor the propensity toward a favorable opinion of American society on the part of Brazilians. In aspects related to human capital and to certain demographic characteristics, recent changes involving social roles and relationships are important so we can measure how the context of reception affects the social and community characteristics of immigrant groups.

Specifically, more egalitarian relationship patterns between men and women, greater recognition of human rights (including children's rights), a growing number of divorces, and an increase in the number of female heads of household are changes that already were seen in the "expulsion context" in the Brazilian case; they therefore precede the migratory process. Considering such changes in the research could contribute to relativizing nostalgic interpretations that describe the countries of origin as stable despite being poor, semi-rural or not very industrialized, with traditional values regarding family and gender, and with a high degree of intergroup loyalty and solidarity.

By calling attention to the topics presented above, in this book I seek to contribute through empirical data and conceptual discussion to a broader understanding of emigration in Brazil and of Brazilian immigration to the United States but also to the exploration of new perspectives in migratory studies no matter what immigrant group is investigated. Among such perspectives I stress the analysis of internal dynamics and forms of solidarity that should be considered objects of investigation and not attributes of ethnicity.

2

Betting on the Future

Scenario One: On an English-made ship with a Spanish name, the *Rosario*, Antonio Della Bianca, his wife, and five children embarked from the Italian city of Genoa. They departed for America, but not for the United States. In January 1895, one month after its departure from Italy, the *Rosario* docked on the Brazilian coast, dropping off hundreds of Italians like Antonio in the south of the country.[1]

Scenario Two: Wagner Silva, Ernesto Macedo, and Cassia da Costa embarked for the United States from the São Paulo International Airport with tourist visas. Each one had come from a different region, and they had never met before. The three planned to work in Boston for two to five years, save money, and then return to the cities from which they departed in 1995.

A century separates the first scenario from the second. Among many differences, there is one particularly salient contrast between the two scenarios. While the first portrays immigration into Brazil, considered a source of national pride, the second portrays emigration from Brazil. The land that used to attract now "expels." Instead of the hope for the future expressed in the phrase "a country of immigrants," there is now a sense of discomfort and a big question: What does this mean? Indeed, Brazil was the third-largest destination for the streams of international populations during the golden age of the "great European migration," when nearly 60 million people left the Old World. Immigration into Brazil grew even more at the end of the nineteenth century, when the county received 5.1 million immigrants, almost 9% of the total number of European immigrants.[2]

Although they were fewer in number, the country continued to receive massive streams of immigrants after World War II; these continued in smaller proportions until approximately the end of the 1970s. After that, the arrival of new immigrants stagnated, and a new picture took shape. From having been the third-largest destination for European immigrants,

Brazil came to be considered a country with a "closed population" (Patarra 1996, Fusco 2002). Nevertheless, the sociodemographic reversals are not limited to this phenomenon. Indeed, the 1970s represented merely one moment in a long-term change that in the 1980s came as a real shock. And it was precisely shock that the first disclosures about Brazilian emigration by the press caused in the country. Many questions were soon directed to the academic community. Who are the emigrants? Where are they leaving from and for what reasons? And above all: How many Brazilian emigrants are there? José Alberto Magno de Carvalho, one of the most important Brazilian demographers, in his search for answers to explain this new picture, carried out a comparative study of the Brazilian population (1995), which he surveyed in 1980 and again in 1991; he concluded that, given the projections determined by his study, the Brazilian population would decrease between 1–2 million and 5 million people. The data were fundamental to the calculation of the importance of the phenomenon that had begun quietly in the previous decade.

The Continual Increase

The 2000 U.S. Census recorded the presence of 231,270 Brazilians in the United States. As the great majority of these Brazilians are undocumented, the census numbers tend to be underestimated. The same holds true for the results of the 1990 U.S. Census, which recorded the presence of 94,023 Brazilians in the country. The numbers are underestimated because there was no category of "Brazilian" either in the 1990 Census or the 2000 Census, which made the exact quantification of this population impossible. In addition, although undocumented Brazilian immigrants can be counted in the census, it is less likely that they will be because they have to make statements to a government agency. The 1990 Census counted 37,817 Brazilians in New England, 12,000 of them in Massachusetts. In the 2000 Census, however, the number jumped to 36,669 in that state (Margolis 1994, 2002). What can be concluded by comparing the results of the two censuses is that although Brazilian immigrants' numbers may be underestimated, the data indicate a large growth in their numbers in the United States during the 1990s.

Again according to the official numbers, 22,310 Brazilian immigrants were legally admitted into the United States between the 1966 and 1979. In the 1980s this number rose to 33,475.[3] In 1990 the U.S. government granted amnesty to immigrants who were working illegally in agriculture through the Seasonal Agricultural Workers (SAW) program promoted by the Immigration Reform and Control Act of 1986. Only 1,200 Brazilians filed applications for U.S. citizenship under the auspices of this program (De Biaggi 1992). However, almost ten years later, 61,850 Brazilians were granted permanent legal residence between 2001 and 2005, surpassing the official limit of 50,000 green cards granted in the previous five-year period.[4]

The first unofficial data regarding the Brazilian population in the United States were supplied by the Catholic Church. According to the Boston Archdiocese, 150,000 Brazilian immigrants lived in Massachusetts at the end of the 1990s. The first estimates from the Brazilian government made use of the numbers published by the Catholic Church: 800,000 Brazilians lived in the United States, 150,000 of them in Boston. Thus the New York metropolitan area, where there are believed to be 300,000 Brazilians, and Miami, where there are believed to be 250,000, had greater concentrations of Brazilians than Boston had. If the numbers from the last U.S. Census seem much lower than the actual numbers, those from the Catholic Church and the Brazilian government itself may be higher. What is certain is that no research has been done with sufficient methodological rigor to ensure the reliability and validity of the data. This being the case, the number of Brazilian residents in the United States as a whole and in the Boston area in particular is really unknown.

The hypothesis regarding the increase in the Brazil-U.S. migratory flow also can be confirmed through the analysis of other available data such as the number of visas granted. Between 1980 and 1998, the number of U.S. non-immigrant visas granted to Brazilian citizens grew continually. Until the end of the 1990s, it was with that type of visa, more specifically with a tourist visa, that the great majority of Brazilians who intended to immigrate entered the United States. The 935,000 non-immigrant visas issued to Brazilians in 1998 put the United States into the top four countries in the world in terms of the number of this type of visa granted to Brazilians that year. However, the number of visas granted in the non-immigrant category decreased continually from 1998 to 2003, when a slight increase was again observed.

Even so, Brazil remained among the top nine countries in the number of visas granted in the non-immigrant category in 2000, although the number fell to 734,000 visas issued by the U.S. government that year.

Table 2.1. Non-Immigrants by Country of Citizenship, Brazil and Total

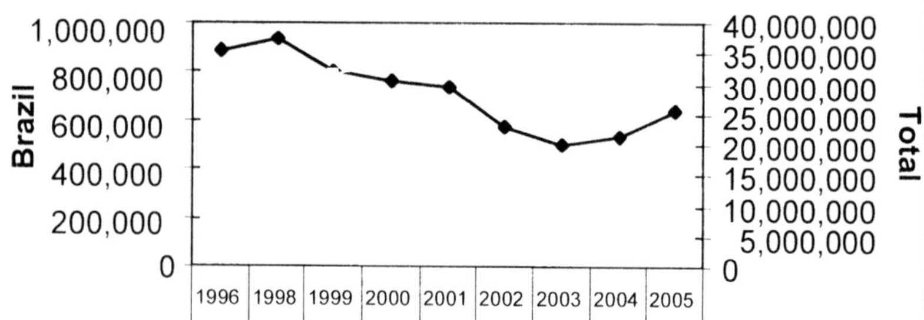

	1996	1998	1999	2000	2001	2002	2003	2004	2005
Brazil	882.9	934.6	802.1	761.9	733.9	576.4	497.0	534.1	636.1
Total	24.84	30.17	31.49	33.66	32.82	27.90	27.84	30.78	32.00

Source: U.S. Department of Homeland Security 2006b.
Note: Non-immigrant visas are all those that do not fall into the category of visas granted by the government for immigration purposes.

The number of non-immigrant visas granted for all countries and the number granted to Brazilian citizens generally have remained proportional. In other words, since 1998 the total number of visas granted by the United States has declined, and the number granted to Brazilians follows this tendency (Table 2.1). Due to the increased restrictions on entry into the United States after September 11, 2001, Brazilians began to use illegal means to enter the country, especially by illegal border crossing, as will be discussed later.

From the available data regarding the granting of visas, it can be observed that the legal immigration of Brazilians into the United States increased, rising from 22,000 in the 1970s to 33,000 the following decade and reaching a total of 92,000 by 2004 (DHS Office of Immigration Statistics, 2006a). Although there was a small decrease in 2003, possibly related to the September 11 attacks, in 2004 the number of immigrants legally admitted again rose, reaching 10,504, the largest number recorded to date.

Paradoxically, it is perhaps possible to conclude that the impact of September 11 made voluntary return to Brazil more difficult than the entry of Brazilians into Massachusetts (Margolis 2008b). This difficulty increased but not to the point of stopping the migratory flow, although obviously the entry strategies changed and the risks increased greatly. In the face of the denial of visas, the long and dangerous crossing through Mexico became the only possible means of access into U.S. territory. This can be seen clearly in the number of arrests made of those attempting to cross the Mexican border into the United States, which in 2004 reached a total of 2,444 Brazilians (*Folha de São Paulo*, February 27, 2007). In 2005 the number rose to almost 30,000 Brazilians arrested trying to enter through Mexico (ibid.). Deportations continued throughout the 2000s. To illustrate this simply, according to the consul general of Brazil in Boston, in early 2007 the number of Brazilians detained awaiting deportation was 150 in Massachusetts, and that number increased to 200 by the middle of the year. The average number of Brazilians deported each month increased from 37 to 45 in the state of Massachusetts (Agência Estado, March 16, 2008).

Despite the deportations and the U.S. economic crisis, the data collected by the present research corroborates the hypothesis that Brazilians continue to arrive in Massachusetts in large numbers. The survey conducted in 1996 found that of the 300 people interviewed, 40% arrived in the United States during the 1980s and 58% arrived from 1990 on (2% did not respond). Of the 300 people interviewed in 2005, 35% had arrived before 2000 and 64% from 2001 on. This means that almost 60% of the interviewees had lived in the United States for fewer than six years in 1996 and that 64% in 2005 had been living in the United States for no more than four years. And there is yet another consideration. Since 2003, government estimates of the number of Brazilian emigrants have almost doubled. The Brazilian Ministry of Foreign Relations indicated that there were 2.5 million Brazilian emigrants worldwide and 1.5 million in the United States alone. However, no research conducted to verify this data has yet been presented. What happened was simply that from that time on, Brazilian newspapers began to take these numbers as official data.

In 2009 the same ministry published on its Internet site three estimates of the number of Brazilians abroad. The highest estimate counted 3,735,826 Brazilians abroad and the lowest, 2,059,623. The estimate of the consulates and embassies throughout the world indicated that there were 3,044,762 Brazilian emigrants in 2009 (Brazil, MRE 2009).

The Country That Expels Still Attracts

Brazilians are leaving Brazil. However, in Brazil the phenomena of emigration and immigration occur simultaneously. According to the São Paulo Pastoral Letter on the Immigrant (Giannini and Guedes 2005), the number of recently arrived immigrants to Brazil is about 1 to 1.5 million, the majority of whom live in the state capital of São Paulo, a city that has for many of them the same significance that the state of Florida does for Brazilian immigrants to the United States. They include Bolivians, Peruvians, Chinese, South Koreans, Lebanese, and Africans coming mainly from Portuguese-speaking countries; the majority of immigrants live and work without documentation. Some are recruited while still in their countries of origin by the promise of employment and are guaranteed board and work when they arrive in Brazil.

Constant allegations are promulgated in the media that a proportion of this labor force is working in conditions of near-slavery, especially in the city of São Paulo. Being generally economic refugees, these immigrants subject themselves to long hours of poorly compensated work. Those who work in the clothing industry in small, illegal sweatshops receive the equivalent of $140 per month on average. They often arrive at 7 A.M. and leave at 10 P.M. each day and work in unhealthy conditions that lack adequate ventilation and light. Nevertheless, the wages most could earn in their countries of origin were less than $50 per month. Everything indicates that they have less purchasing power than do the Brazilians who go to the United States, but they are not in a position to pay the costs necessary to get there (Giannini and Guedes 2005).

The Bolivian presence in Brazil in particular has increased beginning in the 1980s due to the crisis in the mining sector in that country. Currently the majority of Bolivian immigrants are young people of both sexes who come from the cities of La Paz, Cochabamba, and Oruro and who have modest levels of formal education. They are attracted by the offer of employment in small clothing factories whose owners are not necessarily Brazilian but principally Korean and Bolivian immigrants who are already established. Despite the low salaries, the majority of these immigrants manage to send $100 to Bolivia every two or three months (Silva 2006). The Brazilian Ministry of Justice estimates that about 80,000 Bolivians, both legal and undocumented, are living in the country (ibid.).

The migratory flow of Colombians and Peruvians to the Brazilian Amazon region also intensified in the 1980s, especially to the Tabatinga region about 700 miles from the city of Manaus. The points of origin of that flow are the cities of Santa Rosa in Peru and Leticia in Colombia, which are known as drug-trafficking centers. These are flows of undocumented immigrants characterized by family groups and consisting of unskilled laborers with little formal education (M. Oliveira 2006).

In general, the most recent immigration is primarily voluntary, with Korean immigration being one of the few exceptions. In the 1960s the officially sanctioned landing of thousands of Koreans in Brazil began gradually. The political and socioeconomic interests of the South Korean government led it to encourage emigration not only to Brazil but also to other Latin American countries. This emigration emerged as a means of getting around demographic problems (overpopulation) and unemployment, as well as to gain allies in the noncommunist world (Giannocaro 2006, Azevedo 2005, Galetti 1995). Choi (1991) noted 50,000 Koreans from the regions of Kyungsan-Do, Seoul, and Kyungki-Do living in Brazil. This population is concentrated in the city of São Paulo and works in clothing manufacturing, an industry traditionally dominated by Jewish immigrants (Truzzi 2001).

In addition to other categories of legal and undocumented immigrants, Brazil takes in African political refugees, especially from Angola and Liberia, as well as Colombian, Palestinian, and Asian refugees largely from Afghanistan. With the exception of African immigrants, the rest are predominantly family groups. Some of the Africans use Brazil as a bridge to the United States, where they in fact desire to stay. Many embark clandestinely on ships and, upon docking in the United States, present an official request for refugee status, alleging that they are victims of tribal warfare.

There is one final observation. Considering the estimated number of recent immigrants indicated earlier, from 1 million to 1.5 million, and the estimated number of Brazilian emigrants between 1.5 million and 2.5 million, it can be inferred that Brazil does not experience a significant population deficit. The economic dynamism typical of the border regions and the informal economy of the city of São Paulo still appear as factors that attract new immigrants.

Beyond the U.S. Border

Brazilians have immigrated not only to the United States in the past few decades. Although this has been the principal destination (38%), many Brazilians are leaving for Paraguay (30%) and Japan (13%) as well (IBGE 2009). The European continent also receives Brazilian emigrants, whose most common destinations are Germany, Italy, Portugal, England, France, and Spain.[5] Many of these are return immigrants who are not necessarily legal.

Brazilian immigration to Paraguay, which represents the country's second-largest migratory movement (350,000 Brazilians), began slowly in the 1970s. It can be divided into three basic categories, according to Tomás Palau (2001): small and medium-size family entrepreneurs leaving from the south of Brazil who wish to acquire land at a lower price; small-scale tenant farmers; and day laborers in Brazil who emigrate as agricultural employees or landless agricultural workers. In general, these constitute rural and border flows and are marked by constant accusations of exploitation, poor treatment, and even forced labor. These are unskilled and uneducated workers who are predominantly undocumented.

Although the flows Brazil–United States and Brazil–Japan both arose in the 1980s, they constitute different types of emigration because the latter case involves return migration that has institutional support from the Japanese state. On one side, Brazil has 1.3 million descendants of Japanese immigrants, and the city of São Paulo has the greatest concentration of ethnic Japanese in the world outside of Japan itself. On the other side, approximately 200,000 second- and third-generation Japanese Brazilians currently reside in Japan. The Japanese-Brazilian immigrants, called *dekasseguis*,[6] receive a regular entry visa under the category of temporary workers and are generally recruited while still in Brazil to work in the Japanese automobile industry. Return immigration to Japan in the same period affected other South American countries, especially Peru. However, Brazilians of Japanese descent currently represent the third-largest contingent of recent immigrants into Japan. The provinces in which Brazilians are concentrated are Aichi (41,000), Shizuoka (31,000), and Nagano (15,000) (Sasaki 1999, Kawamura 1999).

Brazilian Immigration to the United States

Brazilian emigration branches out to various countries; particularly in the United States, Brazilians not only continue to arrive in large numbers but also are spreading throughout U.S. territory and diversifying their destinations, as Table 2.2 shows.

According to U.S. Census Bureau figures, in the 1980s and 1990s Brazilians were concentrated in two states: New York and California. The 2000 Census records concentrations of Brazilians in five states: Florida, Massachusetts, California, New Jersey, and New York. The other states have a total of almost 76,000 Brazilians, and the total number of Brazilian residents rose from 48,000 in 1980 to 247,000 in 2000 (Goza 2004).

Margolis observes (2009) that the vast majority of Brazilians surveyed by the U.S. Census are still attracted to the same five states. Since 2000, however, 25% of Brazilians sought alternatives to the traditional areas. Margolis finds that Brazilians are departing for Washington, D.C., Philadelphia, Chicago, Houston, Los Angeles, San Francisco, and San Diego. Earlier studies showed Brazilians and other immigrants to the United States in the 1990s heading for regions not traditionally associated with foreign immigration (Dillon 1997, Christian 1998). Researcher Cassandra White (2010) has estimated that 40,000 to 50,000 Brazilians live in the Atlanta metropolitan area.[7] In addition, there is evidence that a second phase of migration is occurring, as when, for example, Brazilians from New York or Boston move to Florida (Burger 2001; Margolis 2002: 55).

In 2002 an estimated 100,000 Brazilians were living in Miami and 200,000 in the entire state of Florida (Capuano 2002). Particularly in the areas of Pompano Beach and Miami-Dade County, Brazilians are known

Table 2.2. Brazilians by U.S. state, 1980–2000

	1980	1990	2000
California	8,688	15,304	29,640
Florida	3,024	10,301	49,153
Massachusetts	2,880	11,674	42,237
New Jersey	4,800	11,870	25,194
New York	8,352	16,677	24,947
Other	20,256	32,275	75,829
Total	48,000	98,101	247,000

Source: U.S. Census of Population, 1980–2000 (extracted from Goza 2004: 7).

to occupy certain niches of the labor market such as housecleaning, delivery, and automobile valet services for hotel chains along the coast. In this there is nothing new because in the other U.S. states Brazilians also occupy positions in the so-called informal sector, or the third sector, of the labor market. What really distinguishes Brazilian immigration into Florida is the presence of a considerable number of entrepreneurs with whom the rest of the Brazilian population rarely interacts (Capuano 2002). Such entrepreneurs are more and more attracted to that region due to the increase in Brazil-U.S. trade relations because, "according to the Brazilian-American Chamber of Commerce (BACC), in 2000 Brazil had seven million dollars in imports (an increase of a million dollars over 1999), and Venezuela, the second largest trade partner, imported less than half that amount. Comparing this with U.S. import figures, in the same year Florida imported more that three million U.S. dollars in Brazilian products and goods" (Resende 2003: 144).

The largest number of Brazilian residents in New England is concentrated in Massachusetts. But in that region the state of Connecticut stands out as well, especially Danbury but also Hartford, Bridgeport, Norwalk, and Milford. Danbury, a city of approximately 75,000 inhabitants, is home to the largest number of Brazilians in Connecticut, representing 10% of the local resident population. Initially Brazilians were attracted to that city due to its community of Portuguese descent. "On Main Street alone—which, as its name suggests, is one of the principal streets of the city—one can find twenty Brazilian commercial and service businesses, two academies, and five churches" (Menezes 2002: 164). Brazilians also live in the states of Rhode Island (East Providence) and New Hampshire (Nashua).

The State of Massachusetts

In the 1990s Massachusetts had the fifth-largest relative concentration of immigrants in the United States,[8] and records show 573,733 "foreign-borns," half of whom arrived between 1980 and 1990 (Lapham 1990). With regard to racial composition, 90% of the state's population was white, 5% black, and 5% of Hispanic origin. In Massachusetts 9% of the population lived below the poverty line; this population was comprised primarily of Hispanics and, to a lesser degree, African Americans.[9] According to the 1990 Census, the state received the fifth-largest population of refugees and the seventh-largest population of recently arrived immigrants.

In contrast to the majority of U.S. cities in which immigrants of the same ethnicity have tended to concentrate, in Boston no one ethnic group was predominant.[10]

Massachusetts experienced great economic growth in the early 1980s when it attracted new immigrants to the point that some aspects of the state's demographic profile were altered. Along with economic expansion came a substantial increase in job openings for unskilled laborers at low wages, especially in the service sector. The state has a long tradition as a safe refuge for foreigners seeking religious and political freedom. In 1980 Puerto Ricans comprised the majority of the Hispanic population in the Greater Boston area (54%), but in 1990 this proportion fell to 42% with the arrival of Mexicans, Cubans, and Dominicans. An economic recession reached the state in the late 1980s, reducing the income of workers in the formal and informal markets and raising the unemployment rate. From the recession of 1988 on, there was a flight of high-technology industries and banks to the southern and western regions of the United States (Halter 1995).

In the first five years of the twenty-first century, the number of foreign residents in Massachusetts increased 15.4% over that in the 1990s, following the trend in the United States as a whole, which experienced an increase of 16%. Almost 14.4% of the population of that state was foreign-born in 2005, and of that total, 37% had come from Latin America. The Brazilian population grew the most (131.4%) between 2000 and 2005, followed by the populations of Africans, Asians, and people from the Caribbean. Europeans were the only group whose population fell during the period, with a decrease of 4.6%.

The cities in Massachusetts that have attracted the most immigrants are Boston, Cambridge, Somerville, Lynn, Lowell, Lawrence, Quincy, and Brockton. In 2005, immigrants comprised 27.7% of the population residing in Boston, up from 25.8% in 2000. However, the greatest increase in the number of foreigners occurred in Framingham, where the proportion of foreign-born residents jumped from 21.1% of the total population in 2000 to 28.1% in 2005 (Levenson and Zeng 2006).

The metropolitan area of the United States with the greatest concentration of Brazilians in 2000 was that of Boston (5,068), followed by Fort Lauderdale (3,342) and Miami (2,212), according to the 2000 U.S. Census. In the Greater Boston area, Brazilians are concentrated in Cambridge, Allston-Brighton, Boston (especially East Boston), Somerville, Marlborough,

Lowell, and Framingham.[11] Outside the Boston metropolitan area, Brazilians live in Cape Cod, the state's famous resort area. The Support Center for Brazilian Immigrants in Cape Cod, an entity created in 1996, recorded the presence of 360 Brazilian immigrants who were residents of the region, especially of the city of Hyannis, and who were working in local bars and restaurants.

Creating Links, Forming Networks

Brazilians began to arrive in Massachusetts in large numbers in the mid-1980s, but it was during the 1960s that the first Brazilians arrived there.[12] According to the statements of some of these pioneers, the number of Brazilian residents in Massachusetts at that time was small, although the exact number is unknown. However, the importance of these early immigrants lies in their initial networks that gave support to the migratory movement that emerged almost twenty years later.[13] Early immigrants have described various social networks that gave rise to and supported this movement.[14]

1) During World War II, American engineers and technicians from Boston went to the Governador Valadares region to work in the extraction of ore and established the first contacts between the two cities.[15] When the war ended, employees of the Morrison Company, headquartered in Boston, went to the Aço River Valley region to work on the construction of the railroad that links the region to the Brazilian state of Espírito Santo. On returning to the United States, some of these employees would have brought with them the domestic workers they had hired in Brazil. The extraction of ore in Governador Valadares at the time of World War II led the U.S. government to sponsor programs to combat malaria in the region as well as to establish water and sewage systems (De Biaggi 1992). Such initiatives contributed to the creation of the Brazilian city's links with the United States.
2) Some Brazilians went to Boston to study and brought relatives who also decided to stay there.
3) After World War II, U.S. entrepreneurs established connections with the Governador Valadares region with the intent of developing trade in the semiprecious stones that were extracted there.

4) During the 1960s, newspapers in Rio de Janeiro and São Paulo published advertisements to recruit women who were willing to go to Boston to work in domestic service.
5) In the 1960s a U.S. entrepreneur organized a soccer team in Lowell, a small city near Boston. About twenty Brazilians from the city of Belo Horizonte in Minas Gerais were contracted by the entrepreneur and later decided to stay in Boston and help family members emigrate.
6) In the late 1960s a group of more than ten young people from Governador Valadares decided to "try their luck" and went to "spend some time" in the United States, the dream country of these young people. They departed for New York and then kept "going up" until they arrived in Boston, going after the jobs offered in the hotels that constituted the New England tourist circuit. Some returned to Brazil, but others remained in Boston and encouraged family members to emigrate to Massachusetts. The veracity of these data collected during interviews was not investigated as part of this research.

Emigration as Part of the Local Culture

In no other Brazilian city is the migratory movement as visible as it is in Governador Valadares. Weber Soares (1995) has noted that 15% of the population of the city has emigrated for other parts of the world.[16] Soares shows how the real estate market had resounding growth throughout the 1980s despite an economic recession that hit the city hard. The real estate market grew surprisingly, Soares finds, thanks to the remittances of dollars sent by the emigrants from that region: "The emigrants were responsible for 36% of the total number of transactions involving land, houses, apartments, and commercial buildings in Valadares: more than one-third of all of the real estate transactions between 1984 and 1993" (1995: 59).

With only 250,000 inhabitants, in 2003 the city had seventy officially registered travel agencies (Resende 2003). Soares notes (2002: 114), "The distribution of these agencies over time shows a correlation between the period in which the greatest number of them were established and the period during which emigration was at its most intense: 60% of the agencies appeared from 1985 to 1989, and 43.6% of the emigrants left Valadares in precisely this same period. In 1991 Valadares, which had approximately 210,000 inhabitants, had a total of 45 travel agencies." From 1990 to 1994, there were reductions in the migratory flow and in the number of new travel agencies, of which only fourteen appeared during this period (Soares 1995: 73, 74).

During my visits to the city, the first in 1997 and the second in 2004, I found that some travel agencies, although not all, financed tickets, had some type of connection with visa and passport counterfeiting networks, rented buses to transport those called for interviews at the U.S. consulate to obtain visas, and provided advice regarding how the applicants should dress when appearing for interviews at the consulate and what they should say.[17] Networks even provided counterfeit receipts, pay stubs, and contacts in the United States in case candidates had no relatives or friends to help them upon arrival. Some financing agents provided these services as a package.

In 1997 an agent would make all of the arrangements for the trip as described above and charge between $5,000 and $10,000 per person for this service. When such an agent was used, the cost of the service was paid in installments, and the candidate left the agent a piece of real estate as collateral. These agencies thus reduced the costs associated with the trip, and in many cases hiring a financing agent was the only way of making the choice to emigrate viable. They performed a function similar to that performed by the employers of immigrants, whom Piore (1979) calls "active agents" in the migratory movements. It is important to remember that even in the 1990s, Brazilians born in the Governador Valadares region who had certain occupational profiles and were between the ages of nineteen and thirty-five had difficulty obtaining U.S. entry visas.

This situation became even more drastic after September 11, 2001, when it became practically impossible for a resident of the city of Governador Valadares to obtain a tourist visa to enter the United States. Such difficulties led many people from Valadares to resort to financing agents (*coyotes*) as the only means of making it possible for them to enter the country. This option involved forged passports, desert crossings, and trips that could last a month and whose trajectory those who undertook them were unable to reconstruct. Under these circumstances, not only did the physical and emotional costs increase, including risk to the emigrants' lives, but also the financial cost. While in the 1990s the prices that the agents charged ranged from $5,000 to $10,000, by the early twenty-first century an illegal crossing could cost as much as $15,000 per person.

Governador Valadares as well as the small neighboring cities have a culture of emigration. The regional newspapers of the Vale do Rio Doce, the Aço River Valley, describe in detail the successes achieved by those who decide to emigrate. This means that the experiences lived in other countries into which local inhabitants are immigrating are transported into the daily life of these cities, generating positive expectations that feed the desire to emigrate and further create strong links between the cities that constitute the poles of the migratory flows (Margolis 1994, Assis 1995). In the northern part of the Brazilian state of Minas Gerais, the Aço River Valley, of which the city of Ipatinga is the regional pole, was home in 1996 to 8% and in 2005 to 6% of the total number of those whom I interviewed.[18] The inhabitants of the small cities surrounding Ipatinga had poorer chances of getting employment with Usiminas, the industry around which the city of Ipatinga was formed. In just two years, from 1991 to 1993, Usiminas reduced its workforce from 13,000 to 10,500, and the reduction of the workforce gradually intensified throughout the 1990s (Costa 1995).

But the migratory movement of Brazilians into the United States is no longer a phenomenon limited to Governador Valadares, nor even one that is limited to the Brazilian state of Minas Gerais. In the late 1990s, in addition to Brazilian state capitals, two other locations began to distinguish themselves as "emigration cities"—Criciúma and Poços de Caldas.

Criciúma is in the south of the Brazilian state of Santa Catarina; unlike Valadares, it is a city of German and Italian immigrants who settled there near the end of the nineteenth century. Assis has found that the grandchildren and great-grandchildren of Italian immigrants began to return to Italy in the 1980s: "Throughout the 1990s, this movement began to change its direction toward the United States. Although accounts collected in the city indicate that there was already movement of migrants toward the United States in the 1970s, it is with the coming of the 1980s that the flow increases. According to the inhabitants of the city, the emigration movement was directly related to the crisis in the coal-producing sector, the main economic activity of the region until the beginning of the 1990s" (2003: 210). The country that most attracts emigrants from Criciúma is the United States (60.2% of men and 58.3% of women), followed by Italy and Portugal. The majority of those who arrive in the United States have the Boston metropolitan area as their destination.

For emigrants from Poços de Caldas in southern Minas Gerais, though, Mount Vernon, Washington, has become the principal destination. One of the local radio stations transmits a weekly program on which Brazilian residents of Mount Vernon talk live with the residents of Poços de Caldas. Poços de Caldas has been portrayed in Brazilian media as a "city of emigration." In 2005, newspapers published long reports about financing agents and *coyotes* who, when they began to be pursued by the Federal Police in Governador Valadares, moved to Poços de Caldas, where a few had previously operated more cautiously. Poços de Caldas has almost 150,000 inhabitants, 56% of whom are below the age of 30. It is a city in the long Mantiqueira mountain range with many tourist attractions, notably nature reserves and mineral springs. Due to its natural beauty, Poços, as it is called, attracts tourists from all over Brazil, especially senior citizens, and it is the headquarters of the multinational corporation Alcoa, a large producer of aluminum. Near Poços, other small cities such as Botelhos, which has only about 10,000 inhabitants, also share in a culture of emigration. In this region of southern Minas Gerais, the emigration that until the late 1990s was mainly directed toward the United States may be slowly moving toward Europe (Spain, Portugal, and Italy) and toward Australia. Such alternative destinations are of particular interest to, and less risky for, those who have or can get dual citizenship due to their European ancestry. There are also those who understand that emigrating first to Europe is a strategy for later being able to enter the United States.

How can it be explained that a city with relatively many natural and economic resources has become a city of emigration? According to one of those I interviewed, a pioneer who emigrated in 1969, it all started "as an adventure." Local middle-class young people merely went to visit the United States but then decided to extend their stay a bit more, encouraged by how easy it was to get jobs that paid well. Later, as with any network-forming process, the flow expanded, pushed along by the poor state of the Brazilian economy in the 1980s. Now, in the beginning of the twenty-first century, it is possible that this city has come to have proportionally as many emigrants as Governador Valadares.

Here I have highlighted only three cities that are departure points for Brazilian emigration. In them can be seen an emerging "immigration industry" that offers services designed to circumvent a series of difficulties inherent in the migratory process.[19] Besides the financing agents are agencies that handle immigrants' monetary remittances to Brazil.

In this region social networks, remittance agencies, financing agents, and the media constitute the set of institutions that lend support to the migratory movement. Through social networks, financing is obtained for the trip to and arrival in the United States or other destination country.[20] The agencies finance airfare and arrange visas and passports. The media, in turn, publish positive accounts of the experiences of Brazilians who have emigrated, thereby encouraging more to emigrate, although some media also explore the dark side of immigrants' lives in America.

A Profile of the Brazilian Immigrant

In its issue dated May 30, 1990, the news magazine *Veja* published an article titled "Brazucas de Boston."[21] The "typical Brazilian immigrant," according to the article, was male, young, and single, or if married, his family remained in Brazil. Other studies at that time confirmed this profile, at least in part (Margolis 1994, Sales 1993, Bicalho 1989).

Supposing this was an accurate portrait years ago, the results gathered in the current study present a much more complex picture. In this study, I intend to show that a typical profile of the Brazilian immigrant does not exist. The data collected in the survey conducted during my investigation in 1996 indicate that although the immigrants were still young (67% of the population interviewed was younger than 34), this contingent included young men and women in equal proportion as well as married and single people in fairly even numbers, and more than half (52%) of those who had minor children lived with them in the United States.

The research was replicated in 2005 under the same conditions as the survey conducted in 1996. The most striking aspect of the results is the absence of any significant change, as can be observed in Table 2.3.

Of the 300 people interviewed in 1996, 60% were men and 40% were women. According to Bicalho (1989), at the end of the 1980s, 66% of the Brazilian population in Boston was made up of men and 33% of women. It can thus be concluded that the number of Brazilian women in Massachusetts is increasing. In fact, the survey conducted in 2005 confirms this tendency, indicating that 43% of the respondents were women.

Most of the Brazilian immigrants (62%) fell into the age range of 21 to 34 years old in 1996, and this finding remained virtually unchanged

Table 2.3. Brazilians in Massachusetts: Comparison of Sociodemographic Data, 1996 and 2005

	1996 (%)	2005 (%)
Age		
15 to 20 years	5	8
21 to 34 years	62	60
35 to 45 years	28	23
46 years and older	4	9
No response	1	-
Place of residence of minor children		
All in Massachusetts	52	55
At least one in Brazil	37	45
No response	6	-
None	5	-
Marital status		
Married	48	45
Single	42	45
Separated/divorced	7	5
Widowed	1	1
No response	2	5
Level of education		
Attended primary school	12	4
Finished primary school	9	7
Attended high school	14	14
High school graduate	31	42
Attended college	12	20
College graduate	16	11
No response	6	1
Stated reason for emigration		
More jobs, higher salaries, more opportunities (for children as well)	30	41
Learning, new experiences, education	14	11
To earn money to acquire assets in Brazil	13	4
Reunite with or accompany family member	10	15
Financial difficulties	15	25
Personal problems	5	10
Lack of safety	-	1
To help family in Brazil	-	3
None	13	1

Source: Martes, surveys 1996 and 2005.

in the data collected in 2005. In terms of marital status, Table 2.3 shows that a relative majority of the total number of those surveyed in 1996 were married. The slight decrease in the number of married individuals in 2005 may indicate a certain instability in the ratio between single and married people.

Family

In 1996, of all those surveyed, 49% did not have minor children, and 50% had at least one minor child. Of these, 24% had only one child, 15% had two children, 9% had three children, and 3% had four or more children. According to the data from the 2005 survey, the proportion of Brazilians with minor children grew to 55%, as did that of immigrants whose minor children lived with them in Massachusetts (also 55%) (Table 2.3).

The 1996 survey showed that among the male population, 28% did not have minor children, and among females, 50% did not have minor children. In the 2005 survey, the ratio between men and women without minor children remained virtually the same. Of the women with minor children, 23% (in 1996) and 25% (in 2005) had left their minor children in Brazil; even more interestingly, among the women in this category, half were married and the rest were separated, divorced, or widowed (less than 6% were widowed). This may indicate that the women emigrated alone and were sending money to their cities of origin, taking at least partial responsibility for the support of their minor children in Brazil. The qualitative interviews show that in general it is the maternal grandparents who become responsible for the minor children whose parents emigrate, providing evidence that emigration is, in many cases, part of a family project. It can be further observed that the separated or divorced women are older than the men of the same marital status. This may indicate an increase in the number of Brazilians who emigrate with their nuclear families as well as suggesting that a process of family reunification may be under way.

Level of Education

Comparing the data from the 1996 and 2005 surveys, almost no change can be observed among Brazilians who stated that they had finished primary school (9% and 7%, respectively). The greatest difference occurs among those who in 2005 stated that they had graduated from high school (42%), that is, almost half of those surveyed as compared to only about a third (31%) in 1996. Along with this, the number of those who stated that they had attended or graduated from college also rose. In the 1996 survey, 12% had attended college, although they did not necessarily graduate, and by 2005 the proportion rose to 20%. The 1996 data indicate a high concentration (45%) of respondents, almost half, who had at least some high school education. The 2005 survey recorded a rise in levels of education among Brazilian immigrants, 62% of whom had graduated from high school and done some college work. Compared to the levels of education in the overall Brazilian population, these data also indicate that the immigrants interviewed had higher levels of education than the average Brazilian. According to Brazil's National Research for Domicile Sampling, PNAD (2004), only 26% of the Brazilian population had eleven or more years of education.

The female interviewees had higher levels of education than the male interviewees both in 1996 and 2005. This is not surprising given that "women in Brazil have an average of a half-year more of higher education than men (7.0 versus 6.8)" (PNAD/IBGE 2004).

Table 2.3 shows that respondents having some college education comprised 28% of the total number of interviewees in 1996 and 31% in 2005. This result is much lower than Margolis found in New York (1994: 147): 46% of her interviewees had attended college in Brazil, and 31% had graduated. As only 24% of Americans have university degrees, Margolis concluded that the average level of education of Brazilian immigrants in that city is higher than that of the U.S. population. However, in my research this did not prove true in Boston.

One piece of data relevant to this discussion is that among those interviewed in 1996, only one was a graduate of a Brazilian public university; that is, all the rest had studied at private colleges or universities in Brazil. This did not change in 2005, when none of those surveyed had graduated from a public university. In Brazil, only a limited number of students are accepted into the free public universities, so competition for admittance to these institutions is fierce. In order to do well on the rigorous entrance examination (the *vestibular*), most students must attend an expensive private secondary school or pay for private tutoring. Consequently, Brazilians from less affluent social classes are more often excluded from public universities. In addition, some programs offered by private colleges and universities in the interior of Brazil have difficulty attracting the most qualified faculty and students. Although there are exceptions, degrees from private schools are less valued in the Brazilian labor market. Having a degree that is less valued in the labor market may be a fundamental variable in explaining why people with levels of education above the average in their native country opt for emigration despite knowing that in the destination country they will have less prestigious occupations than those they had in Brazil.

In isolation, level of education may thus be only part of the explanation and should be correlated with the value or lack of value of a degree from the school attended. Another part of the explanation should be sought in the transformations occurring in the Brazilian labor market. That market increasingly requires professionals with postgraduate studies, more work experience, and proficiency in at least two languages.[22] During the 1980s, under the influence of multinational corporations headquartered in Brazil, the labor market underwent a kind of reversal in the relationship between education and absorption into the labor market. Academic competence appeared as "a necessary but insufficient condition for the development of careers" in the private sector (Grun 1992).

Place of Origin in Brazil

In 1992 the *Boston Globe* reported on a study showing that up until 1987, 90% of Brazilians came from Governador Valadares. Five years later, Brazilian community leaders told the *Globe* they had seen a decrease in the proportion of people from Valadares in the Brazilian immigrant population (De Biaggi 1992). Nevertheless, they confirmed that at least half of Brazilian immigrants still came from that city.

The results of the present study indicate that even in the 1990s, there was great diversity in the points of origin of the migratory flow. In 1996, in response to the question "Where did you live before coming to the United States?" sixteen Brazilian states were mentioned in addition to the Federal District.[23] These states were Ceará, Piauí, Maranhão, Pará, Roraima, Goiás, Rio Grande do Sul, Santa Catarina, Paraná, São Paulo, Rio de Janeiro, Espírito Santo, Minas Gerais, Bahia, Alagoas, and Pernambuco. This indicates that the migratory movement already was spreading rapidly through Brazil. Most noteworthy is that only 17% of the 1996 interviewees responded that they were born in Governador Valadares.

The ten cities with the highest numbers of emigrants represented in the 1996 survey were Governador Valadares (17%), Belo Horizonte (11%), Rio de Janeiro (9%), São Paulo (8%), Ipatinga (6%), Vitória (5%), Goiânia (4%), Anápolis (3%), Brasília (3%), and Criciúma (2%). Six of these cities

Table 2.4. Five Brazilian States Most Often Given as Last Place of Residence of Brazilian Immigrants in Massachusetts

State	1996 (%)	State	2005 (%)
Minas Gerais	47	Minas Gerais	44
São Paulo	12	São Paulo	13
Espírito Santo	10	Espírito Santo	9
Rio de Janeiro	15	Santa Catarina	5
Goiás	8	Paraná	5
Other	8	Other	24

Source: Martes, surveys 1996 and 2005.

are state capitals, and one is the national capital, which indicates that the migratory movement was predominantly urban. Yet if all the cities of origin are taken into account, it can be concluded that the majority (57%) of those interviewed emigrated from cities in the interior of Brazil.[24]

The state of Minas Gerais shows a decline in representation relative to other Brazilian states beginning in the 1990s when the emigrant's last place of residence and not his or her birthplace is considered. Of the total interviewees who arrived in the United States in or before 1989, 64% came from Minas Gerais.[25] On the other hand, the July 1996 data indicate that only 37% of the interviewees who arrived between 1990 and mid-1996 departed from that state.

With regard to last state of residence (Table 2.4), in 1996 Minas Gerais was indicated by 47% of those interviewed, followed by Rio de Janeiro (15%), São Paulo (12%), Espírito Santo (10%), Goiás (8%), and other (8%). The number of states represented in the 1996 survey was surprising, and it indicates that the migratory movement was spreading rapidly throughout Brazil. This tendency seems to be confirmed by the 2005 research. Although Minas Gerais (44%), São Paulo (13%), and Espírito Santo (9%) remained the three states with the highest levels of emigration for Massachusetts, the increased presence of two southeastern Brazilian states is notable: Paraná (5%) and Santa Catarina (5%). As the southeast of Brazil is one of Brazil's wealthiest regions, these states represent quite diverse socioeconomic situations. For some reason, emigration seems to be expanding mainly to the south, from the country's richest states.

Why Do They Emigrate?

What is motivating Brazilians to leave the country? What are the individual reasons for making this decision? A comparison of the answers given in 1996 and in 2005 indicates first an increase in the number of those who stated that they emigrated principally because the United States offered more jobs, higher salaries, and greater opportunities for the emigrants and/or their minor children. In 1996, 30% of respondents fit into this category, and in 2005 they comprised 41%. Justifying emigration as a means of solving financial difficulties also received a greater number of responses in 2005. In 1996, 15% said they had been pushed by their financial difficulties in Brazil, including insolvency as a consequence of the government's new economic plans. A third of these respondents motivated by financial difficulties made a point of emphasizing that they left the country because of the government's poor economic performance and lack of perspective in the face of crisis and economic instability. In 2005 such responses rose to 25%. Among those surveyed in 2005, somewhat fewer cited learning, new experiences, and education as their principal reasons for emigrating; these responses declined from 14% in 1996 to 11%. More significant is the decrease in the number of respondents who stated that they emigrated to earn money by working in the United States in order to acquire assets in Brazil. In 1996, 13% of respondents constituted this category, and in 2005 only 4% did.

Family reunification and/or accompanying a family member accounted for 10% of the responses in 1996 and rose to 15% in 2005. While in 1996 only 5% stated that they were going through personal problems of a nonfinancial nature, in 2005, 10% stated that they had emigrated for this reason. Among these, some cited an "existential crisis," especially the end of a romantic relationship.

It is important to emphasize that the decision to emigrate is usually motivated by several factors; it is difficult to find an interviewee who pointed to a sole reason to justify the decision to emigrate. Besides, such a decision invariably is related to a set of circumstances (perhaps the end of a marriage), to life cycle (being single, for example), to age (such as being young), and so on. Thus, in few cases does a single and clear reason arise for emigrating. It is a decision that involves an element of risk and uncertainty. Emigration means "trying out another life."

The data regarding the stated reasons for emigration are surprising in two ways. Researchers and the leaders of the Brazilian immigrant community often assert that the typical Brazilian emigrant goes to the United States with the objectives of working, saving money, and then acquiring assets in Brazil. This has been held as the principal motivation of the Brazilian immigrants in Massachusetts. The response "emigrated in search of more jobs, higher salaries, and more opportunities" appears as a principal reason for emigration independent of the variables selected (30% of respondents in 1996 and 41% in 2005); still, that response does not exclude the option of "acquiring assets upon return to Brazil" because they can be complementary.

Of the 1996 respondents, 29% gave reasons of a not directly financial nature as their principal motivation for emigrating. That is, the sum of the responses to "learning, new experiences, and education," "family reunification/accompanying a family member," and "personal problems" pertains to almost 30% of all interviewees. This number rose to 37% in 2005. The new category in 2005 of "lack of safety, legal protection, and excessive violence" to justify emigration from Brazil is significant. Although selected by only a small number of respondents (1%), this category did not appear on the 1996 survey, and therefore it possibly indicates a more recent tendency. Although it would be incorrect to conclude that all these respondents had no economic motives for emigrating, they nevertheless indicated that reasons of a strictly economic nature did not predominate in their decisions.

Combining the demographic data with the variable of reason for emigration yields at least three basic profiles; three groups stand out. The first group is made of Brazilians who left the country to raise their incomes and consumer power (for public assets or private goods) and to accumulate savings that would permit them to increase their range of opportunities either in Brazil or in the United States. For this group, emigration is a choice similar to an investment. It includes the so-called target earners (people who emigrate to "earn money" and return to Brazil to acquire assets and businesses) as well as those who emigrate in search of more opportunities or higher salaries or because they were undergoing financial difficulties in Brazil. This is the largest group and the one in which the young-adult Brazilian population of both sexes is concentrated.

The second group includes those who emigrate with the objective of increasing their "human capital" (Becker 1993). In other words, for this group emigration represents a form of investment in new skills and knowledge. The present study finds direct references to learning the English language and to the experience of becoming acquainted with and immersed in a new culture. This group includes a larger number of young and older women with higher levels of education and some of the young men.

The third group is composed of Brazilians who departed for Massachusetts with the objective of family reunification or of accompanying at least one nuclear-family member. Included in this group are people who are situated at two extremes of the age groups: young children and adolescents on one end and senior citizens (especially women) on the other.

Sociodemographic Diversity and the Dispersion of Networks

The profiles of Brazilian immigrants revealed by the present study do not correspond to the profile asserted by Brazilians who live in Massachusetts nor to the profile that is frequently published in the press, because "the Brazilian" to whom these sources refer is, possibly, the Brazilian who arrived in Massachusetts at the beginning of the migratory flow in the mid-1980s. It is possible to present another profile that is more representative of a supposed majority, but it is also necessary to consider the diversity within the Brazilian immigrant population in Massachusetts.

With due recognition of that diversity, the general profile of the Brazilian immigrant described in this research is young (up to 34 years old), equally likely to be a man or a woman, and an individual whose minor children live with him or her in the United States and not in Brazil, as previously was assumed. Although the immigrants came from almost all Brazilian states, most were from Minas Gerais and were motivated to emigrate by the possibility of taking advantage of the opportunities, jobs, and higher salaries available in the United States.

Two important characteristics of this migratory movement are its voluntary nature and the urban origin of the Brazilian immigrants. Nonetheless, it is not infrequent that a farmhand whose father was a cowhand leaves the Vale do Rio Doce region and takes a seat on the same airplane that brings the children of elites from the cities of the interior Brazilian state of Minas Gerais to the United States. Some immigrants are professionals with college degrees, but those who asked for help in filling out the research questionnaires because they barely knew how to write cannot be forgotten. In Massachusetts it is common to hear one Brazilian commenting to another, "I'm from there" and smiling. What is implied is, "I'm from Governador Valadares," like many other Brazilians who reside in Massachusetts. Nevertheless, only 17% of those interviewed responded that they were born in Valadares.

Migrants depart from Minas Gerais (including from Governador Valadares) en route to other regions of Brazil, and it is possible that some immigrants leaving from other Brazilian states have connections with migrants from Minas. Some immigrants are natives of northeastern capitals, and some are from rural Rio Grande do Sul in southern Brazil. Within the states are independent focal points of the flow, not merely in the capitals but also in cities like Anápolis in the state of Goiás and Criciúma in Santa Catarina.

Other evidence shows that Brazilian immigrants to the United States have come from many different areas of Brazil. For example, the soccer team mentioned earlier that was formed in Lowell in the 1960s with players from Belo Horizonte had no connection at all with the flow between Governador Valadares and Boston. The oldest Brazilian resident of Cape Cod lives there because he is married to a Portuguese woman whose family lived in New Bedford; thus, his case involved a process of family reunification related to Portuguese and not Brazilian immigration into that area. Other examples could be given to illustrate that the networks supporting this migratory movement seem to have many branches and different points of origin. The data indicate that the places of origin of Brazilian immigrants, whether using the basis of birthplace or last place of residence in Brazil, are quite diverse and therefore do not support a belief in the predominance of the city of Governador Valadares and the state of Minas Gerais.

The migratory movement of Brazilians to Massachusetts cannot be expressed exclusively in terms of the Valadares–Boston flow. It involves a broader movement that includes Brazil and the state of Massachusetts, not only Boston. The 2005 survey indicates that the points of origin of the extensive migratory network have penetrated throughout the vast Brazilian territory over the past twenty years, especially toward the south, a region that along with the southeast is responsible for 74% of the Brazilian GDP (IBGE 2009).

The Backslide of the Brazilian Middle Class

Despite the many causes underlying migratory movements, a few socioeconomic factors are critical to understanding Brazilian emigration: the decline of social mobility, a decrease in the availability of regular employment, and a decline in salaries. A parallel configuration of social networks is fundamental to sustaining the flows, as will be seen at the end of this chapter.

The decline in Brazilian social mobility provoked by the recession of the 1980s and by the impact of world economic restructuring (which has affected Brazil since the 1990s) was identified by Brito (1995) and Margolis (1994) as a driving force in Brazil's migratory movements to the United States as well as to Europe and Japan. Some of those previously attracted by large Brazilian cities are now departing for other countries instead. Internal migration and displacement have decreased to the center-west and toward the north of Brazil. It has become impossible for the majority of migrants to translate their spatial mobility into greater occupational and social mobility in Brazil. The restructuring of world manufacturing has affected the labor market, and along with the process of globalization, the media have helped to create a "mental image favorable to emigration" anchored in a kind of idealization of the receiving countries (Brito 1995).[26]

Patarra and Baeninger (1995) similarly have connected Brazilian emigration "to the current impossibility of internal migration any longer guaranteeing the social mobility achieved in past decades, principally by interregional migrants. The inability of the São Paulo metropolitan area to retain migratory flows as a function of the strong economic crisis and metropolitan unemployment mirrors the new economic and social configuration of the country, inducing a significant portion of middle-class young people to seek new horizons" (72).

The decline in social mobility of the Brazilian middle class, which had a significant rate of growth until the beginning of the 1980s, is a driving force in the migratory movement. In 1981 the number of job openings in urban areas began to decline (Pastore 1990). According to José Pastore (1990), reduction in opportunities for employment inhibits structural social mobility. From 1981 through 1983, an annual decrease of 2.8% occurred in the number of job openings in the formal market. In the same period, about 4 million new positions arose in the informal market; this market employs workers without formal contractual work relationships.

Nevertheless, informal employment has little impact on social mobility: only one-third as many workers in the informal market have a chance to move up socially as workers in the formal market. The 1980s were marked by a reduction in job openings in the industrial sector as well as by an increase in turnover and unemployment. In 1981, unemployment officially reached a rate of 10% (Pastore 1990).

It is not coincidental that upward social mobility is a strongly shared value among Brazilian immigrants, which obviously conflicts with the absence of good job prospects that they experienced in Brazil. In the United States, Brazilians are not seeking prestige in the traditional sense of the term. By exchanging the occupations they had in Brazil for those they will have in Massachusetts, prestige is set aside in favor of new values that are linked to an increase in consumer power and to a lifestyle and citizenship of greater equality, as will be seen later. The motives for emigration and the justification for remaining in the United States analyzed in the conclusion of this book clearly indicate this tendency toward adopting new values.

Brazilian immigrants express a feeling of failure that should not be attributed to them personally but rather to the political and economic situation in the country. When they departed for the United States, many of them brought with them a family story of upward social mobility that mainly focused on their parents or grandparents leaving the countryside for the city but that suffered an interruption precisely in their generation. It is important to point out that the middle class emigrates because it can afford the cost of the trip. When the Plano Real stabilized Brazilian currency in 1993,[27] the cost of international airfare fell, which made Brazilian international tourism rise to unprecedented levels. In the same period, the cost of living in Brazil fell for the poorest segments of the population while it rose for the middle class. I believe these two factors, a rise in the cost of living for the middle class and a decrease in airfares, may have favored the increase in the number of emigrants. I believe this because during my trip to the city of Governador Valadares in August 1997 I was able to interview various people who said that if they had enough money to buy a ticket, they already would have gone to Boston.

In her book *Little Brazil* (1994), Margolis points out that the economic policies adopted by then president of Brazil Fernando Collor de Mello were mentioned by her interviewees as having been a deciding factor in the motivation to emigrate, especially the freezing of bank accounts. In

Boston I interviewed several Brazilians who arrived in the early 1990s and mentioned this event. However, in my interviews this did not come up as a central theme as it did for Margolis' interviewees in New York.

And what about employment and income? There is nothing to indicate that the scope of the economic stability of the 1990s, especially the containment of the high rates of inflation inherited from the 1980s, contributed toward reducing the volume of the flow. This is above all because the unemployment rate in the large metropolitan regions of the country that previously received a large number of internal migrants grew from 3.3% at the end of the 1980s to a level above 7% in the first six months of 2000 (Goza 2004). The economic recovery after the implementation of the Plano Real in the mid-1990s did not cause a reduction in unemployment primarily because modernization in manufacturing reduced the demand for labor in that sector. Then the crises in Mexico (1995), Southeast Asia (1997), and Russia (1999) led to higher interest rates,[28] which in turn exacerbated the decrease in formal-market jobs (Gremaud, Vasconcelos, and Toneto 2002: 103).

The new millennium brought a phase of expansion in the world economy. The dizzying growth of China and India in the world market generated an increase in demand for products from Latin American countries. A boom in Latin American exports began in 2002 that was fueled by the increase in demand and the rise in international prices for products such as soy, petroleum, and minerals. Thus, the growth of the combined Latin American and Caribbean GDP went from -0.6% in 2002 to 1.9% the following year and 5.0% in 2004 (OIT 2006: 4).

This economic dynamization generated positive effects on the labor market, especially in those sectors related to exports. Between 2003 and 2005, approximately 3 million formal-market jobs were created in Brazil. The recently employed workers had a higher level of education than the previous average, as the majority of the new positions were filled by people with eleven or more years of education, and these workers had to accept longer working hours. Even so, salaries remained at the same level (ILO 2006: 6). In fact, the data found in this research indicate that some of the Brazilians emigrants interviewed occupied positions in Brazil that are considered low level (such as salespeople, office workers, construction workers) or mid-level (such as laboratory technicians or bookkeepers). Only a small number of upper-level professionals were found. The qualitative interviews reveal that these upper-level professionals received their diplomas from private colleges or universities that are little valued in the Brazilian labor market and in disciplines that have an excess number of professionals, such as engineering, law, business administration, and journalism. Similarly, a contingent of university students was found, but they were students whose studies are not valued in the Brazilian labor market, for example, literature or teaching.

Returning to the 1980s, the period in which emigration rose, one should consider the possible impacts of the restructuring of manufacturing on employment and compensation in jobs the Brazilian emigrants held, particularly for metal workers and mid-level technicians. Given the profound changes in the labor market, it was no longer possible for these workers to find satisfactory or stable work. This situation was aggravated because the number of available workers in these sectors far exceeded the demand in Brazil. During the 1980s the real income of persons employed (measured in multiples of the minimum wage per worker) in the manufacturing industry suffered a 15.5% decrease.

Over the past twenty years, salary reduction in Brazil has been linked to slower economic growth and to the restructuring of manufacturing; technological innovations affected not only those directly employed in production but also traditional office workers such as secretaries, office assistants, and bookkeepers, as well as workers in the financial sector. The unemployment that hit mid-level technicians and low-level skilled workers is associated with the crisis situation of the 1980s and with advances in robotics, information technology, and so on, that is, with the introduction of new technologies into the manufacturing process and into workplaces in every sector.

The information obtained from the interviews further indicates that the poor performance of the Brazilian educational system may be partly responsible for the migratory movement. The restructuring of the labor market in Brazil has not coincided with educational policies oriented toward the changes in the labor market and the manufacturing sector. Added to this is the proliferation of colleges and universities whose diplomas are not valued in the labor market. For many of the Brazilians interviewed, this situation represents an open invitation to leave the country because it frustrates their professional and salary expectations.

Social Networks and the Reasonableness of the Gamble

It is within this scenario that the choice to emigrate acquires a specific meaning: that of escaping the circumstance of declining social mobility in Brazil, even though, paradoxical as it may seem, this means a change, albeit temporary, from working as a secretary to working as a maid or from being a bookkeeper to being a dishwasher. But among the trade-offs implicit in these changes, besides higher pay, living in the United States is considered "chic" in Brazil and may elevate the perceived status of middle-class Brazilians in the eyes of their peers.

To understand the extent and meaning of these trade-offs, we must take into account that most Brazilian immigrants move into the category of "low-wage family" after they emigrate. By Brazilian standards, these families do not consider themselves and are not considered by others as poor in Brazil. The Brazilian poor rarely have the means to emigrate, although it does happen on occasion. Several authors have shown that immigrants in general do not belong to the poorest social strata of their countries of origin (Portes 1995). The majority of these families belong to the Brazilian lower middle class. It is a social sector that has been losing its consumer power over the past two decades and is threatened with poverty; many are entering into a spiral of downward social mobility. The results of the research presented here point to great economic diversity in the regions of origin of Brazilian immigrants and show that they generally do not come from the poorest areas of Brazil.

Social networks, generally based on kinship or friendship or even on religion, are fundamental in explaining how Brazilian immigrants arrive in the United States, above all because they help reduce the psychological and economic costs of emigration.[29] Nevertheless, the ties that link immigrants to various networks can be tenuous. The address of the acquaintance of a friend, of the relative of a relative, or of a priest "who helps Brazilians go there" can be sufficient. In a general way, it is through networks that the information and opinions that establish the conditions for the choice in favor of emigration are propagated. Brazilians who have arrived recently in Massachusetts prove to have little information about the United States and at the same time have high expectations about what they will find there.

Looking at social networks can explain why immigrants head for one country and not another and how they arrive in the destination country.

The networks stimulate the migratory process, giving it a mass character once the flow has begun. Social networks are also important in explaining why those groups or individuals who do not have access to the networks do not emigrate although they are subject to the same socioeconomic conditions as those who do.

Beyond family, friendship, neighborhood, and religious networks, other institutions foment migratory movements, among which print and broadcast media, local financing agencies, travel agencies, and remittance agencies stand out. Together, these constitute what may be called the "emigration industry," such as that found in the cities of Governador Valadares, Criciúma, and Poços de Caldas.

In local contexts that are marked by a culture of emigration and that have ample access to the networks that constitute the emigration industry, how are microeconomic factors reflected in the day-to-day lives of potential emigrants? Certainly, they strengthen the decision to emigrate, either at the individual or the family level. The majority of those interviewed admit having left the country feeling like people who do not have a lot to lose. They were frustrated with Brazil when they departed, with the jobs they had, with the salaries they earned, with the schools where they studied, and with the economic crisis and the successive failed attempts at economic stabilization. They also experienced a schism in Brazil between the expectation of at least maintaining the family's social status and the reality of an economic crisis whose end was unforeseeable.[30] This experience is particularly costly for those who have not managed to reach the level of education necessary for a satisfactory position in the labor market. On the other hand, the loss of daily interaction with relatives and friends who remained in Brazil is cited as the greatest loss arising from the decision to emigrate. In the face of the prospect of impoverishment, emigration becomes a less risky choice of a temporary nature and is considered similar to an investment leading to the accumulation of monetary and/or human capital.

The economic factors are fundamental, but they should be kept in perspective. Underlying the economic oscillations of the 1980s and 1990s, a process of social change occurred that gave new meaning to emigration: for a group of Brazilians, going to Boston might be easier and more advantageous than going to Tocantins.[31] For example, in Governador Valadares there is a much greater volume of information and more facilities for financing and airfare for those who are preparing to go to Boston than to the current internal Brazilian destinations of migratory flow. Besides, life in Boston has charms with which the Brazilians who emigrate are familiar: greater security, more modern and accessible consumer goods and services, and better schools for their minor children. These are important factors in understanding the motivation for emigration that a purely economic approach would not encompass. In other words, along with economic motives, others of a cultural nature are driving the migratory movement.

As most Brazilian immigrants are young, emigration is seen as a low-risk choice: if their expectations are not met, they still will be within an age range that will permit them to return to Brazil and begin over again. The money needed for the trip is within the reach of the Brazilian middle class. The majority of those interviewed financed their trips themselves or arranged for loans from family or friends. They understood that if they did not manage to return with any money, they at least would have lived in another country and learned a little English.

Only since the beginning of the twenty-first century have many Brazilians begun to enter the United States through Mexico or other routes that place their lives in danger. Most disembark in the United States with tourist visas and remain in the country after the visa expires. Disembarking with counterfeit visas or passports of course carries greater risk, but even so, the worst that can happen is that the prospective immigrants would be obliged to return immediately to Brazil. Thus for the great majority, emigration is a choice similar to an investment either of an economic nature or in human capital.

Emigration signals a clear bet on the future. Living in another country, learning a second language, taking advantage of the public assets and private consumer goods available in the United States, and getting to know a new lifestyle are experiences counted as benefits that reduce the cost of emigration and drive the migratory movement of Brazilians toward Massachusetts.

3

Organizational Resources in the Salvation Market

The participation of churches in international migration movements is a millennial phenomenon. This topic, however, only begins to receive particular attention in the studies of post-1965 migratory flows in the end of the 1990s (Warner 1998: 15). Viewing them as key institutions in the community life of newcomers, various authors seek to understand the ways in which churches and religious affiliation affect the processes of identity formation, belonging, and associativity (Ebaugh and Chafetz 2000, Kim 1981, Levitt 2003, Menjivar 2003, Warner and Wittner 1998).

Churches are, by definition, expansionist institutions: it is necessary to bring God's word, whatever that may be, to the farthest corners of the earth. The dislocation of populations involves loss, anxiety, and abandonment, factors that also have caught the attention of scholars and that were viewed as variables capable of explaining the reasons immigrants seek to participate in religious organizations in the destination country. In this vein, authors like Herberg (1960) and Handlin (1973) have sought to highlight the psychological benefits of the exercise of faith and of religious practice as means to alleviate the trauma arising from the migratory experience.

Those who are abandoned and afflicted constitute one of the target audiences of churches. Especially for recently arrived and first-generation immigrants, "the combination of culturally attuned spiritual comfort and material assistance heightens the attractions of membership and participation in churches for new immigrants to the United States" (Hirschman 2004: 1208). It is no different for Brazilian immigrants: Brazilian churches prosper and multiply abroad as emigration expands around the globe. If previously it was foreign missionaries who came to Brazil accompanying the European and Asian diasporas, from the 1980s on it has been Brazilian missionaries who have gone out into the world following the flow of emigrants from that country. According to the U.S. Embassy in Brasilia, between 1998 and July 24, 2007, 651 religious visas were granted to applicants in that city. Of those visas, only 13 were granted in 1998, while 83 already had been granted in the first six months of 2007, which constituted a 538% increase. The U.S. Consulate in São Paulo also saw an increase in the same period, although it was considerably smaller. Between 1998 and July 2007, 2853 religious visas were granted to applicants in that city. In 1998, 160 of this type of visa were granted and in the first six months of 2007, 178 were granted, which constituted an 11% increase, according to data given to the author by the U.S. Consulate in São Paulo.

If on one hand churches have an important chapter in the history of Brazilian emigration, U.S. religious tradition has been developed alongside the long historical process of immigration into that country (Herberg 1960, Hirschman 2004). This means that the institutional role of churches organized around migratory flows is fundamental, regardless of the destination country or the country of origin.

Despite the great importance churches exercise in the life of immigrant communities, answers to basic empirical questions are still being sought. What activities are effectively developed by religious organizations? Are such activities differentiated for each ethnic group, or are there significant variations within the groups themselves when separated according to denomination? What are the borders and intersections between religion and nationality or ethnicity?

Several authors have approached the role of churches in the adaptation of immigrant groups in the United States. For Hirschman (2004), churches are not merely fundamental agents in the immigrants' adaptation process, an aspect emphasized by Herberg (1960) and Handlin (1973). Rather, as Hirschman notes (2004: 1207), the immigrants themselves are also agents of transformation for the churches:

> Churches and other religious organizations also play an important role in the creation of community and as a major source of social and economic assistance for those in need. . . . Members in many religious bodies, similar to members of a family, do not expect immediate reciprocity as a basis for friendship and social exchange; the

> idea of community—of shared values and enduring association—is often sufficient to motivate people to trust and help one another, even in the absence of a long personal relationship.

In the Brazilian case presented here, we will see that churches connect and allow the transposition of borders that are, above all, symbolic and institutional. This bridge becomes evident by merely citing a small but significant example from the official calendar of Brazilian churches in Massachusetts. On it one sees "Natal" and not "Christmas." However, Dia de Ação de Graças appears on the calendar as "Thanksgiving" and Dia dos Namorados as "Valentine's Day" (although in Brazil the Dia dos Namorados is not celebrated on February 14). In Brazil the Dia de Ação de Graças does not have the same importance that Thanksgiving has in the United States, even though it involves the same celebration on the same day. Valentine's Day is not part of the Christian calendar and has a slightly different connotation ("Boyfriends and Girlfriends Day"); however, Brazilian churches in Massachusetts have begun to celebrate Valentine's Day. The day of Our Lady Aparecida, the patron saint of Brazil, is still very much celebrated, as are the June holidays known as *festas juninas*, which are rural in origin and dedicated to Catholic saints. Thus, if religious participation in Massachusetts reinforces connections and identification with Brazil (Levitt 2003), the church also clearly appears as a "bridge institution," that is, as an intermediary between the cultures of the destination country and the country of origin.

Perhaps churches can be interpreted as a kind of translator of the two cultures, specifically of what they judge to be fundamental values and practices to demarcate the ways in which the destination country and the country of origin function. As Herberg (1960) and Janowitz (1966) have observed, religion makes it possible for the immigrant to find a place in American life. Without a doubt, for Brazilian immigrants as well, "religion plays a critical role in identity construction, meaning making, and value formation" (Levitt 2003: 851).

Despite the commonality in the role played by churches regardless of denomination, important intergroup variations can be found as, for example, Chen shows (2006a,b). Among the Taiwanese in the United States, churches are not precisely bridges between cultures but rather above all act to reinforce the traditions of immigrant groups. Because they have their own traditions, Chen concludes, religious beliefs and practices cannot be viewed as a mere extension of ethnicity.

Recent studies of international migrations have investigated different aspects of the role of religion and of churches: their influence on the process of decision making and agreements (Myers 2000, Hagan and Ebaugh 2003); the effects of migration on religious life (Massey 1990); assistance and support in the destination country (Min 1992); and the configuration of the organizational context of transnational migrants and transnationality (Levitt 2003).

Churches' aid work and assistance to co-nationals is very similar regardless of immigrant group or religious denomination. Hirschman asserts, "The most visible manifestation of the impact of new immigrants on American religion has been the establishment of thousands of new churches and temples that serve the particular needs of immigrant communities" (2004: 1227). In this way, the social function of Korean churches in the United States, for example, is similar to that of Brazilian churches, that is, the social integration of co-ethnics, support and social assistance programs, the organization of recreational activities, counseling and information about employment, business, housing, legal assistance, health care, and so on (Min 1992).

However, in this study it will be seen that within a single immigrant group, important transformations can be observed over time, especially with regard to religious work, which highlights the need to carry out longitudinal studies. Longitudinal analysis is complemented by a comparative analysis of the work performed by religious denominations. This research strategy enables understanding of the competition among churches supported by immigrants of the same national origin, notably when the group is comprised of different denominations, as is true in the Brazilian case analyzed here.

Indeed, comparative dissension is proving to be promising in studies of religion and migrations (Ebaugh and Chafetz 2000). According to Menjivar (2003, 22), "This approach permits us to hold constant certain factors and examine the effects of those that vary; it also allows us to bridge insights gained from recent scholarship in the field of religion and immigration with those from immigration research more generally."

In this chapter I present an analysis of the work and the services rendered by three individual Catholic churches,[1] that is, of three Catholic communities (those in Somerville, Framingham, and Allston) and three evangelical churches (Christ the King Presbyterian Church in Cambridge,[2] the Brazilian Baptist Church of Greater Boston in Charlestown/ Massachusetts, and the Assembly of God in Somerville).[3] In referring to the Baptist church, Christ the King Presbyterian Church, and the Assembly of God, I will use the term "evangelical," following the designation utilized by Pierucci and Prandi et al. (1983), to refer to adherents of more traditional Protestant sects,[4] as well as to Pentecostals.[5] For simplicity's sake I will use the generic designation Catholics, albeit the Catholic Church has various lines of religious observance.

Overview of Churches and Religious Adherence

To a careful observer, the rapid growth of Brazilian churches in Massachusetts, especially evangelical churches, will not go unnoticed.[6] This observer will easily tend to infer that the number of converts from Catholicism to Protestantism among Brazilian immigrants is quite significant. By 1993, thirty Brazilian Christian churches had been registered in the state (Emmanuel Gospel Center 1993). In 2005 the number rose to fifty Brazilian churches, both Catholic and evangelical (Emmanuel Gospel Center 2009).

In the results of the two sociodemographic surveys I conducted in 1996 and 2005, in addition to the four Catholic churches that offered masses in Portuguese for Brazilians the interviewees mentioned participation in the following Brazilian evangelical churches: Presbyterian, Baptist, Assembly of God, Brazilian Evangelical, Quadrangular Gospel, Christian Community, Brazilian Christian, Shalom Baptist, Maranatha, Missionary Baptist, Good News Evangelical, Methodist, Seventh-Day Adventist, and Universal Church of the Kingdom of God. In fact, Table 3.1 reveals that the number of Brazilian evangelicals is proportionally greater in Massachusetts than in Brazil. However, two factors must be taken into consideration.

The first consideration has to do with the fact that among evangelicals, the establishment of new churches and the expansion of existing churches follow a different process than that established by the Catholic Church. A small group of laypeople with the help of a pastor can form an evangelical church. And in contrast to Catholics, evangelicals do not give priority to their unity; it is easy for them to separate, and for this reason it is

Table 3.1. Religions of Brazilians in Massachusetts and Brazil

Religion	Massachusetts 1996 survey (%)	2005 survey (%)	Brazil 2000 census (%)
Catholic	60	44	74
Evangelical	22	38	15
Nonreligious	13	11	7
Other	5	4	4
Total	100	100	100

Sources: Martes, surveys 1996 and 2005; IBGE 2000.

not feasible to establish a correlation between the number of evangelical churches and the number of evangelicals. This explains why the number of evangelical churches is much greater in the United States, although the number of Catholics is not small.

The second consideration has to do with the greater visibility that evangelicals manage to achieve thanks to their integration into the media. On cable television channels in Boston one can easily watch worship services, meetings, and preaching broadcast in Portuguese or *portuñol*, a mixture of Portuguese and Spanish. These programs are noteworthy for the degree of excitement with which healings and emotional testimonies about favors are given and received and the eloquence of the pastors as they refer to the church's miracles, especially those having to do with cures. In this sense, no differences appear in the conduct and strategies used to achieve visibility by the evangelicals in Massachusetts and those in Brazil. Ruben César Fernandes notes, "Evangelicals (in Brazil) do not hide themselves. They prefer to establish their churches in prominent places, they boldly speak about Christ to neighbors and strangers, they evangelize in the public square and in stadiums, they invest mightily in the media" (1996: 32).[7] In Massachusetts it is no different.

But it is no less important to consider that this visibility also is related to the evangelicals' identification as "different" by other Brazilian immigrants in Massachusetts. Being different means they present themselves as a religious alternative in the midst of a traditionally Catholic population, but it is not merely this. Their lifestyle, conduct, and way of dressing is easily observed, and I believe that the perception of these differences is encouraged (and desired) by the evangelicals themselves.

The data presented in Table 3.1 confirm what any superficial contact with Brazilians in Massachusetts would be enough to reveal: the proportion of evangelicals in that state (22% in 1996 and 38% in 2005) is higher than the 15.5% found in Brazil by the 2000 Brazilian census. The presence of evangelical churches among Brazilians is actually one of the most visible characteristics of this migratory movement.

Of all the interviewees in the 1996 survey, 20% arrived in Massachusetts having already converted to Evangelism, while in 2005 this proportion had risen to 38%, almost double. The cases of conversion from Catholicism to Evangelism after immigration involved only 5% of the 300 Brazilians interviewed in 1996; no data are available for 2005. However, the pastors of the Christ the King and Baptist churches said the majority of church members arrived from Brazil already having been converted. In recent decades, the Catholic Church has been losing adherents to evangelical churches all over Brazil. According to Pierucci and Prandi (1995), Catholics represented 74% of the Brazilian population in the 1990s. By means of comparison, in the Rio de Janeiro metropolitan area, the region with the greatest evangelical population in Brazil, 28% of that population had been converted in just three years, from 1992 to 1995 (R. Fernandes 1996). In the beginning of the twenty-first century, "of the 15.3 million Brazilian ex-Catholics who had converted to another religion (who represent 9.06% of the Brazilian population), 73% belong to some evangelical church" (Ceris 2004). In 2002 Brazil was considered the largest Pentecostal country in the world, with 24 million faithful. By way of comparison, the United States had 5.8 million Pentecostals. Brazil was simultaneously considered the largest Catholic country in the world, with 138 million faithful (World Christian Database 2009).

Yet a decrease in the number of Catholics in Massachusetts can be observed. Table 3.1 likewise indicates a significant increase in the percentage of Brazilians who stated that they were nonreligious as compared to the 2000 Brazilian census but a slight decrease when the results of the 1996 and 2005 surveys are compared. These results thus raise the following question: Why is the proportion of evangelicals in Massachusetts greater than the proportion of evangelicals in Brazil, independent of whether their conversion was prior to or after emigration? It is a difficult question to answer, but I believe I can suggest an approach.

In the past thirty-five years Brazil has been noted as one of the most significant examples of the expansion of Evangelism in the world. Some authors raise the hypothesis that this country, like the rest of Latin America, is abandoning Catholicism to become Protestant (Stoll 1990, Martin 1990). According to the 1991 Evangelical Institutional Census, every two days a new evangelical church opened in the Rio de Janeiro metropolitan area (in R. Fernandes 1996). The 2000 Brazilian census recorded that from 1991 to 2000 the Catholic Church lost 9.4% of the faithful, and the number of evangelicals grew by 6.4%. This increase and the annual growth rate of 7.9% among evangelicals—larger than that in previous decades—show in the 1990s an acceleration in the expansion of the number of evangelicals in the country (Mariano 2004).

Although Brazil is a traditionally Catholic country, Pentecostal and other evangelical churches have grown rapidly, particularly among segments of the lower middle class (R. Fernandes 1996).[8] This is possibly the social segment most representative of the Brazilian immigrants in Massachusetts, according to the data in my survey. Therein lies, I believe, one of the explanations for the existence of a proportionally greater number of evangelical Brazilians in Massachusetts than in Brazil.

Two additional factors can help explain the presence of a greater percentage of evangelicals in this U.S. state. Could the Brazilians connected with evangelical churches be receiving differential aid and incentives to immigrate to the United States? According to data collected in the 1996 survey, evangelicals showed greater interest in bringing their nuclear families to the United States. While 20% of the Brazilian Catholics who immigrated to Massachusetts left their families in Brazil, 11% of the evangelicals did so. This may indicate that they likewise strive to attract their fellow church members.[9] As I will show later, evangelical discourse values and encourages the upward social mobility of members of the church that may result in a kind of symbolic encouragement for emigration.

Another point that cannot be confirmed but about which I found various clues is that a significant number of pastors charged with carrying out international evangelization missions are departing from Governador Valadares as well as from Baixada Fluminense—the places from which the two largest populations of Brazilians in Massachusetts come. These pastors would be following precisely the route taken by the emigrants and would in this way reinforce the emigration of evangelicals.

Despite the growth in the number of evangelicals, the majority of Brazilian immigrants are still Catholic (Table 3.1), though not all of these are practicing Catholics. Among the Catholics interviewed in 1996, 35%

placed themselves in the category "nonpracticing."[10] They justified their abstention as due to a "lack of time," "a lot of work," or "I was always this way." But as Pierucci and Prandi observe (1987), the nonpracticing Catholic is one of the constituent features of Brazilian Catholicism itself.

Just as in Brazil, women tend to have greater participation in religious networks among Brazilian immigrants. But what is notable is that adding the numbers of those who stated that they had no religion and those who did not attend any church (including nonpracticing Catholics), it can be concluded that the majority of the immigrants, 58% of the interviewees, were connected to some religious network. In fact, Brazilian churches, along with family networks, friendship networks, and associative organizations, constitute the principal support networks of Brazilians in Massachusetts.[11] Like other churches organized to serve immigrants and especially the recently arrived, the Brazilian churches are called "ethnic churches." In the same way in which one speaks of "Brazilian churches," one speaks of "Haitian churches," "Korean churches," and so forth. Important in this definition is not merely the language used for the services but also maintenance of the religious culture of the country of origin.

1980 to 1990, The Assertion of Difference

Each of the local units of the six religious communities studied conducts its work with Brazilian immigrants in a relatively autonomous manner. And although there may be a set of general directives about institutional work, those directives, due to their generic nature, are not sufficiently detailed that they intervene directly in the day-to-day work the religious perform for the immigrant group.[12] These six communities likewise promote two types of work: that which is, strictly speaking, religious in nature and individual aid. The private aid is performed by the six churches in the same way; the pastors, priests, and nuns give individual assistance to the members of their communities. They act as interpreters and translators in hospitals, in schools, or in the justice system; they help spread information about available employment and housing; they promote activities for the warehousing and distributing food and clothing. Various services also are offered in the churches and performed by the clergy, religious activists,[13] or professionals.

Where this type of aid work is concerned, the activities promoted by all of the churches studied are similar. This seems to be an important point, for it permits a distinction between the individual aid work by the Catholic Church in the two countries in question. In the evangelical churches greater value is given to these tasks, and the churches are better equipped to pursue them in a more frequent and far-reaching manner.

During the 1990s it was in the religious work that a more significant difference could be found between the Catholic and evangelical churches in Massachusetts in three areas that strike me as fundamental: the notion of the role that the church should exercise, the objectives of the work, and the construction of the identity of the community. These three areas are connected to the theological base of each of the churches (bases that here will be considered only insofar as they refer to the concrete practices studied). Although the individual aid work is similar, it is not all conducted in the same way, with the same intensity, or with the same objectives; as we will see later, the institutional organization and the religious presuppositions that guide the work differ among these churches.

The churches play an important role in promoting the immigrant's adaptation. The pastor of the Assembly of God, who is himself Brazilian, presents his church as an alternative for those who seek to participate in a community guided by moral values and thus distinguish themselves from the rest of the Brazilians:

> The Bible says, "You will know the truth and the truth will set you free," so actually, they come because they do not want to put themselves into the world of drugs, the world of drunkenness, of orgies. They are honest people, so they want a place because they know that the church is a safe place for socializing, for family.
> Q: Do you think that the fact that they feel alone also favors their approximation to the church?
> A: Yes. When people feel alone, they seek out an environment where they feel good. As they don't want to mingle in certain environments, they come to attend the worship service.

The pastor of the Brazilian Baptist Church of Greater Boston, also a Brazilian, reaffirms the idea expressed in the previous interview that evangelicals "do not want to mingle" because they are "different," because they reorient their conduct to adhere to evangelism:

> The evangelicals came, and they are different. The church plays a role in family education. The Catholics are ritualists, they were

> never educators. When the mass was in Latin, the people went there to smell incense and say amen . . . The Evangelist produced a new man, and in the woman, a new woman . . . The majority of the Brazilians who are here are very good. But there are people who dirty Brazil's name as well. We tried to help a young man, a drug addict, who ended up robbing us. There is someone here who just ripped off $16,000, there are many swindlers, but there are a lot of fantastic people.

Catholics also identify evangelicals as being "different" and just as in Brazil, the process of conversion to evangelism implies a behavioral change. It is necessary to be "born again" to become a member of the church (R. Fernandes 1996, Machado 1996, Pierucci and Prandi 1995). Hence it is very rare that evangelicals join the social networks of Catholics. The division between evangelicals and Catholics constitutes one of the most significant among Brazilian immigrants in Massachusetts and accentuates the heterogeneity of this population. Non-evangelicals tend to characterize "believers" as being fanatics (because "they don't leave the church" and "they can't drink or dance"), credulous and ignorant (because they believe in miracles), and fools (because they give money to the pastor). Others associate believers with honesty, thus positively reinforcing differences on a moral level:

> Q: Did you go to this church for some special reason?
> A (Joel): I just went there one day. I like the believers' line. I think they are closer to being honest than the other churches, than the Catholic Church, because I was raised in the Catholic Church.

In any event, as one evangelical woman, Elisa, says, "believers and Catholics don't mix."

Although the assertion of difference by evangelicals remains fundamental as an important selling point in the struggle to attract the faithful, a curious approximation can be observed between the denominations at the turn of the twenty-first century. In recent years the Catholic Church has gone through a process of institutional isomorphism. The abandonment of the principles of Liberation Theology in favor of the Charismatic Renewal Movement did not affect the institutional organization of the Church, but it changed the style of religious celebration and the discourse regarding the condition of the immigrant, as will be seen below.

The Institutional Organization of Churches

A look at the formation process of the churches from the mid-1980s to the early 1990s helps in understanding the significance and importance of the institutional organization of each of them. The formation process is a particular focus of the statements given by the church directors and highlights the relationship between religious doctrine and institutional adaptation. Therefore, along with the presentation of data about the formation of the churches, I transcribe some passages from the interviews given by their principal directors.

The Brazilian Catholic Church

During the 1980s the Catholic Church initiated a program specifically directed toward Brazilian immigrants in Boston. The first Brazilian Catholics who arrived there naturally turned to the Portuguese Catholic churches. However, the manner in which Brazilians participated in the mass began to generate conflicts with established members of the congregation. A parallel can be drawn of the Portuguese and Brazilians with earlier Italian and Irish churchgoers. When they immigrated to America, Italians found another Catholic Church in the United States. It was organized by the Irish, and Italians considered it more distant, formal, cold, and Puritan (Nelli 1980: 1218).

The account of a Brazilian Carlist priest involved in attempts to integrate Brazilians into the Portuguese Catholic churches in the United States is quite enlightening:[14]

> The Brazilians wanted a more participatory celebration, happier songs, and the Portuguese wanted to continue in that rhythm in which the priest was there and did everything for them. The Portuguese exerted pressure from one side, the Brazilians from another . . . The only solution was to form another community, a space in which the Brazilians could have celebrations as they liked them . . . But we made it very clear that there wasn't a Portuguese mass and a Brazilian mass. The mass was open to all, to whoever liked the style of the group that was there, but it was open to all. It was then that the Brazilian community began to grow; we began to hold Bible courses, and afterwards couples' encounters and other activities.

In the same period, around 1984, an American priest who worked near Fenway Park in Boston where Brazilian immigrants were initially concentrated, began to hear in the area "a Spanish with a French accent," in his words. When he discovered that Brazilians were arriving in Massachusetts, he decided to learn Portuguese and prepare himself to work with them. Later, this priest became the coordinator of the Brazilian Pastoral in 1990 and visited Brazil "in order to learn about Brazilian culture" and thus improve his work.

The two experiences clarify the importance of maintaining the religious culture of the country of origin so that the Church's message can attract and keep the faithful. The majority of the Catholic clergy who work with Brazilians are North American, and some of them have participated in religious missions in Brazil. This may in itself generate a series of problems. It is not coincidental that the American priest quoted above went "to get to know Brazil, in order to understand Brazilians and their culture" and that he had his trip partially financed by the Brazilian Catholic community itself.[15] Later we will see that in working with the Brazilians in Massachusetts, the Catholic Church adopted the pastoral practice of Brazil initially in the 1990s as a kind of "adapted transposition" of the practice of Ecclesial Base Communities (Comunidades Eclesiais de Base, or CEBs), an orientation that was later replaced by the Charismatic Renewal Movement.

Christ the King Presbyterian Church

The organization of this church was begun in 1987 by a group of ten people who had been members of the same denomination in Brazil. At that time, there were few Brazilian evangelical churches in Massachusetts, and this group simply met to pray. According to the founding pastor of the church, a husband and wife began to participate in the group, and the wife was the daughter of U.S. evangelical missionaries who had worked in Brazil. Previously, the couple had attended one of the U.S. Presbyterian churches. Later, the whole group joined the American church attended by the couple. Together they formed the first Brazilian and American church in the United States, called Christ the King Presbyterian Church. Its founding pastor described his early involvement:

> This couple went to the American church, and through their intervention, we began to go, too. One day they asked for authorization to

> form a Sunday class in Portuguese on Sunday mornings. The group grew and asked to hold services on Sunday nights. I was invited to be the first pastor of the church. I was pastor for three years, but I had to stop when I began my doctorate at the University of Boston.

The account mentions the theological formation of the pastor and emphasizes selectivity in the choice of members. The church "begins little by little," and its members have roots in the evangelical tradition. These two aspects are characteristic of traditional evangelical churches like the Presbyterian Church.

The Baptist Church

A group of Brazilians who had belonged to the Baptist Church in Brazil asked a Brazilian pastor from the Baptist Church of New York to assist the group twice a month. Later, they decided to establish a church in Boston and invited five pastors from Brazil so its future leader could be chosen from among them. This procedure arose from the fact that the Baptist Church is congregational, that is, its decisions, including the choice of pastor, are made by the members gathered in assemblies.[16] The main pastor of the Brazilian Baptist church in Boston described its origins:

> Brazilians came here and didn't adapt to the American church because English is spoken there. A large portion of the evangelical churches in Boston are in decline. Due to the presence of universities, Boston worships culture, knowledge, intelligence. Boston has forgotten God and is going to pay a very high price for this. The Ph.D. from Harvard can say what he wants, but what rules is the Bible . . . no little professor who sets himself up as an intellectual will knock down the Bible . . . In the case of the Baptist church, the group I lead, this group of people began to meet in homes with ten people, and the group grew until there were thirty-five people. They marched into an American church and asked for the Metropolitan Baptist Church in Cambridge to open its doors to the group.

In this account, the pastor emphasizes the belief (of a fundamentalist nature) in the infallibility of the word of God as expressed in the Bible and of the faithfulness to its teachings characteristic of the Baptist Church. The same pastor reaffirmed God's preponderance over science and reacted in a conservative way against a kind of "modern morality" in the

United States that accepts homosexuality. In the face of these "excesses," the pastor reaffirmed his intervention on the normative level; in contrast to the merely ritualistic character of the Catholic Church, he said the Baptist Church has a didactic role.

The Assembly of God Church

Evangelicals consider this their largest Brazilian church in Massachusetts. It had close to 1,000 members in 1996 and 4,000 members in 2005, according to the pastor who leads it.[17] A pastor from Pará, the state that gave rise to the establishment of the Assembly of God in Brazil, began to organize the Boston church in 1980. It began to operate in a small hall in a former shoe store. In 1985 the church had fewer than twenty members, and it was only in 1988 that it managed to become registered.[18] In 1990, the head pastor said, the church acquired its own building for the price of $1 million, raised exclusively from the Brazilian faithful residing in Boston. More than $300,000 was spent on renovations, and the church's main building was inaugurated in 1992.

From that year on, the church became the headquarters of the missions of the Assembly of God of Brazil (AGB), which expanded to other U.S. states and to countries with large numbers of Brazilian immigrants (Australia, Japan, and Canada). By 1996 there were forty AGB churches in the United States, in Washington, D.C., as well as Florida, Pennsylvania, New Jersey, Connecticut, Illinois, Georgia, and California. The highest concentration of AGB churches is in Massachusetts (twelve churches). Also according to the pastor, the AGB has three million members in the United States, a third of them in Massachusetts. In that state there are almost forty Brazilian Evangelical pastors from this church alone.[19]

The emphasis in the pastor's account of the church's formation is on its rapid growth and its accomplishments: the building, the training of pastors, and the attraction of new members. In fact, this is the church that is most focused on forms of "recruiting." To cite one curious example, when I went to interview the pastor, he asked that I give him ten minutes to "speak with me about God." Then he tried to move me toward a possible conversion by means of two strategies. The first was by trying to awaken in me a feeling of guilt ("at this moment you are being given a chance in your life that will be remembered by God on the Judgment Day"). The second was that of offering the "security of the Church" to my family, especially to my son ("In this church, your son will be safe from drugs, from this ever more dangerous world"). These two points (the threat of hell and family security) are used systematically and repeatedly as resources in the process of conversion in general.

Organizational Structure and Religious Practice

At the beginning of this chapter I asserted that the churches' practices are left in the hands of the religious who work directly with the immigrant populations. Despite this common pattern, the Catholic Church has a more rigid and centralized hierarchic organization than do evangelical churches.

In what way does the institutional organization of the church affect the work that each of them does among the immigrants? The institutional evolution of the Catholic Church, marked by increasing hierarchization and centralization, was historically called a process of Romanization. The transformation of Christianity into the Catholic Church, which has the seat of its hierarchy in the Vatican, was the fruit of a long process that is still controversial today. My objective here is limited to studying how the hierarchical organization of the Church may intervene in its particular work with Brazilian immigrants.

The structure organized by the Catholic Church to render assistance to immigrants is complex. At the national level, there is the National Conference of Catholic Bishops, with its headquarters in Washington, D.C. It is specifically oriented toward matters related to immigrants and political refugees, and the Pastoral Care of Migrants and Refugees is a part of the conference. At the state level, Catholic Social Services (or Catholic Charities) are organized. These offices are coordinated by a local bishop and have the objective of providing legal aid services and clarification regarding documentation, registration, and legalization of immigrants and refugees. Work with immigrants is held as one of the priorities of the Archdiocese of Boston, and according to members of Catholic religious orders, it is quite esteemed by the bishop. It is not by chance that this archdiocese created an organizational jurisdiction called the Ethnic Apostolates to centralize the pastoral work with each immigrant group, including Brazilians.[20]

The Brazilian Apostolate, established in 1990, unites the priests and nuns who work with immigrants from Brazil. When it was created, eight "local communities" made up this apostolate in Massachusetts:

Somerville, Cambridge, East Boston, Allston, Buckland, Framingham, Marlborough, and Lowell. These communities met monthly to discuss the Brazilians' problems and promote joint actions. The apostolate also has as one of its objectives the development of action strategies with its specific target populations. To this end it organized groups for youth, families, catechism, liturgy, and tithing as well as courses in religious guidance and spiritual retreats. The Brazilian Apostolate organized a Social Action Team to coordinate social aid and information about the needs of each Brazilian Catholic community in Massachusetts for purposes such as providing assistance during court proceedings related to legalization and translation in hospitals. From a strictly religious point of view, the Brazilian Apostolate promotes activities that follow the directives of the Brazilian Catholic Church. All of the materials used during these activities are made in Brazil (notes, bulletins, and so on), and the events follow the Brazilian Catholic calendar in celebrating, for example, the feast of Our Lady Aparecida, Brotherhood Campaigns, and Family Christmas. A member of a Catholic religious order said, "The Pastoral is another way of living the church [has] that is different from the American way." This "other way" is an attempt to approximate, insofar as possible, customs Brazilians observed in Brazil, thus avoiding possible disagreements.

With regard to evangelical churches, since the pastors are Brazilian and the connection to U.S. denominations is similar to a partnership, problems arising from the differences between Brazilian and U.S. religious cultures are practically nonexistent; the U.S. evangelical churches do not interfere with the Brazilian churches that belong to the same denomination. AGB churches are affiliated with the Convention of Portuguese Language Assembly of God Churches of the United States, but the headquarters of the AGB in Boston has complete autonomy to conduct the administration of the Assembly of God churches that are connected with it as well as the authority to open other local units anywhere in the United States.

This does not imply a lack of hierarchy. The AGB matrix has local autonomy, but the churches affiliated with it work according to the planning and objectives stipulated by the Boston headquarters. According to the head pastor, "All of them render accounts here, [and] restrictions come out of here, from the commissioning of pastors." From a financial standpoint, they have a "controlled autonomy," the pastor said; the purchase of real estate, for example, cannot occur without the prior authorization of the seat. The responsibilities are hierarchically established from the AGB matrix in Boston and must be followed by the local units subordinated to it, with interference neither from the Assembly of God in Brazil nor from the U.S. Assembly of God:

> The pastors in Massachusetts have autonomy to do work, to spend funds on television programming, radio programming, and evangelism . . .
> Q: And what is the connection between the Brazilian Assembly of God and the American Assembly of God?
> A: They have the same principles, the same doctrines, norms and customs . . .
> Q: But is there a hierarchy among you?
> A: No, this church is affiliated with the Convention of Portuguese Language Assemblies of God of the United States . . . the church is autonomous, with authority to begin work in any place in the United States and in the world.

This type of organization offers greater agility and flexibility so the church can conduct its activities.

One of the preponderant factors in this flexibility, besides institutional decentralization, is the evangelical churches' means of financing: each local community is responsible for financing the church with which it is connected; each church is financially dependent on the local members. In the Catholic Church, in contrast, a large part of the financing of the local units comes from the Church hierarchy. Evangelical pastors tend to take their pay from cash donations and tithes collected from the faithful they lead, while priests' salaries come from a different source. Priests' room and board expenses are paid with money from offerings, not from tithes, and although there is no fixed rule, generally half the salary of the Catholic clergy is taken from offerings, and the other half is paid by the local parish. The parish priests with whom individual priests are connected and to whom they must render accounts are from the United States and only have an indirect connection to Brazilians through the intermediation of the priests. Individual priests are linked to parish priests who in turn must render accounts to and seek authorization from the bishop of the diocese to which they belong for changes they may perhaps seek to implement.

The U.S. Catholic Church does not collect tithes, but Brazilian Catholic churches have both types of collections because the way the faithful participate follows the Brazilian model.[21] Even so, the major emphasis is on offerings and not tithes. Evangelicals, in contrast to Catholics, place greater emphasis on tithing for the purpose of financing the churches. The tithe collected in Brazilian Catholic churches is used to help the neediest members of the community, while the offerings, generally collected during mass, help with maintenance of the churches. In 1996, for example, the Catholic Church of Somerville sent $500 to a needy family in Brazil and to a priest who aided street children in Rio de Janeiro. The money collected during special events (fairs, dances, bingo games) constitutes another source of income for the Catholic Church. A member of the Brazilian Apostolate said one function of the collection of tithes is to increase the responsibility of the faithful for their own community. The tithe is used as an instrument to intensify living in community, and money collected by this mechanism does not go toward financing the local units.

Despite the Catholics' concern with promoting a stronger community life among Brazilians within the church, evangelical churches manage to create more intense social interactions and more active participation than the Catholic Church. To understand evangelical churches' success, it is important to analyze how they are transformed into the prime locus of sociability of their members. The remarks of the pastor of the Baptist church are incisive in this regard:

> Our church is already prepared to help the Brazilian as soon as he arrives. We help with moving, we give free English classes from Tuesday to Thursday evenings, we donate clothing, especially winter clothing, when he arrives. We support pregnant women, guiding them with regard to the hospital and other resources; we buy cribs, layettes, clothing, shoes, and furniture. There is social assistance carried out by the church. When a member of the church becomes unemployed, we also help with food, and other members help find him employment so that he does not suffer hardship.

Thus, although the Catholic pastoral agents attribute greater emphasis to ideal of participation, it is the evangelicals who manage to promote a more active religiosity and sense of community. In fact, the institutional structure of the evangelical churches is more decentralized than that of the Catholic Church. In the former, the pastors exercise a powerful controlling role over their communities. The pastors thus have a fundamental role with which to compensate for the weakness of the hierarchical structures. They centralize information about the personal affairs of each member of the church and give economic, conjugal, and family advice or even counsel regarding migration. Along with this controlling role the pastors often play a paternal role toward the members of their communities and frequently are called to act as arbitrators in conflicts between members of the church. A large part of the pastor's authority is based on personal charisma, but the exercise of this authority is considered by the church as a mission delegated by God.

Brandão has observed (1988) that individual religious "militancy" is one of the principal characteristics of Evangelicals. In contrast to Catholics, the category "nonpracticing" evangelical is nonexistent: they all participate regularly in the church's activities. However, Catholic communities also organize a significant number of activities, including social activities, that have a more festive and sporadic nature than those promoted by evangelicals. Examples include *festas juninas* in June and bingo games to raise money. There are also dances to celebrate Valentine's Day, September 7 (Brazilian independence day), and the feast day of Our Lady Aparecida.[22] It is important to note that the number of activities offered by Catholic churches depends on the personal efforts of each priest. Saint Tarcisio Church in Framingham, for example, was more active than the rest in the 1990s. However, the church in Allston became equally active when it organized Charismatic prayer groups in the following decade.

The way each church is financed influences the kind of use that the faithful make of it. Buildings of the Baptist Church of Greater Boston and the Assembly of God feature lunchrooms where refreshments are served every Sunday. These weekly gatherings become an important time of religious and social fellowship and demonstrate that the faithful can build their own community spaces within evangelical churches. Catholic as well as Protestant leaders relate church participation to the promotion of forms of sociability, and the manner in which the physical spaces of the churches are used does not go unnoticed, as an Assembly of God pastor explained:

> The first thing that we seek is the comfort of the people; immigrants, seeing that they are far from home, depend on a place in which they feel comfortable along with their compatriots or relatives. Then we provide a social hall, and we provide rooms for children with toys and nurseries. .

Evangelical church buildings are renovated to accommodate members' activities, while a significant area of the Catholic Church building is conceived as serving the priests who reside in them. In fact, all three evangelical church buildings researched here were being renovated. Their pastors said the renovations were intended to address their communities' needs, such as dining halls, nurseries, and meeting rooms. The way church space is used is similar to a club, which demonstrates that evangelical churches provide the faithful with greater involvement in the daily life of the church by means of more regular and constant activities.

The Catholic Church buildings belong to the Church hierarchy and are not for the Brazilians' exclusive use. The evangelical churches (except Christ the King Presbyterian, which is associated with the United States Presbyterian Church) are attended almost exclusively by Brazilians. This does not preclude participation by people of other nationalities, but it offers Brazilians a sense that this is a space constructed especially for them.

The data suggest that the evangelical churches employ a discourse and religious practice of exhortation to work and incentive to socioeconomic upward mobility.[23] This general consideration is valid for the three evangelical churches studied here, but it is important to note that each pastor stresses the meaning of upward mobility in a different way.[24] In the Pentecostal churches, there is greater encouragement for increasing the individual incomes of the members and involvement in the determination of family budgets. A similar position can be seen in those Pentecostal churches in Brazil that adopt a "theology of prosperity."[25]

Besides providing for the intensive use of the physical space of the churches, financial dependence on local communities reinforces the idea that the members should seek to achieve economic success. Potentially, the socially upward mobility of those who attend the church may contribute to increasing the volume of contributions through both tithes and offerings. The diverse ways in which the pastors take a special interest in following the trajectories of the socioeconomic upward mobility of the members of their communities are easily identifiable. A statement by the head pastor of the AGB is illuminating in this regard:

> Q: Are the majority of women who come to the church cleaning women?

A: No, up to about five years ago, the people worked mostly in cleaning. Today, there are many other professions because people came and began organizing. Today many are owners of firms or travel agencies, of currency exchanges . . .
Q: But you believe that participating in the church helps [financially]?
A: More than 200% . . . [Here] one is blessed from the marital perspective and blessed in financial life, because you stop spending money on *carnaval*,[26] on cigarettes, on drink, on drugs, in bars. All of this you save for your home.
Q: In opening a firm, a business, does the church give some encouragement?
A: It does. First, we have a very large group in the church that is always praying for your blessing, for your prosperity . . . We have people who own restaurants, who work as managers in influential jobs, and others who work in import-export.
Q: Then your followers are different, a lot wealthier than the average of other Brazilians? Because the people I interview deliver pizzas; they work in construction.
A: Our church has a large congregation; besides that, it has God's blessing in the midst of all this . . . It is common for a person to arrive here and a few months later have a good job, be earning well; you even receive papers from the government.

When questioned about the professions of church members, this pastor overvalued the "more noble" professions, emphasizing the business owners, and established a hierarchy of occupations. The interviewee outlined a kind of evolution from house cleaners to businesspeople in which his church played an essential role as facilitator on one hand and as a controlling force on the other. He said the church facilitated the upward social mobility of its members to the extent that it reaffirmed such mobility as a religious value: earning money is the expression of a divine recognition of one's effort and merit. The church institutes mechanisms of control over personal conduct that promise an increase in saving because, he said, "believers do not throw money away."

The encouragement of upward social mobility, clearly expressed in the theology of prosperity, is also present in Pentecostal churches in Brazil.

Yet, in the context of immigration the reaffirmation of this value on a religious level finds more fertile ground and becomes powerful since to varying degrees emigration is strongly motivated by the possibility of an increase in income.

The idea that in the church everyone can "improve his life" takes on special meaning when its members come to recognize or believe that the growth of the church, whether in the number of members or the acquisition of assets, depends on their personal efforts. For this reason, the acquisition of their own building is a kind of epic in which all participate and in some way feel themselves to be owners, or at the very least responsible for the acquisition. They speak with pride about the church center and frequently inflate the actual price of the property.

It is easy to deduce, therefore, that having charisma, being a good communicator, and being "anointed by the Holy Spirit" are not sufficient personal characteristics for becoming a prestigious pastor. In addition to these attributes, the person must have a proactive profile. Being a good administrator assures the pastor's authority in the eyes of the church's members. It is noteworthy that in only five years the Baptist church purchased a building valued at $760,000, and the pastor was proud that this whole sum was collected exclusively from the faithful; the building previously belonged to the Catholic Church, which for him was also a motive for great joy. In 1995 Christ the King Presbyterian Church bought a building for its headquarters that had a value of $800,000.[27] The Baptist church broadcasts a cable TV program in Portuguese and offers a telephone service called TeleCristo (Tele-Christ) to spread messages of "faith and solidarity"; the phone service has the objective of "attenuating loneliness," which the pastor considered the biggest problem Brazilian immigrants faced. The Assembly of God Church owns a building valued at $1 million; it spent more than $300,000 on renovations, and it broadcasts radio and TV programs.

A good pastor who is also proactive promotes the involvement of the church community in these "victories." In so doing such a pastor leads members of the congregation to interpret (and feel) the growth of the church as a collective effort to which they personally contributed.

Religious Community Work

One characteristic of the religious work evangelical churches performed in the 1990s differed from that of the Catholic churches, particularly with regard to how they constructed their respective communities. This difference was more salient before the arrival of the Brazilian Charismatic movement in Massachusetts and results because in evangelical churches the emphasis falls on the religious faith that the group should share. Rarely is the status of being an immigrant directly broached by the pastors during worship services. The assistance given to the immigrant as such and problems related to housing, employment, and so on are dealt with as "personal problems" and thus should be solved with individual help from the pastors or other church members. In the Catholic Church, making the Brazilian aware of his or her status as an immigrant is a fundamental part of religious work, as a nun explained:

> For us, the Church—the Bible—is an instrument so that the people can grow personally and in community and transform their reality. It has to reflect their reality, their life experience. All that we do has this goal; this is our methodology.

In the 1990s the raising of political consciousness was emphasized as a fundamental part of pastoral work. Three of the five members of Catholic religious orders who were interviewed spontaneously stated that they sought to awaken the social and political consciousness of the faithful, at least in part so they could act politically when they returned to Brazil. One described the goal:

> The group that I work with here . . . I made them feel very at ease . . . in order to see what they wanted to study, to talk about. In the beginning, they wanted to know about the churches. Many only began participating in the Church here because they feel isolated. They want to belong to something meaningful. We study the Gospel of Mark, and now that of Luke. Because of my experience in Brazil, I said to myself: "This is an instrument for me, a tool for self-discovery and discovery of their role in transforming the world. How is this group of people going to become engaged?" I thought. "Is it possible that this will go somewhere?" What makes me happy

> is seeing their reflections on their analyses about Brazil, and they grew in their commitment to become engaged when they returned to Brazil.

Similarly in the Catholic church in Framingham, discussion groups not only about religion but also about the Brazilian political situation and the condition of immigrants in the United States were organized to raise participants' consciousness and cultivate relationships of solidarity. The priest in charge said immigrants overvalued "the idea of earning money, and they only look at themselves in order to reach this objective . . . This doesn't lead to anything; it's worse for them who should support each other in order to be able to improve the living conditions of all Brazilians."[28]

This ideal of raising consciousness that underlay religious activities in the 1990s is closely related to liberation theology, a movement begun mainly by Catholic clergy in Latin America based on a proclivity toward the poor.[29] From a theological point of view, such a preference is based on the "belief that the salvation of man is inseparable from his development in the struggle for the radical transformation of the social structure that perpetuates poverty and repression" (Adriance 1986: 2). From a practical point of view, this proclivity led to the creation of Ecclesial Base Communities in Latin American countries. The CEBs promote, through meditation and prayer, a socially and politically engaged religious ideal, and thus they emphasize popular participation not only in the Church but also in sociopolitical institutions (Mariz 1994: 17).

The main goal of the pastoral agents of the CEBs is to raise participants' consciousness regarding social justice and inequalities including their own condition of poverty. This goal requires a political and religious stance in the face of factors that favor such inequalities. In this broader sense the work of CEBs in Brazil is similar to that of Catholic Brazilian immigrants in Massachusetts.

The transposition of pastoral community practice from Brazil to the United States produced a dislocation in the notion of how one should raise the consciousness of the faithful. Self-identification as poor (promoted by the CEBs in Brazil) is replaced by construction of the identity of the immigrant worker. It is not by chance that the Brazilian residents of Massachusetts are defined by the Catholic clergy as belonging to the "world of work." The roles of worker and of immigrant are the two aspects through which Catholics seek to construct the collective identity of Brazilians. Nevertheless, self-identification as an immigrant is, for the immigrants themselves, a source of great ambiguity. The idea of identifying oneself as an immigrant worker tends to be strongly rejected, largely because many Brazilians believe their stay in the United States is temporary. Going to America represents the intention to change their lives when they return to Brazil. Many Brazilians understand that they may be able to pass from their former status as an employee to the position of boss when they return to their cities of origin with the money they will manage to accumulate in the United States.

The message preached by evangelicals is therefore more compatible with the aspirations of many Brazilian immigrants because the attempt to promote self-identification as an immigrant worker has proven to be a difficult task and one that causes problems similar to those confronted by CEBs in Brazil.[30] Several studies demonstrate that the poor in Brazil tend to deny their condition of poverty, or at the very least they avoid accepting poverty as the principal focus of their identity (Cardoso 1978, Zaluar 1985). Following a similar line of argument and referring to CEBs in Brazil, Mariz concludes that "the attempt by the CEBs to create a collective identity based on the condition of poverty creates a rupture with the cognitive presuppositions of popular culture and its values" (1994: 74).

Evangelical pastors establish greater harmony between the Brazilians' immediate aspirations and their own religious messages. Evangelical sects propagate messages of encouragement for upward social mobility. In the Assembly of God church, for example, one of the words most often uttered during the worship services is "victory." During the services, participants pray and sing with their hands raised and their fingers in a "V." When compared with the proactive practices of evangelical pastors, priests tend to have a calmer personal style.

In Catholic churches the emphasis on autonomy and popular participation in the 1990s were complementary to the Catholic clergy's ideal of raising consciousness. Social networks are valued by priests and nuns as resources that Catholics ought to create and expand with a view toward strengthening their communities. As a means of encouraging the autonomy of participants, laypeople are called on to decide what kind of religious and social work will be carried out. In this way, the faithful are valued as active elements in the work of the Church.

The importance given to the values of consciousness-raising, participation, and popular autonomy among members of the Brazilian Apostolate in Massachusetts has as its "font of inspiration" the methodology developed by educator Paulo Freire.[31] But to be able to make use of Freire's methodology, the religious strive to adapt the methodological principles to the new context. To this end, while Paulo Freire's approach to literacy is to provide reflection about reality based on the everyday life experiences of those who are to be taught to read and write, pastoral agents attempt to promote the raising of their members' political consciousness by means of reading the Bible. They believe that in this way they can provide those who read the Bible with an interpretation of its messages that must always be compared to the reader's life experience. The following statement given by a nun illustrates this point:

> Our way of working comes from our time in Brazil . . . This experience speaks with respect to a methodology, a way of relating, a pastoral vision, the Bible based in the life of the people . . . Our pastoral here is defined by the work in Brazil, but the work here doesn't even come close to that done there. The rural people from the Northeast [of Brazil] are perhaps the most beautiful people and the easiest to work with in the world, and we saw results every day. That was growth. How do we attempt to do that in this country? Here it is difficult even to recognize who the enemy is, everything is so entangled. There it was easier to raise consciousness.

This statement shows that the communitarian ethic is valued in a way analogous to the CEBs in Brazil. Raising consciousness means organizing for action and acting to transform important aspects connected with the living conditions of a whole community. According to Prandi (1992), the CEBs attempt to reproduce an idea of communion with the sacred that is filtered primarily through the value given to the ethical principle that leads the faithful person to think of himself not as an isolated individual who appeals to God but as part of a subject that is constituted collectively in order to experience the presence of God. The basic social actor making the reference to sacredness possible is the group, the community, and not the individual. The very notion of politics, Prandi argues, is founded "on an ethic oriented toward systematic rationalization between God and the world" (1992: 83).

This is clearly another point of contrast with evangelicals, who tend to keep problems of an economic nature circumscribed to the individual sphere. This does not mean that such problems are kept outside of the orbit of the church or the domain of the pastor. On the contrary, this is precisely what assures the place of individual economic problems on the plane of religiosity because, in contrast to Catholic communities that tend to prioritize collective problems to the detriment of individual ones, evangelicals see individual problems as a priority and hence not subjugated to collective matters.

It is not by chance that the pastors' messages appeal directly to each one of the participants, making them responsible for their own economic circumstances, whatever they may be. Economic success, as already mentioned, is also attributed to personal merit but with the church's help in each case. I believe that a sort of accommodation between evangelical churches and the aspirations of Brazilian immigrants is reinforced by the capitalist ethos in the United States that was brought about in part by Protestant colonization. Evangelical discourse seems to find more fertile ground in a country where social relationships are strongly marked by capitalist values of upward social mobility and personal accomplishment and at the same time provide workers with ample access to consumption. In this way, there is not merely greater harmony between evangelical churches and Brazilian immigrants but also between these churches and U.S. society.[32]

Reorientations and Confluences in the First Decade of the Twenty-First Century

The adoption of a multicultural discourse and a more professional organization of community aid work characterize the recent institutional evolution of religious work among Brazilians. But what turns out to be most surprising in following the changes in the religious communities of Brazilian immigrants in Massachusetts since the 1980s is the shift from an initial situation of emphasizing differences among the four churches to a more recent situation in which they churches have come to act similarly in many important respects. This unexpected rapprochement of the churches lies mainly in the fact that Catholics have come to adopt a type of religious celebration and a discourse about the situation of the immigrant that was previously typical of evangelical churches.

The set of transformations that has occurred in the Brazilian churches in Massachusetts at the beginning of the twenty-first century cannot be understood without taking into consideration the arrival in that state of two important religious movements: the Charismatic Renewal Movement (Catholic) and the evangelical movement called G 12.[33] Although neither of these two movements originated in Brazil, they were brought to the Brazilian churches in Massachusetts by religious and lay Brazilian immigrants.

The Charismatic Renewal Movement originated as a lay movement in the United States in 1967; it arrived in Brazil in the following decade and began to attract a large number of Brazilian Catholics in the 1990s, reaching a total of almost 4 million followers (Souza 2005).

Just as in Brazil, the Charismatic Renewal Movement grew in Massachusetts in exact proportion to the decline in the concept of religious work based on the CEBs. In fact, there no longer exists any vestige of the discourse of liberation theology in Brazilian Catholic communities, neither among the laity nor among the clergy. The Church abandoned the discourse that marked its pastoral practice in the most mobilized communities in the 1990s.

Liberation theology came to be severely criticized by the hierarchy of the Catholic Church after the election of Pope Karol Wojtyla (Pope John Paul II) in 1978. In Brazil the theologians began to suffer persecution and punishment; more importantly, the naming of bishops and new priests came to implicitly adopt the criterion of non-adhesion to that doctrine (Prandi and Pierucci 1996). The division between conservatives and progressives intensified up to the critical moment of this dispute when Brazilian priest Leonardo Boff, one of the principal exponents of liberation theology, renounced the priesthood. It was at that moment, marked by the internal reaction against the "progressive wing" of the Church, that the Charismatic Renewal Movement gained ground in Brazil and received incentives from the institution's hierarchy.

Parallel to this, the expansion of neo-Pentecostalism in Brazil came to represent a serious challenge to the comfortable hegemony of the Catholic Church. The data recorded by the Church between 1989 and 1996 raised a kind of alarm. To cite one example, the number of marriages performed by the Catholic Church in Brazil dropped by half. An evasion movement from the Catholic Church became evident in the face of which the Church hierarchy of the largest Catholic country in the world began to reveal its concerns publicly: a frank expansion of neo-Pentecostalism was in progress in the country. However, in the wave of expansion of the

Charismatic Renewal Movement, curiously, neo-Pentecostals ceased to be openly criticized and soon began to receive praise for no longer being merely admired but also imitated. Happiness in the liturgy, direct and facilitated communication, miraculous cures, magical practices (pilgrimages, *novenas*—characteristic of the rural Catholic tradition) began once again to be religious practices that were valued by middle-class Catholics of Brazil's large urban centers (Souza 2005).

It is interesting to note that if the hierarchy of the Catholic Church represents an obstacle to the flexibility that the condition of emigration demands, as were the organizational conditions of the 1990s found in this study, the purpose of the Charismatic Renewal Movement is capable of offering an alternative and efficient answer. This is because it is a movement in which laypeople assume hierarchical charges of coordination in the parishes and dioceses. The idea of priests and nuns playing the role of tutors and no longer of active agents fits like a glove with the situation of the Brazilians in Massachusetts because it opens a more flexible organizational space for bypassing the rigid hierarchy of the Catholic Church's organizational structure. As a result, assistance centers for Brazilian immigrants were created in various locations, as will be seen.

One of the characteristic features of the Charismatic Renewal Movement is that it affects the religious practices in Massachusetts with regard to the conception of and resources used in the design of the mass. The mass is transformed into an act of liberation, with active participation of those present. Music has always been used to attract the public to Catholic churches but without recourse to choreography, as is common in evangelical churches. With the Charismatic Renewal Movement, the mass takes on the format of a show, a spectacle that features "singer priests." In Brazil the masses officiated by Father Marcelo Rossi, the greatest expression of the Charismatic Renewal Movement in the country, began to attract thousands of people in the Santo Amaro neighborhood of São Paulo in the late 1990s. In 2002 Father Marcelo's CD won the U.S. Latin Grammy award in the category of Best Religious Album. If in Brazil the Charismatic Renewal Movement is winning ground and popularity by presenting itself as an alternative to the Pentecostals and incorporates many of their resources, the situation was no different in Massachusetts.

Up to the 1990s, glossolalia (speaking in tongues) was a common practice in the Brazilian services of the Assembly of God and the other Pentecostal churches in Massachusetts. With the arrival of the Charismatic

Renewal Movement, it was introduced into Catholic celebrations. The moment of catharsis that follows—songs and choreography, the words to the music shown on a screen, and musical groups—are highlights of the celebrations. Thus substantive changes can be seen in the Catholic celebrations that made them very similar to evangelical services.

The Charismatics arrived and quickly organized themselves into prayer groups and rapidly achieved a noteworthy place in the internal organization of the Church and legitimacy in the eyes of the apostolate. The website of the Brazilian apostolate has a link to "Charismatic Renewal" that presents especially the actions taken by the communities in Boston, with articles and schedules of events in the city.

G 12, Group of Twelve

The Charismatic Renewal Movement arrived in the United States at the same time that the immigrants also brought with them the neo-Pentecostal evangelical movement called G 12. This is a movement created by the Colombian pastor César Castellanos Domínguez, the leader of the church called the International Charismatic Mission, founded in 1984. The G 12 organizational principal is oriented as a growth strategy for the churches that adopt it. Castellanos was inspired by the model used by South Korean pastor Paul Yonggi Cho and his Church of the Full Gospel. In 1991 Castellanos claims to have received a prophetic revelation directly from God that guided him to organize the church in twelve member cells, adopting the same number as that of the apostles of Jesus Christ. Each of the cells should gather in prayer in the homes of the participants under the guidance of a leader with the goals of evangelization and the proliferation of groups. As soon as a cell reaches a sufficient number, it is divided into two cells with twelve members each, and so on.

The G 12 arrived in Brazil through the leadership of pastors Valnice Milhomens and Rene Terra Nova, who are considered disciples of César Castellanos. Valnice Milhomens is a television-program host, and Rene Terra Nova is the leader of the First Baptist Church of the Restoration in Manaus, the capital of the state of Amazonas. Both belong to the Brazilian Baptist Convention (Romeiro 2009). Although it is an evangelical movement, the G 12 has great similarities with the Catholic Church's Christian Cursillo Movement. The Cursillo Movement has existed since the 1930s and was created by the Spanish monk Don Escrivã, a precursor of Opus

Dei. In the system created by Escrivã, the number 12 is used as a reference. The Cursillo Movement, like the G 12, features the periods of pre-Cursillo, Cursillo, and post-Cursillo for each group that is formed. In the G 12, the church is divided into small groups (cells) in which the people are evangelized (AGIR 2010).

During the Cursillos,[34] which are three-day retreats, a vow of silence is taken, just as in the G 12. That is, the participants are prohibited from communicating with each other, and secrecy is required regarding what occurs during the events, in accordance with the statute of the Cursillos (Movimento dos Cursilhos da Cristandade do Brasil 2010).

Since the arrival of the G 12 movement in Brazil, there have been nine national G 12 conventions. At the 2007 convention, in the city of São Paulo, Pastor Castellanos and his team of twelve were present in addition to the Reverend Tommy Tenney, author of the book The God Chasers, as well as other national and international leaders (Ministério Internacional Restaurando Vidas 2009).

Thus the Pentecostal and Catholic churches' activities coincided on two fundamental points in the first decade of this century: performances in the church services and organization of the faithful around prayer groups. It is important to understand that these changes took place within the church and therefore do not affect the discourse of differentiation in the 1980s and 1990s, which was oriented toward the Brazilian community in general. With regard to the individual and community aid work, there are two points to emphasize as important transformations in recent years: the emphasis by evangelical pastors on the formation of social networks and their vibrant action in the face of the immigrants' social problems, and the creation of support centers by the Catholic Church in the form of NGOs.

The pastor of the Brazilian Baptist Church of Greater Boston said,

> There is a clash between the church's discourse and the immigrant's situation. What is the Brazilian's ethic before his own group, and how does he dialogue with American culture? Brazilians should seek a life of dignity in the United States. How? By organizing. They should do as the Hispanics, who are organized here as a class, have done: they communicate with the government, they vote, and so on. The role of the church is to help this dialogue, to encourage the believer to participate in Brazilian organizations. We brought the

> Center for the Brazilian Immigrant, for example, to speak with our friends from the church about women's health.

The pastor of Christ the King Presbyterian Church similarly speaks with pride about its participation in events that relate directly to immigrants. An important change took place in the pastors' attitudes that reveals engagement in movements and causes related to civil rights that was not seen in the 1990s.

In the Catholic Church, greater professionalism can be observed in the organization of aid work as well as a change in locus of the exercise of this function from the Church to NGOs, albeit still under the guidance of priests and nuns. Six NGOs were organized in the early 2000s to guide Brazilian immigrants on issues related to access to employment and education, telephone and utilities services, health care (including Free Care) and psychological services. The centers offer English classes at all locations as well as assistance in reporting automobile accidents, filling out insurance forms, and finding attorneys. They are located in Allston, Framingham, Lowell, Stoughton, Marlborough, and Worcester. One of the nuns responsible for directing the centers said,

> Services are given on a voluntary basis by Catholics; it is part of the work of the Church, but it was understood that opening an office outside the Church would be better so as not to restrict the aid work. Here we don't ask about religion. All the work is done for free. The Center is a nonprofit; its work is to welcome and support Brazilians who ask for help.

Two points must be emphasized. First, organizing aid through NGOs permits an "end run" around the rigid Church hierarchy and gives greater mobility and agility to the work. Second, this organizational structure allows the aid to expand beyond the limits imposed by religious affiliation. We found a situation in Massachusetts similar to one found by Menjivar (2003) in relation to Salvadorans: she concludes that although the aid work of Catholics and Protestants is similar, evangelical churches operated on a smaller scale.

The most sought-after service of the Catholic NGOs is help finding employment. A register of available jobs is compiled as well as a list of those who are seeking work. The spokesperson for the unit in Allston indicated the importance of this service: "Today, for every twenty people who seek us out, one is assisted because there aren't many available openings . . . We try to help with what the Brazilians seek most: work. . . ."

Over the past decade the Catholic Church reduced its emphasis on raising political consciousness about the immigrant's situation in order to adopt a discourse that seeks to "lessen the pain, bring hope, and encourage life in community so that all feel like part of a family," in the words of a nun. The religious discourse of evangelicals generally underwent a kind of updating by introducing the multicultural component to its main concerns in the early 2000s, although this change does not apply to the Assembly of God.

The pastor of Christ the King Presbyterian Church explained that its work follows two lines: worshipping God and making an "attempt to correct the distance of prejudice in order to offer the immigrants connections with Americans, to provide them with material necessities." The church went from being bicultural (Brazilian and American) in the 1990s when it was created to being multicultural when it began to add Canadians, Japanese, Koreans, and Europeans. If previously this was a bilingual church, "today, seeking convergence with Cambridge's nature as a multicultural city, we have expanded," said the pastor.

The exercise of official leadership of the Presbyterian church does not reflect the multi-ethnic composition of the faithful, for there are only two Brazilian pastors and two American pastors on its board. Its institutional vision is expressed on the church's official website (www.presbiterianacristorei.org): "We wish to be a church that is welcoming to the suffering, especially to immigrants, capable of proclaiming the Gospel in a joyful, relaxed, and intelligent way in the most secular region in the world (Boston—USA)." It is rare that the faithful of different nationalities attend the same events at Presbyterian churches in Boston. But one such event is Easter. No study has been done of the multiculturalism of the services, but there is information regarding the pastors. The tithes are not managed by the pastor but rather by the "church government," that is, by the council, which is divided between Brazilians and Americans. The pastors are not full-time employees of the church who dedicate all their time to religious work, as are the priests in the Catholic Church.

The pastor of the Baptist church linked multiculturalism to the attraction of new members and the celebration of cultures. He said it is necessary to change from a "temple mentality" to an "auditorium mentality":

> The church of Jesus did not use a temple in the Old Testament. In the New Testament, yes, because the idea was to sanctify the space for the activity of worship. Our building doesn't look like a temple. The word "church" represents something that is outmoded. Therefore, we make the church into a place of celebration.

More important than evangelizing are celebrations that involve cultural appeal.

The pastor's goal is to reach not only Brazilians who immigrated to work but also those who came to study and feel dislocated. Following the multicultural orientation, soccer tournaments are organized among students of various nationalities and from various denominations: "We have to be more inclusive, to welcome people in order to love them, not in order to change them. We have to promote cultural events in order to attract everyone."

Church Expansion after 2000

In 2005 Massachusetts had a total of fifty Brazilian churches: twenty-six evangelical and twenty-four Catholic communities. Services are celebrated in Portuguese and oriented toward Brazilians in both the Catholic and evangelical churches. The twenty-six evangelical churches are distributed throughout various areas of the state: Winthrop, East Boston, Cambridge, South Dorchester, North Dorchester, Fenway/Kenmore, Allston/Brighton, Back Bay/Beacon Hill, and Charlestown. They are connected to the following denominations: Assemblies of God, Missionary Church, Church of the Nazarene, Presbyterian Church in America (PCA), Seventh-Day Adventist Church, Presbyterian Church (USA), Lutheran Church Missouri Synod, Conservative Baptist Association, Southern Baptist Convention, Episcopal Church, American Baptist Churches, Free Methodist, and Roman Catholic Church, as well as assorted independent and interdenominational congregations not formally affiliated with larger groups (Emmanuel Gospel Center 2009).

From 1995 to 2005, the number of Catholic churches jumped from eight to twenty-four, and concurrently the Central Office of the Brazilian Apostolate was organized in the state, with its headquarters in Everett. The Catholic Brazilian communities are in Acton, Allston, Amesbury, Cambridge, East Boston, Everett, Fall River, Falmouth, Framingham, Hudson,

Hyannis, Leominster, Lowell, Marlborough, Milford, Nantucket, Peabody, Pittsfield, Plymouth, Rockland, Somerville, Stoughton, Vineyard Haven, and Worcester (Apostolado Brasileiro 2009).

But great growth can be observed also in the evangelical churches studied. In the 2000s, Christ the King Presbyterian Church grew from one to four locations: New Life Presbyterian Community in Framingham, Bethel Presbyterian Church in Marlborough, and City Life Presbyterian Church in East Boston, in addition to the original church in Cambridge. Almost 600 members of various nationalities and ethnic origins participate in its services and religious activities, and it is the largest Presbyterian church run by Brazilians in the region. The Baptist church did not increase its number of locations like some others, but the pastor said the number of faithful grew and Sunday services in Spanish were introduced.

The Assembly of God church was renamed the World Revival Church of the Assembly of God in 2003. But that transformation is not reflected in the official discourse of the organization, as can be deduced from its website: The World Revival Church–Boston Ministry is an evangelical ministry founded in 1985 by its president, Pastor Ouriel de Jesus, who "felt a strong call from God to leave his country and immigrate to the United States of America" (de Jesus 2009). The split between the founding pastor and the Assembly of God became public after the publication in 2003 of the book *O triunfo eterno da igreja* (*The Eternal Triumph of the Church*), which was written by de Jesus and a group of workers from the World Revival Church in Boston.

Antonio Donizeti Romualdo, co-pastor of the Assembly of God Church in Tampa, Florida, wrote in 2004 that the book is the result of a revelation of paradise that occurred in a supposed scripture hall. Romualdo describes how the authors reported being in this paradise in an "ecstasy of feelings." He writes that the book's publication caused the Portuguese-language evangelical church in the United States to be shaken by the "theological aberrations it described." The reaction of the General Council of the Assemblies of God in the United States, with which the church was affiliated, was immediate. As soon as its members detected deviations from the scriptures in their reading and analysis of the book, the council, as a precautionary measure, made the radical decision to remove de Jesus from its membership registry and to dissolve the Portuguese Language District (Donizeti Romualdo 2004). Since then, the founding pastor of the Assembly of God has given his church another name: the World Revival of the Assembly of God (WRAG).

Despite this schism, the WRAG can be considered the most successful Brazilian "business" in Boston. The church building has undergone several renovations since its purchase and the church's foundation. The organization owns a television studio where videotapes of the services are edited for later broadcast on a gospel cable-television channel in Brazil. The tapes are also sold in a small shop next to the main entrance of the church building. The hall where the services are held doubled in size in 2003. In the back are television screens and a stage, which is very wide and tall. On the other side is a special space for the orchestra that was formed by church members. In the back of the building, rooms are under construction, some of which are already used by members of the youth orchestra for rehearsals.

A Safe Space for Sociability

Dulcinéia and her family have belonged to the Presbyterian Church since they lived in São Caetano do Sul in the Brazilian state of São Paulo. Since 1992 she and her family have lived in Everett, in Greater Boston. Dulcinéia works as a housecleaner and earns income by making savory snacks that are sold to the members of her church. Her husband runs a home day care, and some of the parents of the children in his care attend their church. In Dulcinéia's house "there is no want." A perfectionist, she made the master bedroom the most decorated room in the house, full of colorful curtains, a television set, and a large silver picture frame holding their wedding portrait. It was there that she brought me to give me the interview, and we sat on the double bed, which was covered by a bedspread made of the same fabric as the curtains.

> My friends are all from the Presbyterian church. I was already a Presbyterian when I came here. When I arrived here, I got in contact with an evangelical church, although it was Baptist, because it was already there. [Later] we planned to open the Brazilian Presbyterian church.
>
> Q: Do you help Brazilians who arrive here?
>
> A: Oh, yes! The churches welcome the immigrants, helping them with whatever they need . . . They arrive in debt, without any money.

> The first thing they need is employment. The church makes contacts to arrange for a job, [and] it holds a shower to get them things for their home.

This account underscores the importance of the religious network in advancing immigrants' access to the labor market and in welcoming the recently arrived. This perception is shared by many who make up the churches. Whatever the religious affiliation may be, the churches are presented as a "safe place" where the members can confide in one another. In a complementary way, the interviewees highlight the psychological support these institutions provide. One of the priests from Framingham, for example, was a psychologist, and he confessed that he frequently acted as one. The life experience within the church is positively valued, whether it be for the friendship or the material and spiritual help provided by its members.

Knowing that they will be able to depend on support, including material support, in times of difficulty provides the church members with a feeling of greater comfort and security. Even for those who do not attend them, the churches represent the strengthening of the bonds of solidarity.[35] The environment of fraternity, support, and aid is fundamental to attracting new members and keeping those who already participate. Internal solidarity is one of the keys to guaranteeing the church's success, as the pastors and the priests, like this one, are aware:

> We have to create a fraternal environment, where the person feels good. After celebrating the mass, we have a get-together, a coffee. [Previously] the mass ended and each one went his or her own way . . . With the coffee, the people have a moment to get together . . . there they create a spirit of solidarity . . . What we do, in the first place, is help in the spiritual sense so that they can feel at home, not feel like strangers . . . feel that people can help them in every sense, from the material and the social point of view as well.

The interviews demonstrate that Brazilians tend to seek out churches when they feel lonely, when they miss Brazil and/or want to socialize in a safe, protected, trustworthy environment. That is why individual religious choice is more easily explained by friendship or family connections than by the doctrinal principles of each denomination, as the Presbyterian pastor explains:

> After all, why do Brazilians seek out churches? Because it is a Brazilian environment, it's the opportunity to speak Portuguese with people who are from their people, their culture. This alone brings comfort, support, encouragement, equilibrium. This puts an end to loneliness, isolation. The church also has spiritual, religious functions. The messages that they hear are of encouragement, of hope.

The priests as well as the pastors tend to transform personal problems into an incentive to participate in the church: family discord (between parents and children), alcoholism or drugs, and lack of legal documentation are issues that, they say, lead people to seek out churches.[36] Thus, it is important to observe how the "Brazilians' problems" are perceived by the religious leadership and how the pastors and priests attempt to promote the sociocultural adaptation of Brazilians to the new context.

The pastors tend to give the topic a more dramatic tone and magnify the moral basis of the problems people confront in the process of adaptation. But they stress that the immigrants should not adapt to everything in their new environment. Especially in matters concerning family values, sex, and drugs, they should keep following Brazilian practices:

> The Brazilians who are here are running away—running away from the marriage that failed, others from debts, others from fights, others from a son, a daughter, the police . . . And the great majority are sincere, honest, and are running away from a lack of resources because they have understood that even working honestly from dawn to dusk, they will not manage to realize their objectives . . . the women, in general, were housewives. This causes many crises and here, for this reason, we have a biblical family orientation. Of course, if they both work, when the husband comes home, he cannot stay alone on the sofa watching TV while the woman does everything in the home. We do not support that. But we also don't accept some aspects of the American family. The family is in decay here.

The comments on the preceding pages garnered from interviews conducted from 1994 to 1996 still remain valid today. The following excerpts from interviews conducted in 2005 reconfirm the same kind of motivation, that is, solidarity but also opportunities—including employment and income—in a space that is protected by religious precepts and that therefore favors safe sociability:

> Here I feel good, at home. I have friends, and if I need something, I can count on them. Life here is hard and the church gives me peace. (Raquel, single, 46)
>
> The first houses where I worked I managed to buy here from a sister who was returning to Brazil. I was very lucky. God blessed me. My best friends are here in the church, here I have what I need and the blessing of God. I am no longer alone. (Rosa, divorced, 31)

The principal motivation for Brazilians to attend church, whichever church it may be, continues to be the same: they believe that in church they will be able to enjoy a space marked by solidarity, familiarity, and mutual assistance. Meanwhile, as first-generation immigrants, Brazilians seek out the churches in Massachusetts especially because they wish to socialize with other Brazilians.

Fry and Howe (1975) found no differences on a religious level (of theology and doctrine) that justify individual adherence to one denomination or another. The functionality of the church with regard to the necessities of Brazilian immigrants is an important attraction insofar as it can facilitate sociability. In the 1990s, evangelical churches enjoyed a comfortable advantage over Catholic churches in this sense. But I believe what is fundamental is the way each religious community promotes personal aid and solidarity among its members, constructing identities on religious and community levels to demarcate protected spaces of socialization. The cultural dimension, the symbols and values pursued by immigrants in the United States, especially that of upward social mobility, also help in understanding religious choices. Evangelical churches act in a manner more in sync with the way Brazilians value U.S. culture, which includes valuing economic individualism, but this individualism should nevertheless be balanced by community involvement, which the churches offer.

Being temporary residents and sometimes undocumented immigrants awakens in many a strong feeling of insecurity and transience. This situation obliges them to live constantly with an uncomfortable feeling of uprootedness. The uncertainty is added to their unfavorable opinion of the extended community to which they belong,[37] as is readily evident in the constant complaints about the low degree of trust and solidarity among Brazilian immigrants. It is within this context that religious discourses express the attempt to reorder the chaos, attributing meaning—be it on an emotional or a cognitive level—to individuals' perceptions and life experiences. By incorporating them into the religious field, churches redefine limits and parameters capable of reinterpreting those life experiences, in this way reinforcing, whether in the pastor or the priest, the figure of the father, the boss, or the charismatic leader who institutes norms and performs a pontifical role.

Spatial mobility facilitates cognitive and normative modifications and contributes to increased sensitivity toward a set of issues in the face of which churches make their religious appeals. The welcoming environment of the churches contrasts with the situation experienced "out there," which is perceived as being competitive, lacking solidarity, and having little community spirit. This example can explain why, even today and despite the incontestable advancement of the process of church secularization, religion still teaches one how to live, just as Émile Durkheim observed at the beginning of the twentieth century.

If the prime function of religion is to help one live, the church is a privileged locus where values are reaffirmed and meanings are not merely instituted but also ritualized so they can be lived collectively in an emotional way.[38] I believe it is for this reason that churches, either Catholic or evangelical, transform distressing—and often ambiguous—life experiences and perceptions into the raw material to be reworked by them.

As the year 2000 approached, churches demonstrated a vigorous capacity for offering people a way of classifying and ordering the world, of orienting and codifying human conduct on the level of a pragmatic morality. Yet, by establishing themselves as an alternative to unsettling life experiences and perceptions, churches contribute, albeit indirectly, to reinforcing the pessimistic vision that Brazilians express about their community in Massachusetts. Evangelical churches are more aggressive than their Catholic counterparts in this regard because by establishing themselves as a religious alternative for Catholics or for skeptics, they emphasize difference, reinforcing the polarization between solidarity (here inside) and competition (out there). The struggle between churches to attract new members generates a kind of "market of identities" and of organizational resources that in turn attributes a specific meaning to the self-identification of evangelicals as different. Being different, in this case, reinforces a belief in the ability to construct a more vigorous community ethos so that, by responding to Brazilian immigrants' expectations of sociability, evangelical churches present themselves as a protected space of reciprocity.

Photo 1. A Brazilian restaurant on Cambridge Street in Cambridge, Massachusetts. Photographer: Ronaldo Porto Macedo Jr.

Photo 2. Entrance to a Brazilian restaurant in Cambridge that features *moqueca*, a dish from the Brazilian state of Espírito Santo. Photographer: Ronaldo Porto Macedo Jr.

Photo 3. Street view of the Brazilian *moqueca* restaurant in Cambridge. Photographer: Ronaldo Porto Macedo Jr.

Photo 4. A market in Cambridge that sells Brazilian, Portuguese, and American products. Photographer: Ronaldo Porto Macedo Jr.

Photo 5. A clothing store in Somerville, Massachusetts, part of the Brazilian clothing chain Moda Brasil that specializes in women's fashions from Brazil. Photographer: Ronaldo Porto Macedo Jr.

Photo 6. Two Brazilian businesses—a market and a restaurant—on the same corner in Somerville. Photographer: Ronaldo Porto Macedo Jr.

Photo 7. Novelties for sale in a Brazilian store in Somerville. Photographer: Ronaldo Porto Macedo Jr.

Photo 8. A juice bar inside a Brazilian store in Somerville. Photographer: Ronaldo Porto Macedo Jr.

Photo 9. A Brazilian boutique in Somerville. Photographer: Ronaldo Porto Macedo Jr.

Left: Photo 10. Sandals and clothing in a Brazilian store in Allston, Massachusetts. Photographer: Ronaldo Porto Macedo Jr.

Below: Photo 11. A Brazilian hair salon in Allston. Photographer: Ronaldo Porto Macedo Jr.

4

The Social Arena of Employment and Businesses

In Chapter 2 I sought to show that demographic and socioeconomic diversity cannot be ignored when using the generic term "Brazilian immigrant." In this chapter I draw attention to the manner in which this diversity is reflected in the workforce. First, I intend to show that the labor market to which Brazilians have access in Massachusetts, although quite limited, does contain some mobility and job diversity. Second, when the jobs that Brazilians had in Brazil are compared to the jobs that they come to have in the United States, a certain continuity is evident. A large number of Brazilian immigrants are employed in the informal sector of the U.S. economy, but even in Brazil they carried out activities connected to the informal economy. I believe this is a relevant point since researchers tend to give greater emphasis to differences when they analyze the jobs held in the two countries, emphasizing the Brazilian immigrants' lower occupational status in the United States.

Two niches of the workforce merit particular emphasis in this chapter: housecleaning and the small businesses begun by Brazilians. In both cases, a significant church presence can be found, and thus a few pages will be dedicated to the description and analysis of religious networks in the world of work. Housecleaning and small businesses are spheres of activities that are strongly affected by the exogenous/endogenous binomial, not as intrinsic sociocultural characteristics of the group but as a sign of its situational condition. In the current phase of Brazilian immigration, small businesses are organized in such a way that they are oriented inward within the community, and employment, especially housecleaning, is that branch of activity that expands outward to a broader market. Therefore, emphasis will be given to the process of building a client base and to relationships with clientele, variables that have not been the focus of studies of ethnic businesses. From this perspective, the nature of housecleaning as a social arena organized by Brazilians in the United States parallels the patterns conventionally associated with businesses. Conversely, stores, the traditional sphere of business as places of profit and rational conduct, cannot be understood unless sociability is taken into account as a central characteristic.

I believe the analysis of job selling presented here permits a new perspective on the ways various U.S. authors have emphasized the role played by ethnic solidarity networks in advancing immigrants' access to the labor market. Here again I call attention to the role of churches in the struggle to organize and standardize the social arena of housecleaning and businesses. This role has been transformed over the course of almost thirty years of Brazilian immigration into Massachusetts and includes efforts to eliminate job selling or define fair prices for the sale of jobs, provide assistance in building a clientele, and encourage self-employment and entrepreneurship.

Finally, in the daily battle for the remuneration that feeds the dream of "making America," one can observe more than markets, labor niches, and problems of information and access alone. The opportunity to earn a living involves the complex interplay of individual and collective compensation, always mediated by intricate social networks that join strong and weak links and whose dynamics are imposed not only by solidarity but also by competition and profits, symbolic or material.

Access to and Integration into the Labor Market

The theory of the dual labor market, by relying on macro and institutional bases as central elements for explaining the means of incorporation of the immigrant workforce in the United States, on one hand liberated the socioeconomic approach and on the other raised a series of limitations on the then-predominant economic explanations of the topic. The work of Michael Piore, particularly his book *Birds of Passage* (1979), became an obligatory reference because it initiated a profitable debate with proponents of the version of neoclassical economic theory regarding the means of incorporation of immigrants into the United States and the forces that attract and repel workers.

In *Birds of Passage*, when analyzing the segmentation of the labor market in the United States, Piore presents the division of this market into a primary sector and a secondary sector. The first sector is presented as subdivided into two strata: the *upper* is comprised of workers who perform management functions and occupy highly specialized professions; the *lower* is composed of white-collar workers, the working class, and unskilled laborers. The strata are defined by the ways workers learn and understand their jobs. In the upper stratum the worker is prepared before entering the workplace (abstract apprenticeship), while in the lower stratum the worker is trained on the job (concrete apprenticeship). The two sectors, like the two strata of the first sector, exhibit a hierarchy of salaries, working conditions, levels of security and stability, and required qualifications. In contrast to the first sector, the second has the following characteristics: low salaries, precarious working conditions, little job security, a high degree of voluntary turnover, no possibility of a career, no required skills, and the predominance of highly personal relationships between employer and worker, that is, the absence of the mediation of formal work rules and high dependence on supervision in carrying out tasks. The workforce in this sector encompasses groups whose identity comes predominantly from outside the workplace: women, adolescents, migrants, and temporary immigrants (Piore and Berger 1980: 2).

This model had vast repercussions on studies of the incorporation of immigrants into the labor market. It presented an alternative to the explanations of the neoclassical approach, calling researchers' attention to the relationships among the sociocultural dynamics, and not merely the economic ones, that act to segregate groups (especially blacks and immigrants) and to promote specific relationships within each sector. From a macro-structural standpoint, the theory of market segmentation helps in understanding why immigrants who arrive in the United States come to occupy certain niches of the labor market. Which niches they occupy is a function of the structural barriers imposed on them that impede them from crossing from the secondary sector into the primary sector of the labor market (Piore 1979).

Beginning in the 1980s, researchers began to question this model.[1] They charged it with being both overly generic and overly rigid for overemphasizing the discontinuity between the sectors (Nee, Sanders, and Searnau 2002). What is certain is that the explanations presented by the market segmentation model remain limited to the macro-structural dimension. This means that they are not very useful when the task at hand is conducting a case study or when it is necessary to differentiate and characterize the labor markets in terms of specific occupations, particularly in the service sector, precisely the sector in which many Brazilian immigrants are concentrated.

However, another observation can be made. I believe segmentation theory is especially useful in understanding the integration of immigrant manual laborers into the labor market. This group in fact represents the largest contingent of recently arrived immigrants in the United States and almost all of the Brazilians I was able to interview. Yet it cannot encompass the professionals who already have positions when they arrive in the United States. This flow, also known as brain drain, is not widely applicable to the Brazilian case but is very significant in the United States. In the face of the acceleration of the restructuring of manufacturing that was in progress in the 1980s and the subsequent transformations of the U.S. labor market, a group of researchers began to question the scope of the market segmentation model, proposing the informal economy as an alternative model.

Initially the informal economy model was strongly influenced by the Latin American theory of marginality that posited a radical separation between the formal and informal economies. According to that theory, Latin America would be excluded from the economic dynamic of the pivotal countries and therefore would tend to become increasingly marginalized, creating its own market: production by the poor for the poor. In the late 1970s researchers began to reconsider the marginal or residual nature of the informal economy when they investigated the growth of informal activities in the dynamic sectors of the economies of the so-called developed countries in North America and Western Europe and revealed the connections between the formal and informal economies. In the 1980s the informal labor market began to incorporate highly skilled professionals by means of outsourcing and subcontracting labor, and this contributed to weakening the dualist interpretations that supposed there was a radical separation between the two sectors.

The principal point of divergence between the informal economy model and the market segmentation model is that while the latter identifies the root of segmentation in the discontinuity of social structures, the informal economy model proclaims the interdependence between formal and informal activities. According to Portes, Castells, and Benton (1989), the informal economy is intrinsically linked to the formal economy, and it is therefore not a matter of two autonomous spheres but of interdependent spheres: "There is not a clear duality between the formal and informal sectors, but a series of complex interactions between the two that arise from distinct relationships between the economy and the State" (26). The goods and services produced by the informal economy result from demand in the formal economy. These authors find that the relationships established between the two sectors depend on the institutional and social arrangements articulated in each society. Nonetheless, their interpretation of the division of formal versus informal differs from what is indicated by the segmentation model (between monopolistic capital and competitive capital); according the former model, small businesses operate in a captive market like extensions of the large companies for which they produce goods and services.

The informal economy model thus offers an alternative path to the theory of dualism and marginality: informality is a particular kind of production relationship. It is not a matter of economic activities that are necessarily linked to poverty or marginality, since informal activities may expand in cyclical circumstances of crisis and unemployment as well as in the midst of periods of economic growth. Their development may be a consequence of an increase in available labor, as is the case in California and other U.S. states that have a large contingent of immigrants; on the contrary, it may come about as the consequence of a reduction in available labor due to emigration, as is the case in Uruguay (Fortuna and Prates 1989: 70).

The Informal Economy

Despite having been used for almost a half-century, the concept of an informal economy is polemic even today.[2] The meaning, nature, and scope of the informal economy are also controversial from an analytical standpoint. Its scope can include activities that involve fraud and tax evasion, outsourced production units, paid domestic services, or micro-businesses with a maximum of five employees. In addition to these factors, the informal economy assumes very diverse forms according to regional or national economic dynamics.

Some researchers have adopted the definition of informal economy recommended by the International Labor Organization (ILO). According to the organization's Fifteenth Conference on Labor Statistics, held in January 1993, the unit of analysis of the informal economy is the unit of production; that is, analysis should begin with the characteristics of the units of production and not the characteristics of individual workers or of jobs. The emphasis should fall on how the units of production perform and are organized and not on the legal status of the workers, although the two factors may be related. Production activities may be continuous or not (in seasonal work, for example). Such units should produce goods and services for trade, not for the producers' own consumption, and on a small scale. They should have a low level of organization and operate without a distinction between capital and labor as production factors. The owner of the unit of production must participate in the production process, and the number of employees in each unit cannot be greater than five. In summary, workers employed in the informal sector are all those assigned to units with the characteristics indicated above. I believe this definition is useful because it clearly posits that this is a labor market in which the possibilities of professional advancement are very limited.

The definition of informal economy adopted by the ILO likewise may aid in understanding the integration of Brazilian immigrants into the labor market at the two ends of the migratory flow, Brazil and the United States. Brazilian immigrants are being integrated into the labor market in Massachusetts similarly to any other group of recently arrived, nonprofessional immigrants. They hold jobs reserved for unskilled workers, and many of them are involved in activities connected to the informal sector. The majority of Brazilian immigrants, although not exclusively immigrants from Brazil, work in the service sector and not in the industrial sector. In Brazil prior to emigration, many of these workers already worked outside (or were never in) the formal labor market.

Table 4.1 presents a comparison of the jobs Brazilian immigrants held before and after they emigrated. The data collected in the 2005 survey differed little from those collected in 1996, as can be seen in the table.

Beyond the data shown in Table 4.1, I should add that information obtained through the qualitative interviews indicated that the majority of interviewees who had jobs in offices and retail establishments were employed in micro-businesses. This figure, when added to the number of self-employed workers, may indicate that the number of Brazilian emigrants who worked in the informal market while still in Brazil is quite significant.

Complementing the data collected in the 1996 and 2005 surveys, another survey was conducted in 1999 to determine what jobs were held

Table 4.1. Jobs Held by Brazilian Immigrants in Brazil prior to Emigration and in Massachusetts, 1996 and 2005

	Brazil		Massachusetts	
Occupation	1996 (%)	2005 (%)	1996 (%)	2005 (%)
Domestic service worker	—	1	15	19
Small-scale farmer	1	2	—	—
Construction worker	1	2	8	16
Homemaker	1	2	1	1
Bar or restaurant worker	1	2	8	10
Health care worker	2	1	2	1
Manager	2	2	3	3
Service worker, not self-employed	3	2	7	9
Public servant	4	3	—	—
College-educated professional	5	7	2	3
Laborer	5	6	3	3
Bank worker	6	5	—	—
Teacher	6	6	2	1
Mid-level technician	6	8	1	3
Small-business owner	7	10	5	4
Self-employed service worker	8	6	10	12
Retail worker	11	12	9	5
Student	13	10	2	4
Office worker	15	11	4	3
Unemployed	1	1	1	1
No response/none	2	1	17	2
Total	100	100	100	100

Source: Martes, surveys 1996 and 2005

Notes: n=300

Although individual percentages may be low, I opted to group the occupations to show their heterogeneity.

in Brazil by a sample of 100 immigrants before they immigrated (Table 4.2).

It can be seen that 22 of the 100 interviewees stated that they were unemployed in the period immediately preceding their departure for the United States. Of these, 68 had been unemployed from two to six months.

In fact, in the 1980s and the early 1990s, an increase in informal economic activities in Brazil can be observed. According to Freitas and Montagner (1997), between 1988 and 1996, there was a large reduction in the

Table 4.2. Jobs Held in Brazil Prior to Emigration by 100 Brazilian Immigrants, 1999

Self-employed	28
Small-business owner	9
Salaried contract worker	35
Salaried noncontract worker	13
Student	11
Homemaker	2
No answer	2
Total	100

Source: Martes, survey conducted in 1999.

number of positions in Brazilian industries, particularly in metalwork and mechanics, chemical and pharmaceutical, textiles and clothing, and construction and infrastructure. In the service sector, job growth occurred only in those areas whose activities had a close relationship with the process of outsourcing of auxiliary or specialized services. The growth in job openings in this sector along with the decrease in industrial jobs, which are traditionally more formalized, helps to explain the increase in informality during the same period.

From 1990 to 1992, a 19% reduction in the level of salaried formal employment can be seen in the private sector alone, alongside an increase in the number of self-employed workers and domestic workers. The economic recovery that occurred from 1993 to 1995 was insufficient to alter this trend in the Brazilian labor market so as to promote more intense absorption of labor into the economy (Baltar and Dedecca 1997).

In the 1990s a relative decrease in formal salaried employment occurred in favor of informal employment and self-employment. This last category arises as an alternative to unemployment or to the instability of integration into the labor market, especially for workers having scant human capital: a low level of education but some experience acquired on the job (Caccamali 1997). In that same decade, there was a further reduction in the number of formally contracted employees due to the reorganization of industrial activities and the public sector:

> The short-term strategy adopted by business in the 1990s, especially large industrial corporations, combined intensive reduction in the demand for labor with an increase in the use of alternative forms of subcontracting—of labor, services, and products. This practice was

> encouraged by the growing openness of the economy and facilitated by three factors: 1) the existence and forms of non-salaried integration, which involve extensive regulation; 2) a reduced level of union organization, and 3) differentiated legislation for micro- and small businesses with regard to taxes and other practices, which in theory favors subcontracting and, therefore, the transferal of a significant portion of labor costs from large to micro and small businesses. (Freitas and Montagner 1997: 2–3)

The informal economy grew alongside the restructuring of manufacturing that began in the late 1990s. However, it is difficult to establish any more direct relationship between the restructuring of manufacturing in Brazil—and its impact on the reorganization of the internal labor market—and the beginning of the migratory movement. This is because Brazilian immigration to Massachusetts intensified in the mid-1980s, and the impact of the restructuring of manufacturing on the Brazilian economy occurred beginning in the 1990s. The banking sector, which began to reorganize in the second half of the 1980s, is an exception. It is not a coincidence that 6% of those interviewed in 1996 and 5% of those interviewed in 2006 were bank workers (Table 4.1). But the fact that economic restructuring did not affect the beginning of the flow does not mean that its effects are not reflected in the continuation of the migratory process beginning in the 1990s.

The data available for the first decade of the century does not change this picture. Studies of the evolution of the informal urban economy in Brazil point to sustained levels of informal employment over the past decade. In October 2003 the Brazilian Institute of Geography and Statistics (IBGE) counted approximately 10.5 million small manufacturing units that participated in the informal urban sector, while in 1997 the number was 9.5 million enterprises.[3] Thus, an increase of 10% can be seen in this period. The most significant increase, however, can be seen in the number of job openings in these businesses—in 2003 an increase of 8% compared to 1997; by 2003 informal urban businesses employed nearly 13.5 million people. An important complement to this picture is information on the value of the receipts of these businesses, which tends to be decreasing. In 1997 they invoiced on average more than in 2003, a year in which the average receipts were 6,033 Brazilian *reais*. I believe this general picture reveals the existence of at least 13.5 million potential Brazilian emigrants.

Obviously, due to the very nature of the data, small-scale landowners and rural workers are excluded. Although few in number, some in this group already have begun to emigrate from various regions of the country.

I want to draw attention to the fact that Brazilian emigration and the expansion of the informal market in Brazil are two parallel phenomena. That is, Brazilian emigration coincides with the expansion of the informal economy in that country. As I see it, the decrease in formal employment helped to feed emigration, although there is not necessarily a causal relationship between them. This is because the jobs available in the informal labor market present very limited prospects for upward social mobility, and in this case emigration can become an alternative for those workers who do not manage to integrate themselves into the formal labor market. Although Brazilian immigrants are also included in the informal labor market in the United States, the income levels that they manage to reach are much higher, almost three to four times more, according to the qualitative interviews.

The growth of the informal economy and the increase of the migratory movements allow for comparison of the two ends of the flow, Brazil and the United States, because in the same period, growth of the informal economy is seen in the United States as well. There are, therefore, similarities and not only economic differences such as employment opportunities and better salaries and jobs between the two countries that receive and send migrants. Since the "new migratory wave" coincides with the expansion of the informal economy in the United States, various studies have begun to research the relationship between the two phenomena. Is it the case that immigrants are attracted to work in occupations provided by the expansion of the informal economy in the United States? Or are they bringing with them to the United States the forms of economy activity typical of their places of origin?

Saskia Sassen-Koob (1985) criticizes the association usually established between expansion of the informal sector and the growth of Latin and Asian immigrant populations according to which the immigrants replicate in the United States the survival strategies developed in their native countries. In fact, although immigrants tend to make the most of the opportunities arising from informalization, such opportunities are not necessarily created by them. They are the structural result of the current trend in advanced industrial economies. The growth of the service sector and the introduction of new technologies had a large impact on the urban economy in restructuring the labor market. Sassen points out two central characteristics of the economy of New York City: an increase in both low-wage jobs and the number of highly paid workers. The growth of both categories contrasts sharply with the expansion of labor in the post–World War II period, when an increase in mid-level jobs was seen. The economy now is moving in the opposite direction of that period of mass production and the growth of the middle class in the United States. Alongside the expansion of the market for extremely high-priced products can be seen increased availability of products whose prices are surprisingly low, in the service sector as well as in manufacturing and retail. In this context, the informal economy emerges in the United States as an alternative to reduce costs and to make production more flexible (Sassen-Koob 1985).

Alejandro Portes (1995) finds that the informal economy has become stronger, especially in the clothing industry, electronics manufacturing, and retail trade. The clothing industry, one of the industries most affected by economic globalization, began to contract small businesses (including sweatshops) that employ workers in unstable circumstances.[4] In New York City a large proportion of these businesses moved to neighborhoods where a high concentration of immigrants reside (such as Queens and the Bronx) to reduce the costs associated with the unionized workforce. In the electronics industry, direct manufacturing and assembly of goods that do not require skilled labor have been employing predominantly Latina immigrant workers. Small retail trade establishments, a niche that is more and more suited to immigrants, offer products such as clothing, food, decorative items, and perfumes that are imported from every place on the planet.

To what point, however, does the restructuring of manufacturing in the U.S. economy help to explain the integration of Brazilian immigrants into the labor market in Massachusetts? If Table 4.1, which presents the jobs held by the Brazilian immigrants in that state, is observed more closely, it can be concluded that the sectors in which Brazilian's are employed are not affected directly by the restructuring. The jobs Brazilians hold are concentrated in the service sector and specifically in the informal service sector.

The expansion of the fast-food sector of the food service industry, the increase in job openings for cleaning women—a job that thirty years ago seemed destined for extinction in the United States—or even the increase in openings in nursing homes are more readily associated with changes in lifestyle, in patterns of consumption, and in gender relationships, particularly as related to the growing integration of women into the U.S. labor market. This means that sociological and not only economic variables merit the attention of researchers so that they may consider the recent demands of the host society that immigrant labor meets.

Three Ways of Making Money

Brazilian immigrants in Massachusetts hold jobs and exploit niche markets that can be classified as low-wage workers, self-employed workers, and small-scale entrepreneurs. I will discuss each of these categories, highlighting their principal characteristics and differences, the forces that drive them, the meaning that Brazilians attribute to each category, and the role that each plays in the internal dynamics of the group. First, however, it should be emphasized that although these can be classified as activities connected to the informal economy or to the secondary labor market, these categories are organized hierarchically by immigrants in terms of the social mobility they afford.

Recently arrived Brazilians generally begin by working in hotels, in nursing homes, as cleaning staff in hospitals, or even as dishwashers or housecleaning assistants alongside other Brazilians who have already "purchased" the houses in which they work. A few months later, these immigrants manage to get other jobs that are better paid and less strenuous. The next step may be working as an assistant cook, delivering newspapers or pizzas, working in a fast-food restaurant (especially for one of the big national chains),[5] or busing tables. These jobs function as springboards to the next step: construction work for men and housecleaning for women.[6] Moving from belonging to the middle class to becoming a low-wage worker might seem like a decline in social mobility, but this is true only when considered in terms of prestige, not income. This movement shows that Brazilian immigrants adopt different criteria when seeking their place in each of the two societies.

After earning some money by working hard in construction or housecleaning, an immigrant might open a small business oriented toward the Brazilian consumer. Becoming an entrepreneur is the primary aspiration of most Brazilian immigrants. This possibility is facilitated by the low barriers imposed to either entrepreneurship or self-employment, so they are compatible with the immigrants' human capital. Thus, according to the Brazilian owner of an accounting firm,

> We have more than 500 Brazilian businesses registered here, the majority in Somerville and Framingham. In one year alone, I registered more than 100 businesses as self-employment. In Brazil, the government limits the size of a business, but here a person who does housecleaning can be a business. The U.S. government says that if you work for yourself and pay taxes, you are a business. It is the dream of Brazilians here to be self-employed.

When examining the changes in the social status of Brazilian immigrants, how they interpret these changes, and the value their family members and friends in Brazil attribute to the idea of going to "live in America" should not be underestimated.[7] The departure in and of itself is generally interpreted as a kind of upward social mobility or, at the very least, as a chance to escape the poverty to which they see themselves as susceptible.

Roberto's case is illustrative of this perception. He abandoned his dream of becoming a doctor after several unsuccessful attempts to get into college. His brother managed to graduate from the program that he desired, which made Roberto feel "very inferior." His only remaining option was to open his own business, but he had no investment capital. When Roberto was 23 years old, a childhood friend lived in Boston, and Roberto decided to take a chance. I asked Roberto to tell me what impression the people in his hometown had of him now that he lived in Massachusetts, and he answered:

> "They think that I'm rich. Everyone thinks that anyone who's in the United States is rich, and you're not rich. You spend and earn more than you do there [in Brazil]. It's not my family that thinks this; it's the other people who know me."

Roberto said he did not regret having left Brazil. He was satisfied with his job working in a stockroom. He thought he made a good salary, he went on vacation every year (he already had been to Las Vegas and traveled to Florida), and he had good health insurance paid by the firm where he worked, even though he was there illegally. But it was not always so easy, especially in the beginning when he worked as a dishwasher, a job he managed to get in his first days in Massachusetts thanks to a tip from a friend. Roberto was planning to open a cleaning business with the savings he accumulated.

Self-employment is seen as an option for individuals who belong to social groups marked by a long-disadvantaged place in the workforce (Light and Rosenstein 1995, Tienda and Raijman 2000a,b). For Brazilians, becoming self-employed or having their own businesses represents the highest aspiration of social mobility for the first generation of immigrants who have little cultural capital. Precisely this case is seen in what Ivan Light has described (2004: 8) in other immigrant groups: "For poorly educated adults, business ownership in the informal and illegal sub sectors of the ethnic economy permits more lifetime mobility into the middle class than do all other avenues of mobility together . . . the informal economy rewards this human capital better than does the formal."

Low-Wage Salaried Workers

Undocumented immigrants are the principal source of a low-wage workforce in the United States. They do menial jobs and occupy the lowest positions in the occupational and wage hierarchies. Until about the 1970s, low-wage workers were predominantly rural workers; at that time, they began to concentrate in the service sector of U.S. labor market.

According to the data collected in the interviews, the jobs found in this category share the following characteristics: the work is offered both within and outside of the Brazilian community; a typical employer-employee bond is lacking; weekly wages are paid per hour worked and in cash; the employer pays no benefits or Social Security taxes for the employee; the work is part-time, which makes it "possible" for the worker to have more than one job; the wages are low compared to the U.S. average but for Brazilians are quite attractive; the work requires few skills and no sort of previous training, although many workers have at least some college education in unrelated areas; the type of work is of little social value to locals (with workers lacking status and social prestige) but is valued by the Brazilians due to the pay and work relationships; and there is a high rate of worker turnover, either voluntary or compulsory.

These characteristics are specifically centered on the irregular nature of the employment agreements, regardless of the stature of the business. Brazilians who make up the "low-wage worker" category are employed by national supermarket chains, large international fast-food chains, snack shops and restaurants, or even locally important midsize or small firms, especially as maintenance workers. The following occupations are found in this category: food-preparation workers, buspersons, waiters, pizza and newspaper delivery people, and workers in commercial cleaning firms.

Brazilians, like other immigrants who find themselves in similar circumstances, are contracted as temporary workers although they may stay for years in the same job. A significant proportion of Brazilian low-wage workers are employed by companies that clean commercial buildings, offices, and restaurants. In the Boston metropolitan area, this is one sphere of commercial activity that has experienced tremendous growth over the past forty years. This is because in the late 1960s, large firms began to subcontract maintenance work to small cleaning companies.[8] The greatest growth in this sector can be seen in the 1980s. Between 1982 and 1987 alone, the volume of jobs in this sector grew by 34%. Most of these companies are not unionized and offer part-time employment at wages between $4.25 and $6.00 per hour.

The labor contracted by these firms is traditionally immigrant labor. According to Lado (1994), the Portuguese and Polish immigrants who constituted a substantial part of this labor force up to the 1970s were later replaced by Cape Verdean and Latino immigrants (Guatemalans, Colombians, Haitians, Dominicans, and Brazilians, among others). However, the management positions of these firms even today are predominantly occupied by Portuguese immigrants, which Brazilians say is a source of constant conflict. Several of the Brazilians interviewed complained about the managers' "stupid way of behaving" and mentioned cases of sexual abuse by Portuguese supervisors against their female Brazilian subordinates.

Legally, the candidates for the available job openings in this sector must present proof of residency and authorization to work in the United States (a Social Security number) at the time they are contracted. Companies must report the names of job candidates who present counterfeit documents, but that communication does not occur in reality; on the rare occasions when such information is reported, the "INS admits that it does not have the power necessary to oblige compliance with its legal requirements" (Lado 1994: 33). If the cleaning company is unionized, benefits are established in the contract with the union: paid holidays, retirement benefits, and sick leave. Otherwise, the workers do not receive such benefits, and the wages are lower. Still, according to information given to the author in 2005 by the president of the Brazilian Immigrant Center in

Massachusetts, even companies whose workers are not unionized must pay overtime and include the workers' travel time in their wages.

It is estimated that a greater number of undocumented workers are employed in nonunionized companies. Maintenance workers in Boston are formally represented by Local 254 of the Service Employees International Union regardless of their legal status, since union membership is automatic after 130 days of work, and their union dues are deducted directly from their wages. However, as Lado stresses, this union has the reputation of not representing its members as it should.

When a Job Is Also a Business: Self-Employed Workers

This group is characterized principally by the way its members perceive their work relationships: they have no bosses, but they do have clients to whom they sell their services.[9] Payment is rendered per task and not per hour worked. Their services are offered outside the Brazilian community, and no type of employment paperwork is necessary because there is no formal contact but rather a verbal agreement. This category includes housecleaners and some construction workers.

In brief, these occupations share the following characteristics: the services are offered outside the Brazilian community; there is no employer-employee relationship; payment is rendered per task and in cash after the task is completed; the employer (client) has no social responsibility for the worker; the work is part-time, which permits the workers to serve more than one client on the same day; the work is unskilled, and any training is given as the tasks are performed; and the work is of little social value to locals (the workers have little social status or prestige), but the work is valued by Brazilians due to its independent nature, the positive relationships between worker and client, and the amount of income generated.

As mentioned previously, from the 1970s on, rapid growth in the number of self-employed workers in the United States (people who work in their own businesses or professions) can be seen. Currently, this group consists principally of African Americans, women, Hispanics, and Asians and is especially concentrated in the areas of services and financing, insurance, and real estate (De Freitas 1991: 168).

Of these self-employed workers, those who work in housecleaning constitute the most significant occupational niche of Brazilian immigrants in Massachusetts. Suzanne Model (1993) uses the expression "ethnic niche" to indicate the occupations in which a particular ethnic group manages to gain an advantage in the labor market for some specific reason. In fact, Brazilian immigrants appropriated the housecleaning niche so as to generate distinct advantages relative to other immigrant groups, as will be shown. Also for this reason, housecleaning has characteristics that merit more detailed analysis.

When Housecleaning Becomes an (Excellent) Business

The majority of Brazilians who work in this niche say that they own a business, a *companhia de limpeza* (cleaning company).[10] In most cases the business consists of only one person who is at once the owner and the worker. In others, however, the cleaning company may be formed by a couple, or even by an owner and an assistant, out of which arises a kind of subcontracting. As a general rule, the assistant is also a Brazilian and has arrived recently in the United States. During the periods in which the surveys were conducted, the person who owned the company earned an average of $50 to clean a house that took, on average, two and a half hours to finish. The assistant received about $5 an hour from the owner of the company, or approximately the U.S. minimum wage at the time.

Calling housecleaning a business may be interpreted as a euphemism intended to disguise the lowering of the occupational status of the immigrant as compared to his or her former position in Brazil. As mentioned, a large proportion of Brazilian immigrants had jobs of higher social value in Brazil than the ones they later held in the United States. Although in Brazil as in the United States it is something of an exaggeration to consider a housecleaning service with as few as one or two workers a business, it does not seem to me that this exaggeration is simply a way to deal with the lowering of status. For the Brazilian residents of Boston, housecleaning is not only considered a business, but it is a great business.

Since most Brazilian immigrants presumably intend to return to Brazil, the faster they can save money, the more quickly they will have the opportunity to realize this goal. Michael Piore, in analyzing the situation of other immigrant groups (1979), concludes that the temporary nature of the stay in the United States and the disassociation between the status of the worker in the destination country and in his or her native country, due to this transitoriness, help to explain why immigrants accept jobs that are less valued than those that they had in their native countries. However, among Brazilians, such dissociation is only part of the explanation, for what can be seen here is a valuing of this type of work.

Brazilians generally tend to posit themselves as economic refugees who were driven away by the crises that extended throughout the 1980s and into the 1990s. For this reason, they tend to highlight the presence of "many professionals" among them (doctors, engineers, lawyers, and so on). Where there is a significant decrease in occupational status, the decline is made subjectively relative. That is, occupational status tends to be reinterpreted according to new criteria that permit the revaluing of certain occupations.

Housecleaning is the area in which the revaluing of the work is most significant because it permits the establishment of a business. The arduous side of housecleaning rarely surfaces. It is constantly hidden in the accounts when the principal preoccupation is to ennoble the work, whatever it may be. Housecleaning in Brazil is different from housecleaning in the United States, as will be discussed, but in both Brazil and the United States cleaning houses means cleaning bathrooms and kitchens. Yet housecleaning in the United States is seen also as a means of immersion into the local culture. By cleaning houses, Brazilians enter "the American home."

Various authors stress that first-generation immigrants are the target population in economic ascent and care little about social status (Waldinger, Aldrich, and Ward 2000). Brazilians have transformed housecleaning into a symbol of upward social mobility in the eyes of their compatriots. The housecleaner, even if he or she works alone, is "the owner of a company." Owning a business is a form of promoting oneself before the members of the group. In this sense, one sells not only a house in which to work but also a symbol that identifies those Brazilians who already have "started to make money." This status attenuates the traditionally female nature of housecleaning to the point of incorporating male labor, thus strengthening the business-owning couple as an economic unit. In this way, housecleaning connotes, at least initially, what Brazilians went looking for in America. It is a source of income but also a source of stability and satisfaction.

The valuing of housecleaning derives principally from the income level that a housecleaner can reach in Massachusetts ($20 an hour at the time the research was conducted). A good wage provides dignity. But other factors that contribute to the creation of this valuing must be considered: the meaning of being a housecleaner in Brazil is very different from that of being a housecleaner in the United States. The perception of this difference is so clear that the interviewees confirmed that in Brazil they would never submit to doing this type of work. In Boston, besides good pay and the notion that they owned a business, the nature of the work itself and the relationship between client and employee cause many Brazilian immigrants to value housecleaning. It is important to clarify that a cleaning woman in Massachusetts has set tasks: vacuuming, cleaning bathrooms and the kitchen (with products that permit a "dry" cleaning), and dusting the furniture. In contrast, in Brazil a cleaning woman tends to do whatever tasks the homemaker specifies, which may include anything from washing and ironing clothes to cooking. The job of housecleaner in the United States is therefore considered to involve much less heavy work, and those who do it see it as a different situation than what a cleaning woman in Brazil experiences.[11] The following excerpt of the interview with Dulcinéia illustrates this point:

> I am a cleaning woman. People devalue cleaning women in Brazil. They don't respect them. Not here. I am treated as a person who is important to the family, a trustworthy person. They turn the house and the key over to me, and jewelry and money. In Brazil they are not trusting. In Brazil my salary was viewed as good. But when the rent went up, I had to ask my brother for money just to buy food . . . It doesn't bother me to work at something inferior to what I did in Brazil. I don't know if it's because I think that I couldn't be doing anything better, or if I give great value to what I do. I see people working in offices, they have a work permit and speak English well and earn 200 U.S. dollars per week. I work for myself, I am nobody's employee.

Her remarks confirm a fundamental point regarding the situation of the self-employed worker: relationships between workers and employers in the United States are very different from those typical in Brazil, and these differences permit the immigrants to relativize the submission typical of this job in the Brazilian context. In the United States, housecleaners can view themselves as self-employed workers, while in Brazil they are employees.

The men and women engaged in housecleaning in the United States consider themselves self-employed workers, especially because they have no bosses, but rather *clients*. The employer, they argue, treats workers with trust and respect and assures them a fair wage for the services rendered. Some interviewees emphasize the more formal nature of the treatment they receive from their clients, and this very formality is interpreted as professionalism, a characteristic that is absent in the relationship between cleaning women and homemakers in Brazil. Formality in personal dealings is perceived as a cultural trait, and many of the interviewees made a point of relating the ways they tried to "break the ice" and "win over" the goodwill of the clients by taking greater care in their work, preparing "a little homemade soup" and other friendly gestures that from their perspective made Americans prefer Brazilian cleaning women.

Brazilians perceive this difference as a "comparative cultural advantage," to use the expression coined by Peter Berger (Halter 1995). It is important to note that this is one of the moments when Brazilian immigrants feel a positive affirmation of their national origin.

Analyzed as a whole, these data help explain why Brazilian immigrants tend to evaluate their personal migratory experiences favorably. Although they may be in the extremely adverse circumstance of being illegal immigrants who work in jobs completely devoid of social prestige, the majority of the interviewees said they felt more dignity in their current situation as immigrant workers in the United States than they had in their previous situation as workers in Brazil, a country in which, although they were citizens, they did not exercise full citizenship.

For all these reasons, Brazilian immigrants who manage to get into the area of housecleaning rarely leave it except when they return to Brazil.[12] Because they have started businesses, although this may seem laughable to someone who observes it from the outside, many rise somewhat professionally, a feat not easily accomplished in the immigrants' circumstances. This means that there is some job mobility among Brazilians immigrants.

Like other recently arrived immigrants, most Brazilians gain access to available jobs by information transmitted through their friendship, family, and religious networks. Nevertheless, there is one area in which information about jobs is sold: housecleaning.

Job Selling

Aparecida, age 42, described her housecleaning enterprise:

> Now, after having worked hard and having put together a good schedule of houses, I plan to sell it to a Brazilian. So, I sent several

emails to the Brazilians I know, and I asked them to forward these to as many people as possible. With the money, I'm going to buy a shop in Lowell. Now, fifteen years ago when I went to buy a house [to clean], the house[work] belonged to a woman I knew in my city. I was a friend of hers. I learned about the house and bought it. But here, in any Brazilian beauty salon, or in the shops, restaurants, banquet halls, or in the church, there was always someone who was selling something. And the person who bought it didn't even have to be a friend. It was business, like any other business. And it's still like that today.

How does job selling work? Because Brazilian immigrants who enter the area of housecleaning rarely leave it, when they decide to "sell" the houses in which they work, it is generally because they are returning to Brazil permanently. Information about the sale is primarily spread through friendship, family, religious, and neighborhood networks, but there is no obstacle to selling the houses to Brazilians who are strangers. Advertisements for houses that are "for sale" can be found in Brazilian newspapers in Massachusetts as well as on notice boards in Brazilian stores. The housecleaning trade seems to be so promising that an advertisement was placed in the newspaper *Brazilian Times* for a "housecleaning kit." This is a manual with a set of instructions about cleaning products, key words in English that may be useful when communicating with the homemaker, guidelines for how to treat the homemaker, and information about how to accumulate the largest number of houses to clean in the shortest amount of time. More recently, information about selling and buying jobs, in other words, houses to clean, can also be spread via the Internet, as indicated in Aparecida's account above.

There is no fixed price for the sale of houses, but it is on average the equivalent of three months' work in each house. The price depends, however, on the number of houses put up for sale, the rule of thumb being that a housecleaner cleans two houses per day. When a buyer appears, the seller speaks with the homemaker to explain that she is leaving her job but that she has a Brazilian friend who can replace her. If the employer agrees to meet the friend, the seller promises to train her. Thus the homemaker can determine if the job done by the candidate is satisfactory. This transition is completed on average over a period of about a month, enough time for the homemaker and the candidate to reach an initial understanding. If the homeowner agrees to hire the candidate, the transaction between the buyer and seller is concluded, which means that the house is sold and cash payment is made immediately. From that moment on, there is no going back; the transaction is done, even if the new housecleaner is fired soon afterward.

During the course of my research, I did not find any information about other groups of immigrants that practice job selling so systematically.[13] Mahler (1995) records the occurrence of job selling among Latino immigrants residing in Long Island, but there it happens in a very different way. The author mentions a Cuban who charged $50 to get jobs for recently arrived Hispanics. The researcher refers to this practice as a kind of "recruiting" of employees, which seems strange to me since the one who pays for the employment is the employee and not the employer, and she calls the service provided by the Cuban immigrant "information assistance" (156). This Cuban man, along with a Puerto Rican immigrant, charged recently arrived immigrants for finding them houses to rent and for sending letters. Calling such practices "information assistance" strikes me as a euphemism for referring to the ways immigrants sell information to their peers. In any event, these two cases do not contradict the rule: Latinos, Mahler concludes, get employment through their compatriots and relatives, like all other immigrant groups in the United States.

According to Margolis (1994), Brazilian immigrants who work shining shoes in the streets and parks of New York also sell their positions. In this particular case, however, the sale of a place constitutes a common practice. It is presumed that the person shining shoes has acquired the right to use the place where he works although it is a public place. The unique aspect of the practice of house selling in Massachusetts is in the sale of the right to work in a house that does not belong to the seller and without the owner's consent to the transaction. Access to housecleaning is access to the "American home." It is, therefore, a more closed transaction because it requires trust.

It is even more curious that although the positions are sold, this market functions on a presumption of ethnic solidarity. That is, when the cleaning woman tells the homemaker that she cannot continue working but can recommend "a trustworthy friend" to replace her, the cleaning woman is acting as if she were motivated by solidarity in relation to the other Brazilian. When the homemaker accepts the offer, she is presuming that the cleaning woman is motivated by solidarity and not some economic gain.

By accepting the offer the homemaker is reinforcing the idea of ethnic solidarity. Thus, the trust that she placed in the first cleaning woman is transferred to the one who will replace her (obviously not without some restrictions, since trust requires not only a recommendation but also familiarity). Despite this pretense, the market works well. The new cleaning woman will make every effort to meet the homemaker's expectations and gain her trust because if she does not, she will be let go and suffer a loss at least equal to the amount she paid for the house.

But what factors favor this trade? Not having a good command of the English language and a lack of legal documentation are two factors that make access to the labor market difficult, favoring the buying and selling of jobs. With the exception of the area of housecleaning, there are basically four means of access to information about job openings. Information can come through the Brazilians' social and religious networks, from newspaper ads, from information spread by employers themselves, and, more recently, via the Internet. It is significant that housecleaning is considered a business by Brazilians who live in Boston and the decision to immigrate to the United States as an investment. Except for those who find professional positions, housecleaning is the best-paid work to which Brazilians have access. Some couples earn as much as $4,000 per month. In contrast, job openings are more scarce. In general, the circumstances surrounding job selling have not changed over the past decade except in the stance that churches have taken toward it, as will be discussed.

Why Does Solidarity Matter?

The literature in the United States tends to emphasize the role that ethnic networks play in immigrants' access to the labor market. According to Portes (1995: 12),

> Social capital refers to the ability of individuals to command scarce resources by virtue of their belonging to networks or broader social structures. Such resources may include tangible economic goods, like discounted prices and loans, as well as intangible goods, like information about business conditions, exclusive information about jobs, and generalized "goodwill" in market transactions. The conceptual key that is characteristic of such resources is that they are free. They have the nature of a gift since it is not expected that they

> will be repaid by a quantity of money or another object of value within a certain period of time. The resources acquired through social capital frequently carry an expectation of reciprocity at some future point.[14]

I want to point out the limitations of the concept of social capital centered on a notion of ethnic solidarity in explaining cases like that of Brazilians who work in housecleaning insofar as access to jobs is concerned because this involves a different sort of relationship. This is not because social capital is unimportant in the course of the transaction—since most often the trade takes place between people who are connected by bonds of kinship, friendship, or membership in the same church—but rather because, in this case, access comes through a buyer-seller relationship. The networks spread information about houses that are available within these networks, but sometimes the transaction occurs without the seller even knowing the buyer, even though the trade takes place only between Brazilians.

It is possible that only Brazilians "sell houses," but exactly how this trade began is unknown. It certainly is not a Brazilian custom. However, when one hears about the topic, it is difficult to prevent some Brazilian scenarios from coming to mind, such as the sale of locations for the *jogo do bicho*,[15] a gambling game, or jobs for unskilled laborers on the docks. There seems to be something in common between housecleaning and these examples: the idea of possession. Possession is understood as the control that someone acquires over a job, so that house selling may represent not the entrepreneurial impulse of Brazilian immigrants but rather an archaic vestige of Brazil's culture of inheritance. It is perhaps for this reason that job selling was at times interpreted by the interviewees as a sign of the Americanization of Brazilian immigrants ("In America, everything is about money") and at times as a bruising manifestation of the Brazilian *jeitinho* or of a lack of solidarity.[16] Loaded with ambiguity, this trade generates a series of embarrassments. The interviews reveal a bit of apology in relation to the homemaker and a modicum of exploitation and lack of solidarity in relation to the buyer.

Even if the Brazilians in Boston sell employment recommendations in the area of housecleaning when such recommendations are generally transmitted in other groups as a function of a supposed solidarity, innumerable manifestations of solidarity among Brazilian immigrants appear, particularly within religious communities and among close friends and family members. Brazilian immigrants collect money to send to philanthropic organizations in Brazil, help their compatriots in emergencies, offer support and assistance to their recently arrived family members and friends, and so on. Therefore, nothing indicates that job selling represents the breakdown of good social relations or a lack of solidarity within the group. It is rather a matter of practices having to do with specific contacts that are reached at particular times. Solidarity does not preclude self-interest, and it cannot be forgotten that the immigrants are participating in a highly competitive society and were attracted to the United States for precisely this reason. This is particularly interesting to the degree that sociologists in the United States have highlighted close relationships among solidarity, trust, and the informal economy and include so-called ethnic businesses in this category.

Portes has found (1995) that in order for the informal market to function effectively, the communities it involves must be able to preserve strict dependence on social bonds. Mutual trust between the contracting parties is a precondition for the existence of the market itself. Without a high degree of trust, there would be no way for the informal market to work. Trust, Portes asserts, is generated by shared "identities and feelings" and by the expectation that if deception occurs, the transgressor will be punished by exclusion from the social network to which he or she belongs. That is, the sanction in these cases is exclusion from the network, and the transgressor's punishment is his or her separation.

But are "trust" and "solidarity" correlative terms? I do not believe so. Solidarity involves the notion of community, the sharing of common ideas, and a sense of moral duty, as Portes points out. I believe that trust precedes the idea of community, though, because above all trust refers to a kind of confidence, an expectation that someone has regarding the behavior of another person. This is why cooperation is possible without solidarity. That is, for cooperation to exist, trust alone is sufficient, and solidarity is not necessary. Trust results from a calculation regarding the possibility that the conduct of another will not be opportunistic because such behavior may be disadvantageous for that other person as well. Solidarity, like trust, involves the construction of relationships within groups and therefore also may involve self-interest (Macedo 1998).

From a very broad perspective, making any contract requires a degree of trust. For example, Brazilians have a reputation as being bad credit risks, and in many Brazilian retail establishments neither checks nor credit cards are accepted, or payment is required at the time a service is rendered. Here, the lack of trust does not prevent the market from functioning, but it does require that the agents take care to have certain guarantees. This is also true for the customers. I will give just one example. The illegal remittance of dollars to Brazil carried out by Brazilian agencies in Massachusetts cannot be used as proof of the trust Brazilians place in the owners of these agencies, who are also Brazilians. Rather, it reveals the lack of a viable alternative: there are no Brazilian banks in the state. When sending money illegally through these agencies, a person runs the risk that the money will be misappropriated.

Finally, Portes' argument includes the idea that immigrant populations can be described as if they formed a single large network defined by the term "community." To the contrary, if it is assumed that several networks exist and that they compete with each other, it can equally be assumed that an immigrant who has been excluded from one network would have some chance of becoming integrated into another precisely because of the competition. In the case of Brazilian immigrants, competition among various networks occurs in the commercial sphere (in Brazilian business), as well as in the religious sphere.

Sociability Matters: Brazilian Small-Business Owners

Among the most visible transformations that have occurred since the beginning of Brazilian immigration into Massachusetts, the increase in the number of small businesses that principally serve the Brazilian community merits discussion. In the early 1980s, establishments began to spring up in Somerville (Union Square), Allston, and Cambridge (Cambridge Street) such as a small shop selling a variety of Brazilian products, a beauty salon, and an ethnic restaurant. By the mid-1990s, businesses appeared whose products and services were more varied, such as English-language schools, medical and dental offices, and photography studios, all of which were oriented predominantly toward serving the Brazilian immigrant population. Today, Brazilian businesses are easily found in the downtown areas of other cities that have large concentrations of Brazilian immigrants, especially Marlborough, Framingham, and East Boston, and in East Providence, Everett, Lowell, Arlington, Nashua, and Cape Cod, among others. An interesting record of the evolution of Brazilian businesses can be gleaned from the pages of community newspapers in advertisements, news stories, and society pages. The owner of the newspaper *Brazilian Times* said that almost seventy Brazilian micro-businesses based in the United States placed ads in this newspaper in the early 2000s, and 80% of those businesses were in Massachusetts.

Understanding entrepreneurship as the third type of economic activity to which Brazilian immigrants have access in the United States completes the analysis presented here about the three ways of making a living in Massachusetts. These entrepreneurs include musicians and hairdressers, but they are mainly owners of restaurants, shops, and offices whose services are oriented toward Brazilian immigrants. Such enterprises, which are designated as ethnic businesses, develop specific connections and regular patterns of interaction with people who share a common nationality or a common immigrant experience (Waldinger, Aldrich, and Ward 2000). Therefore, the study of the entrepreneurship of an immigrant group is not limited to a strict analysis of the supply and demand of goods and services. It is more important to understand the relationships that make up the social sphere of business owners, clientele, stakeholders, and broader networks.

What Brazilians Want to Buy and the Establishments That Offer It

Immigrant populations of any nationality generate their own consumer demands; for this reason, neighborhoods where immigrants are concentrated tend to have small retail establishments oriented toward these populations (Halter 1995, Light and Gold 2000, Light and Rosenstein 1995). The recognition of Brazilians' demand for Brazilian products is one of the principal reasons given by entrepreneurs for having opened their businesses. Although immigrants from other countries and native-born Americans frequent these businesses on occasion, most of the customers are Brazilian. As one of the interviewees stated,

> In five years the number of businesses here doubled, and this is due to immigration. More and more Brazilians are constantly arriving. If the clientele grows, the businesses grow. The majority of these are stable; I don't see businesses closing. If the number of Brazilians were to decline, the businesses would also decline.

Halter (1995) notes that when an immigrant purchases a product from his native country, he is not just trying to meet a need. The merchandise that he gets has high symbolic value due to its direct reference to his native culture, and it has no equivalent in an American supermarket. Often, access to some kinds of products has been made possible by the increase in income resulting from immigration. Therefore, sociocultural and economic factors are involved in the consumption of these products. This is illustrated in the following excerpt from an interview with the owner of a Brazilian store in Brookline:

> I have many customers who want to buy Brazilian designer clothes. They're expensive. One of them told me, "Back home, the mayor's daughter used to wear clothes by Fórum, and I couldn't afford them. Here, I buy them because I can."

This statement reveals that the consumer aspirations of these customers still revolve around Brazilian values and consumption patterns.

Chimarrão (a kind of Brazilian tea), *oleo de dendê* (African palm oil, a key ingredient of some Brazilian regional cuisines), coconut milk, *rapadura* (raw brown sugar that comes in blocks), and even pressure cookers (one cannot forget the black beans) and clay pans (used for preparing an authentic *moqueca capixaba*, a kind of seafood stew that has its origins in the cuisine of the Brazilian state of Espírito Santo) are easily found in Brazilian shops. Because these are products related to Brazilian cuisine, it comes as no surprise that they are rarely available in other stores and cannot be replaced by equivalent American products.

Under these circumstances, purchasing Brazilian products is not a purely economic act. In fact, the main attraction of Brazilian retail establishments is not price but rather the kinds of products they offer. However, this is a different situation from that in the retail trade of Latino immigrants in New York City (Mahler 1995: 139). Brazilian restaurants and retail stores do not necessarily offer products or services that are comparatively less expensive. There was empirical evidence for this when, from the mid-1990s to the early 2000s, the U.S. dollar and the Brazilian *real* came to have equal value, that is, a dollar was worth exactly one *real*. It was precisely in this period that the greatest expansion of Brazilian businesses occurred.

Even today, a Brazilian "dental floss"–style bikini is more expensive than a bikini purchased in a department store. Garoto-brand candies may cost the same as a similar American product, the Brazilian soft drink *guaraná* is the same price as Coca-Cola, and so forth. Brazilians purchase some products in Brazilian stores because that is the only place they can find them.

A large variety of Brazilian food products can be found in these establishments (such as Brazilian "cheese bread," savory snacks, Sonho de Valsa–brand chocolates, and sweetened condensed milk), as well as Brazilian-style clothing (bare-midriff blouses and tight pants, for example), airplane tickets, pharmaceutical products (medicines, even antibiotics without a prescription), personal hygiene products (of brands that are popular in Brazil such as Phebo, Natura, Boticário, and Leite de Rosa), and jewelry made with precious and semiprecious stones mined in the Governador Valadares region.[17] Videotapes of Brazilian television programs, especially soap operas, can be found in variety stores. However, video rental is in decline because the programming of Rede Globo (a large Brazilian media network) is broadcast to some U.S. cities, including those in the Boston area.

Almost all of the Brazilian shops handle remittances even though they do not specialize in this service. There is in fact great demand for this type of service since almost 80% of Brazilian immigrants send remittances to Brazil with some regularity, with a total of $6,535 sent annually per remitter (Martes and Soares 2004, Martes 2005a,b,c). Indeed, according to scholars, remittances in general are primarily sent by businesses and not by banks (Suárez-Orozco and Suárez-Orozco 2001). This was also the case for Brazilian immigrants until 2003.[18]

To enhance the significance associated with the products they make available, small businesses and the Brazilian media (newspapers and radio programs) in Massachusetts have a special interest in projecting an attractive image of Brazil to the Brazilian immigrants themselves.[19] Brazilian businesses attempt to recreate a "slice of Brazil" in the United States that can provide what the community tends to appreciate most from its native country: food, clothing, and music, for example. In offering these products, the businesses play a strategic role by enhancing the visibility of Brazilian immigrants, promoting a pleasing image of Brazil, and supporting and disseminating information regarding activities such as Brazilian musical performances, *carnaval* dances, and Brazilian independence-day celebrations. These businesses promote a favorable image of Brazil because they cater to the Brazilian consumer market, that is, to a segment of the market defined by ethnicity and supported more broadly by national origin. Thus, Brazilian businesses and media in Massachusetts foster an ideal image of Brazil at least in part to increase the value of the products they sell.

This promotion of Brazil is readily seen in the photographs of Brazilian cities and calendars from Brazil exhibited in many businesses as a means of immediately identifying the nationality with which they are associated. The names of these establishments, which invariably evoke aspects of national identity, are often posted on signs of yellow and green (the colors of the Brazilian national flag): Salão Brazil, Salão Ipanema, Café Brasil, Valadares Express, and so forth. However, after September 11, 2001, the size and number of some of the Brazilian flags displayed by these businesses were reduced, or the business owners placed U.S. flags next to the Brazilian flags.

In any event, while such national symbols are often seen in retail establishments, I did not observe symbols or objects referring to national culture in many residences of Brazilian immigrants. In only three homes, and more precisely, in three bedrooms, was there a Brazilian flag. Also in the bedroom, the most intimate and hidden part of the home, I saw images of saints and rosaries hanging above the head of the bed. Thus, perhaps in no other context with the exception of churches and, obviously, the offices of societies that seek to represent the community is Brazilian identity expressed as overtly as it is in Brazilian businesses in Massachusetts.

The value attached to Brazil and its culture by Brazilian immigrants is not unlimited. The relationship between business owners and their Brazilian clientele consists of a series of ambiguities that can be explained by an initial attitude of mistrust.

To describe this relationship I will cite two examples. One of the hair salons in Cambridge owned by a Brazilian refuses to take checks from Brazilians. The owner explained: "We've had a lot of checks that have been returned. I don't accept them any more." Likewise, in a store in Somerville, the owner refuses to accept credit cards from Brazilians. In general, it appears that Brazilians do not have a good reputation in this area: "They aren't good about making payments, and they don't honor the due dates." These statements, albeit clearly stereotypical, indicate a low level of trust among Brazilian immigrants in Massachusetts. Relationships of trust are maintained only in family, friendship, and religious networks.

The Role of Small Businesses in Supporting Sociability, Networks, and Community Activities

In addition to retail trade, the simple buying and selling of goods and services, ethnic businesses perform three curious and no less important functions. These three less obvious functions can be called latent functions, as Robert Merton (1968) has named those that result in unintentional actions that are not always (or not entirely) conscious. In the case analyzed here, the role of the businesses as social spaces obviously should not be interpreted as invariably the result of a conscious choice, even though offering such spaces may coincide with the general objectives of the business owners as economic agents. But once the confluence of the formation of a particular social space with the self-interest of the business owner is evident, the social function tends to be reinforced by the owner of the establishment. The first of these functions is that the businesses, especially the shops, provide an open space for sociability. It is an open space because the Brazilian immigrant population in Massachusetts, like any other, is separated into specific networks that frequently compete with one another and are closed to a certain degree. One might consider the divisions between those who came from different places in Brazil. These networks create not only connections and interactions in relationships but also barriers between Brazilian immigrants. In social spaces where more horizontal relationships predominate, these barriers become relaxed, and weak connections—those outside the familiar and intimate circle—can grow. The inclination to horizontalize tends to be reinforced in the friendlier way that some business owners treat their clientele. That approach is a target of criticism from business owners who do not share this approach, as one expressed: "I don't like the practice of camaraderie among Brazilian business people because they aren't very professional. I'm not my clients' friend; I don't go to barbecues with them, etc." For most business owners, though, camaraderie seems to be an ingredient indispensable to the success of the enterprise precisely because these are firms that respond almost exclusively to the demands of Brazilian immigrants.

The second function is that, over time, these establishments promote a place of physical and social contact among individuals and networks. The access, admittance, and inclusion of recently arrived immigrants are mediated when they frequent these establishments; the businesses have a function similar to that of the "structural holes" in Ronald Burt's network theory (1992). Besides, by facilitating contacts, shops and restaurants provide information that the networks spread efficiently about job openings, events, parties, and so on. In summary, the establishments mediate the strengthening of connections among individuals and organizations and increase their chances to better their positions, for example, by making access to information about job openings available.

The third function is that these establishments assist in organizing, or act as facilitating agents for, a "Brazilian community" by promoting solidarity campaigns and mutual assistance initiatives. Among other immigrant groups, businesses play a similar role (Halter 1995, Levitt 1995). According to Halter (1995: 13), Haitian retail establishments in Greater Boston form sociocultural spaces and spaces for political interaction, they act as support networks in the adaptation process of recently arrived immigrants, and they spread and promote the cultural identity of Haitians.

In Brazilian retail stores, throughout the day and especially in the late afternoon, Brazilians of various religions, occupations, and places of origin in Brazil meet to talk. A Brazilian jewelry store in Framingham has a large, round table holding a tray of coffee. Around the table Brazilians sit down to converse, tell jokes, talk about soccer, gossip, discuss life in the United States and Brazilian politics. They help publicize solidarity campaigns for those facing illness and collect money for fellow Brazilians in need due to emergencies. This store, like other businesses, turns mere shopping into a ritual because it mediates social interactions: periodic encounters where above all national identity is affirmed.

Some businesses play an important role in spreading information about artistic events and promoting shows, although few business owners make financial contributions to community events. When asked about his reasons for providing this kind of support, one business owner gave financial reasons: "The return is slow, but it's worth it." Most shops and restaurants have bulletin boards where people can post newspaper clippings, notices about employment and rooms for rent, and information about telephone cards and tickets to social, cultural, and civic events such as the commemoration of September 7, the most important date on the official Brazilian calendar. Thus, Brazilians frequent these establishments not merely as purchasers of the merchandise displayed on the shelves. One described how "there are always people talking to Lurdes, the owner. She likes to chat, even though she has a lot of work to do. This helps explain the success of her shop." Making friends, getting to know those who have arrived recently, hearing the city gossip and the news from Brazil, and getting information about jobs and parties are also "part of the business." This is why Portuguese is commonly spoken in these places and why the clerks should be Brazilian, like almost all of the clientele.

Factors That Stimulate Entrepreneurship

It can be said that of the three types of incorporation into the labor market to which Brazilian immigrants have access, becoming an entrepreneur is the one that tends to have the highest social status within the group and the most coveted income. In the intricate game of individual compensation, it is better to be limited to the home community by opening a business than to work for a large U.S. firm as a low-wage worker.

According to some authors, ethnic businesses open an alternative path to immigrants for adaptation and upward social mobility in the United States. Generally, the literature corroborates a strong connection between social mobility and the number of businesses in an ethnic community (Wilson and Portes 1980, Halter 1995, Light and Gold 2000). The possibility of achieving upward social mobility by means of a business geared toward meeting the demands of Brazilians seems to be at least partially valid as well. The data collected during the present research reveal that workers who managed to keep the same jobs in the United States that they had in Brazil tended to be those who offered services or products of special interest to Brazilians, such as owners of accounting firms and retail establishments. Their social status can be maintained and even increased along with their incomes.

It was mentioned previously that Brazilians believe that by working hard, especially in housecleaning, they can save enough money to open small businesses. In fact, most Brazilian businesses were opened with the owners' savings accumulated by working as immigrants in the United States as housecleaners, painters, carpenters, and pizza deliverers or in other jobs to which Brazilians commonly have greater access. This shows the group's potential, albeit limited, for upward social mobility.

It is also important to emphasize that the start-up capital used by Brazilian small businesses was not brought from Brazil and was not supplied as credit either by members of the community or by members of the extended family, which are the two main sources of financing cited in the literature (Portes 1995; Light, Bernard, and Kim 1999; Stiles and Galbraith 2004). Although the principal motivation for opening a business is to gain some possibility of social mobility, this goal could not be pursued without the initial involvement of the family and a group of stakeholders and religious networks to maintain its development, although the presence of these three groups is not seen consistently or with the same intensity in all cases.[20]

The main point to be noted is that making the creation and continued operation of these small businesses viable requires resources and networks organized both within and outside the community. This is easily verified in the cities where the businesses were started. In 2001, 67 Brazilian businesses in Somerville (48) and Allston (19) were surveyed with the objective of characterizing them and their owners. Of these, 50 were studied, and the results are presented here.

The first piece of data to be noted is that the businesses were mostly new: 80% were started between 1995 and 2000, and the oldest was established in 1984. The start-up capital for most of these businesses did not exceed $50,000. The businesses included restaurants, hair salons, variety stores, remittance and airline ticket agencies, cell phone outlets, and grocery and clothing stores.

Family

The importance of family ties is present from the very beginning of the establishment of a business and in the day-to-day work of these firms. At least one member of the family appears as a business partner and/or as an employee. The main justification for having family members work in the businesses is to compensate for the lack of trust among Brazilians, as is seen in the following excerpt from an interview with Rodney, age 36:

> I have business partners, but only family members. As for trust, I don't trust anyone completely, nor do I trust Brazilians. But there are safe ways of working. Today I have TV cameras, and the worker has no idea if he's being taped, if the boss can see what he's doing, or not. This is what I'm going to do in the branch location that I'm planning to open: put a camera above the cash register.

The level of trust does not change whether the employee is a Brazilian or an American.

The majority of firms are family businesses, but it is important to note that "family" in this case predominantly includes the nuclear family and, more specifically, a married couple, husband and wife, because children have a low level of participation in these businesses. This arrangement is important because, as Roberts emphasizes (1995), family organizational patterns and normative systems differ according to the culture of origin of the immigrant group. Commonly propagated notions about ethnic businesses where cousins, aunts and uncles, and godparents work alongside immigrant fathers, mothers, and children do not hold true among Brazilians, whose family businesses are limited to the nuclear family and do not include the extended family.

Generally, when a wife works with her husband, she participates as a business partner. The division of labor is normally such that the women handle the service part of the business and kitchen work in restaurants and snack shops, and the men handle the bookkeeping, contacts with the bank, and other financial and/or administrative tasks. This division of labor is similar to the pattern of other small businesses run by recent immigrants in Massachusetts (Halter 1995).

Stakeholders

Although the role of the family has been highly stressed in studies of ethnic entrepreneurship (Iyer 2004), a second variable identified here has not received the attention it deserves: the stakeholders. These are generally professionals associated with private firms, public agencies, or NGOs that develop programs oriented toward minorities and immigrant communities.[21] They are partnership assistants, bank workers, business administrators, and more recently, university professors who volunteer their services or who work directly in these three sectors. Their main areas of activity are education and community development, legal assistance, and small-business support.

The role of these professionals is fundamental to the business activities and also to making connections because they know and can navigate the channels necessary to access organizational and financial resources, the politics of getting credit, labor and property law, the payment of fees and taxes, and so on. Even when they work for banks whose interest in the community is primarily economic, the stakeholders function as a kind of broker in network theory, making connections between actors (and actor-organizations) that otherwise would not communicate. Therefore, they act as intermediary agents able to increase and enable action and access to resources through information or direct assistance such as by supporting the development of projects and business plans. They are resources that do not exist within the Brazilian community because, among other possible explanations, this is a relatively recently arrived immigrant population and is still in its first generation or generation 1.5. Some of these agents, but not all, speak Portuguese, especially second- or third-generation immigrants from the Azores.

Researchers have generally stressed that immigrant groups have resources available within the communities to which they belong, especially from their social networks, which make up for their disadvantages in terms of cultural and physical capital (Portes and Sensenbrenner 1993, Portes 1995). Among Brazilians, however, the resources accessed by entrepreneurs are not necessarily only those that their compatriots have and distribute. On the contrary, the stakeholders play a strategic role without which it would be impossible to understand the economic and social dynamics of the enterprises. According to Light et al. (1995), "ethnic resources" stimulate the social capital of the communities and are fundamental to the creation and survival of the businesses started by immigrants. Such resources are created and made available by the community itself and have their origin in the specific characteristics of each group, such as its values, knowledge base, skills, information, and patterns of social relationships, including solidarity and trust. Consequently, ethnic resources make opportunities in the marketplace accessible and minimize risks. Waldinger, Aldrich, and Ward (2000) reached very similar conclusions, although in a slightly different way. The structure of opportunities, access to property, characteristics of the group, and mobilization resources are, according to these authors, the critical variables in ethnic businesses. The structure of opportunities entails market conditions (demand for a particular set of goods that can only be offered by one who is already familiar with them) and open market access (the existence of neglected or underused markets with low economies of scale, along with instability and uncertainty, and the existence of consumers of "cultural" or "exotic" products). Access to property refers to vacant business-ownership positions and governmental support policies. The characteristics of the group that affect ethnic business are predisposing factors such as impeded economic mobility, social selectivity in the migratory process, and the necessary psychology of autonomy and independence. Among the main "mobilization resources" are networks of friends and acquaintances (Zimmer and Aldrich 1987). In this model there seems to be no place for stakeholders, except perhaps with regard to those who implement governmental policies.[22] Churches are not mentioned, and family only appears as a generic designation.

In the Brazilian case, the creation of a binational Chamber of Commerce is an example of the role played by these external agents. A group of community leaders, pastors, and small-business owners led by administrators from the Brazilian consulate in Boston created the Brazilian American Chamber of Commerce of New England (BACCNE) in 2003. This is a nonprofit organization whose principal objective is to facilitate the economic development of the Brazilian community in New England and the development of strategic relationships between Brazil and the business enterprises of this same region. Its foundation was the result of the transformation of an older entity, the Brazilian Business Network (BBN), founded in 1997 and run by a small group of Massachusetts residents, both Brazilian and non-Brazilian (Anglo American and Portuguese American), interested in supporting and promoting the Brazilian community in the region. Because they had no previous experience, the Brazilians had no idea how to do it nor what the U.S. institutional system allows and encourages. Thus, in addition to the support of the administrators from the Brazilian consulate, the participation of a group of non-Brazilian professionals who had experience in similar organizations with other groups or who were connected to special credit financing programs for minorities was indispensable. They were the ones who developed the business plan and made available a considerable number of contacts and much information regarding local business customs that could support such an initiative.

Fligstein (2001) seeks to show the theoretical and empirical relevance of the social skills of groups, organizations, and social movements as a prerequisite for collective action since such skills lead to cooperation: "The idea of social skills is that actors have to motivate others to cooperate. The ability to engage others in collective action is a social skill that proves pivotal to the construction and reproduction of social orders" (3). It is important to note that, for recent immigrants, the ability to use such skills requires an *institutional apprenticeship.* In the absence of such an apprenticeship, unless the skills are understood as resulting directly from characteristics of the native culture, how can their genesis be explained? Social skills necessarily imply a kind of social action that works, that is, skills that lead to collective actions the results of which are reasonably satisfactory for those involved. In the Brazilian immigrant community, such skills are passed to new members from within by the older members of the community or by those outside the community, by the stakeholders. Outsiders are important precisely because the means of access to established, formal channels are unfamiliar. While contact between a well-established native entrepreneur and a lending official might be trivial, contact between an immigrant and an official who lends to minorities is a strategic resource. Therefore, as opposed to what the literature tends to emphasize, the social capital of the group is not limited to the closeness of relationships and strong internal connections within community networks. In the case presented here, everything that goes beyond the cultural, human, and material resources that the Brazilians themselves possess, control, or dominate (or that they brought with them as "cultural baggage") has enormous value because it is more rare and less accessible. Stakeholders are agents who can model the presentation of internal community interests in accord with local customs, which in this case greatly reinforces the internal cooperation of the group.[23]

It thus can be deduced that Brazilian entrepreneurs have little human capital, as is also true of other recent immigrant groups (Butler and Greene 1997). In fact, only 12% of the business owners in Somerville and Allston graduated from college. Few speak English well or know how to develop a business plan. Therefore, the claim that the lower the human capital of the business owners, the greater their connection with the immigrant group (Sequeira and Rasheed 2004), in the sense of greater dependency, can be put into context. Among Brazilians, the connection between business owners and their clientele is one of dependence,[24] but it is not exclusive because they also depend on outsiders who have knowledge of local business customs. Therefore, maintenance of a close connection between entrepreneurs and the ethnic group can vary depending on when they arrived and their generation. That is, recently arrived first-generation entrepreneurs generally maintain a close relationship with the ethnic group, although they also depend on outsiders.

In conclusion, the resources they need and use cannot be limited to the category of ethnic resources or of mobilization resources. In particular, to maintain and expand their businesses, the owners need a set of resources that are available outside the community and the support of external actors who, like the immigrants themselves, constitute the social arena of immigration. In other words, the social capital of a group tends to transcend its borders. The participation of stakeholders can result in an increase in the social capital of the immigrant group, even extending beyond its physical and social borders.

Religious Networks

The third driving force behind entrepreneurship among Brazilian immigrants is religious networks. The association between social capital and higher rates of success of ethnic businesses is stressed time and again (Light and Bonacich 1988; Portes 1989; Portes, Castells, and Benton 1989; Putnam 1996). Although various aspects of the concept of social capital have been the focus of study, the number of works that examine religious affiliation as a component of this capital is surprisingly small (Candland 2000, Greeley 1997, Martes and Rodriguez 2004).

Belonging to a religious network increases a Brazilian business owner's chances of forming a loyal and stable, although limited, clientele. It legitimizes the desire to climb socially, provides support through the participation of pastors in the life of the Brazilian business community, reinforces a communitarian ethos, and makes available organizational resources provided by the church.[25] These are the findings of the present research that help explain why the number of evangelicals is proportionally higher among business owners vis-à-vis the entire Brazilian population residing in the Boston metropolitan area. In terms of religious affiliation, 38% of the Brazilian business owners in Somerville and Allston were Catholic and 28% Protestant. In the latter group, half belonged to the Assembly of God church, the largest evangelical church in the Brazilian community in Boston, while the rest were Baptists, Presbyterians, and Maranatha Christians. The number of Catholics among Brazilian immigrants was much larger, as was seen in Chapter 3.

The owner of a business who is an evangelical stands a better chance (or at least a better chance than his or her Catholic counterpart) of attracting fellow church members. The same is true for wedding photographers, the woman who sells traditional Brazilian sweets and savories, and the *sacoleira* who sells Brazilian-style clothing and lingerie.[26] However, the same cannot be said for Catholic business owners. The great majority of this group's customers have roots in the same Brazilian cities and live in the same Boston neighborhood in which the business is located. A salient point among evangelicals is that when businesses are opened, church members tend to patronize the establishments whose owners are also evangelical.

A greater degree of participation and even leadership roles of some pastors in the activities of Brazilian associations does not go unnoticed either. These pastors have attended meetings and gatherings and taken part in the establishment of networks such as the BBN and the BACCNE. While pastors are interested and involved in the businesses run by members of their churches, including frequenting the establishments and praying for them, priests and nuns remain apart from the process. Evangelicals thus create an ethos that is more favorable to business, and their pastors dedicate time and effort to this end. The desire to "make money in America" finds welcome and reinforcement in the evangelical discourse, as it directly encourages becoming wealthier as a sign of salvation. This kind of affirmation, when it happens at all, is not equally stressed nor does it occupy the same space in the preaching of priests and nuns.[27] Greater harmony is evident between the motivation of the entrepreneurs and the religious discourse of evangelicals because the desire for upward social mobility is pursued with as much intensity or more by the entrepreneurs who see the opening of a business as a better chance to move up socially.

It is possible that religious affiliation may also result from the perception that the social networks formed around certain churches are more favorable to entrepreneurial activities. Some research points out that the support of community institutions by ethnic entrepreneurs may be motivated by individual commercial interests, especially the survival of the business, and not only by solidarity with the group (Boswell 2003). Likewise, Kim (1987) observes that Korean immigrants attend churches in New York in order to get information about available jobs, opportunities, and business contacts as well as loans. Although the association between social capital and religious networks has not been stressed in the recent literature on ethnic entrepreneurship, the connections between religion and economic life consistently merit attention in the pioneering studies on the ethnic economy.[28] According to Bonacich and Modell (1980), each religion stands for a system of social relations in which a peculiar economic shape develops. The crucial issue, therefore, is not to relate theological doctrine to the level of economic propensity but to explain religious affiliation as a result of the social relationships that churches develop and foster. People are more likely to pursue social relationships than doctrines. This means that people who go to church often stand a better chance of reinforcing the social ties expressed by religious affiliation itself.

In this vein, some more recent studies, Light and Gold (2000) and Martes (2000a), raise the hypothesis that the immigrants who are predisposed to participate in churches are drawn by the social networks. Religious affiliation itself may be a dependent variable that is subordinate to the decision to be associated with a network whose benefits, including material benefits, are available to them (Martes and Rodriguez 2004).

Relevant data to support this hypothesis show that Brazilian Catholics spontaneously state that they are nonpracticing, which is very rare among evangelicals. It then follows that social networks are stronger among the latter because Catholics tend toward dispersion and participate with less frequency in mass and other religious activities. Ethnic networks, when sliced according to religious affiliation, can provide their members with advantages coming from an increase in trust because they reduce the incidence of opportunistic behavior and reduce transactional costs (Fukuyama 1995, Nahapiet and Ghoshal 1998, Martes and Rodriguez 2004).

In conclusion, I suggest that the affirmation that "the key connection between social capital and entrepreneurship is efficiency in the use of ethnic resources" (Light 1999) be expanded to incorporate religious resources specifically. It is true that ethnic and religious resources can be mixed in some cases. However, since religion is not necessarily a component of ethnicity, it is perhaps more appropriate to use the concept of spiritual capital (Berger 2003) as a subtype of social capital to explain the association between entrepreneurship and the resources available to immigrants. Berger states that "social capital refers to the power, influence, knowledge, and dispositions an individual acquires by virtue of membership in a network or group. Spiritual capital might be thought of as a sub-species of social capital, referring to the power, influence, knowledge, and dispositions created by participation in a particular religious tradition" (3). Churches and networks create spiritual capital by making such resources available to their members. The following excerpt from an interview with the owner of a successful store in Somerville is worth noting:

> Being a church member helped me in the spiritual sense, including as regards retaining customers and dealing with them. It is difficult

> to deal with all kinds of people. When you know the word of God, it is easier to understand other people and control yourself. I always pray before entering the store. Part of the money I make is dedicated to the Lord. God gives you strength to stand. The pastor always comes around to pray with us. I ask God to teach me how to best use the money I make here.

The Tenuous Border between Employment and Businesses, Profits and Solidarity

In this chapter, I have sought to present the means by which Brazilian immigrants are able to incorporate themselves into the labor market in Massachusetts by calling attention to some common aspects before and after emigration and to points of convergence between the economic conditions in the native and destination societies. In the chapters that follow, I will present the social aspects of incorporation into American society in each of the three categories that are considered principal. Through the presentation of data and discussion of the literature, I have sought to emphasize that although there is solidarity among them, Brazilian immigrants also compete for employment. They are united around a single national identity that they make a point of affirming, but they try to protect their economic interests in the name of a generic distrust among members of the community.

Several authors use the concept of social capital (Bourdieu and Wacquant 2000, Coleman 1990) to refer to sources that generate resources and collective actions that permit the strengthening of internal social relationships within the group and that support collective actions. Even in situations that involve economic interests, whether in the sphere of an "ethnic economy" or an "enclave economy," calculated individual interests are mitigated in the face of the feeling of belonging and the development of solidary actions. Likewise, opportunism is replaced by lasting relationships built on trust because they are anchored in the belief that they share a common past, and the emergence of freeloaders is in turn inhibited by normative expectations, so that active community participation becomes an end in itself.

It is possible that this general picture has resulted to some extent from a reaction to the predominance of economistic approaches that are politically more conservative and tend to ignore the importance of social structures and relationships. As Mark Granovetter (1995) stresses, until the mid-1990s, the ethnic economy was treated as a primitive vestige in which networks, solidarity, norms, culture, and trust still made a difference. These are factors that economic sociology has preserved to explain behavior and economic life. Ethnicity and friendship, continues Granovetter, are not archaic categories that are superseded by the efficiency and impersonal nature of modern economies. Indeed, the results of the present research reinforce Granovetter's conclusions in the sense that it is not possible to understand the "world of work" without them.

However, Brazilians are as "solidary" as they are self-interested, and they are inclusive but also exclusive in social networks. A lack of trust is expressed in various spheres and in various ways: how entrepreneurs treat their clients (not accepting checks despite displaying a friendly demeanor), in the contracting of services and workers, in partnerships with the aim of starting up a business, and so on. Particularly with regard to their clientele, the small-business owners make it a point not to accept checks because they are afraid the checks will bounce, and they never extend credit to Brazilians, as one explained:

> I accept anyone's credit card, but not checks. I've already been shafted. Once I accepted a check from a gentleman who could have been my father and who always ate lunch here. He asked me to cash a $700 check for him. I cashed it and he went to Brazil; the check was returned and I was stuck holding the bag.

This kind of story is not unusual. A climate characterized by distrust also extends to participation in associations but does not stop some of the business owners from being involved in organizations and campaigns. Nothing, however, can be called "convergent cultural baggage" with regard to patterns of normative expectations, as expressed by Marcos, a 32-year-old painter from São Paulo: "I don't want any help from Brazilians, nor for them to create unity in the community because Brazilians only get together to badmouth one another."

It is interesting that the idea of strong ethnic solidarity among the members of immigrant groups is taken for granted by the academy as well as by people in general. In an example presented here, it is a basic presupposition used by a Brazilian housecleaner so her American client will accept the candidate proposed to clean her house next. The results of the present research demonstrate, however, that solidarity should be understood as a social relationship and not as a presupposed attribute of ethnic groups and that the idea of ethnic solidarity, like ethnic identity, can be used when convenient to generate goodwill. Marcelo Suárez-Orozco notes that "the cultural models and social practices that we have come to call multiculturalism shape the experiences, perceptions, and behavioral repertoires of immigrants in ways not seen in previous eras of large-scale immigration . . . In that ethos, racial and ethnic categories became powerful instrumental as well as expressive vectors" (2000: 13). Therefore, solidarity and its absence should be the objects of further research, as should the group's internal rifts and the distribution of social capital that, like any other capital, becomes an object of contention and is distributed unequally among members of the group.

It is possible that the situation described here with regard to Brazilians may be affected by territorial dispersion in terms of the distribution of jobs and places of residence. Even in the case of businesses, their relative concentration does not correspond to an area occupied exclusively by Brazilians or by another specific ethnic or national group. The residential location of this population and that of its businesses is more appropriately called a multi-ethnic neighborhood.[29] It is important to stress that even though there is not a high level of population density or territorial concentration—which means that the formation of an enclave cannot be confirmed—the social arena of Brazilian businesses operates on a practical logic that approximates that of an enclave (Nee and Nee 1986, Portes and Bach 1985); it is oriented inward. This means that sociability, conviviality, expression of identity, and specific manifestations of solidarity are reinforced in these spaces. The social arena of housecleaning, in contrast, seems to have developed a logic that is outwardly oriented for two specific reasons: the clientele is American (or at least not Brazilian), and access is commercialized, even though it is principally provided by social and interpersonal networks. Since they are oriented toward serving a particular community, Brazilian businesses construct strong connections with their clienteles and work for the development of a more far-reaching social pattern that extrapolates the limited buyer-seller relationship. In the area of housecleaning, which depends on a sparse clientele that is difficult to access and outside the social space and interpersonal networks of the groups, Brazilians are guided by commercial logic, establishing a buyer-seller relationship in order to obtain access to employment.

5

Respect, Citizenship, and Solidarity

Contrasting Perceptions

We have, unfortunately, an inexplicable tendency to imagine everything we do not know to be homogeneous.
Gabriel Tarde

When following the course of the transformations of Brazilian immigration from its beginnings, it can be seen that few themes have remained constant. Immigrants' favorable opinion of U.S. society is, surprisingly, one of them. The consequences of September 11, 2001, increased feelings of fear in many of them, especially fear of deportation, but their favorable opinion of U.S. society overall has generally changed little. There have been widespread anti-immigrant demonstrations and in Framingham the creation of a movement called Concerned Citizens and Friends of Immigration Law Enforcement. Some community leaders have even been threatened and harassed, although incidents of this sort have remained limited to certain regions, and Brazilians generally separate "American society" from this type of demonstration. The discourse and the position of community leaders, however, differ from most immigrants' generally favorable attitudes toward the United States; these leaders are more critical and bruising because they consider it necessary to sensitize Brazilians for eventual consequences that may effectively be prejudicial to the community.

In order to understand the meaning, origin, and persistence of most Brazilian immigrants' favorable opinion of the United States, one must consider that identity-formation processes are accomplished through contrasts. This is especially true for first-generation immigrants who, due to having lived part of their lives in their native countries, bring with them when they emigrate memories that will allow them to understand and position themselves with respect to the receiving country.

In migratory movements, there is displacement of labor, but immigrant workers also bring with them vital cultural elements of the countries in which they were born. The manner in which and extent to which they do this has indeed been the subject of a long debate among social scientists. Sociologist Alejandro Portes, currently one of the most important and influential researchers in the area of international migrations, understands that when they emigrate, people bring with them "cultural baggage" from their native countries. For Portes (1995), the culture brought by the immigrants is fundamental in determining the survival and organizational strategies adopted by the immigrants in the country of destination. Because they share a common memory and find themselves exposed to a high degree of discrimination in the receiving society, the immigrants are led to define "who we are" and the criteria that determine their belonging to their respective communities. Still according to that author, the adversities that immigrants are forced to face reinforce the solidarity among them. This solidarity emerges from a common cultural memory brought from the country of origin that includes customs, values, language, and a feeling of belonging that comes from the shared experience of being targets of discrimination. In a relatively short time, these two elements transform the immigrants into an ethnic community.

In this chapter, I will discuss two topics that are interconnected with this approach: the importance given to cultural baggage and to the shared experience of discrimination and hostility as elements fundamental to the determination of the immigrant groups' survival and organizational strategies as well as to their transformation into "ethnic communities"; and the emphasis on solidarity among the immigrants that results from a common cultural memory, a feeling of belonging, and the experience of adversity that they are forced to confront in the receiving society.[1]

With the aim of analyzing these topics, I will initially discuss the notion of cultural baggage in order to then explain why the life experience of Brazilian immigrants permits the construction of a positive image of America, especially with respect to the civic culture of this country. In this regard, I call attention to the notions of respect and citizenship that emerge from these perceptions and to the larger institutional picture that circumscribes such experiences, establishing rights (access to public and collective goods and services) and rules for civic life. Citizenship is addressed here not in its formal political dimension (rights of participation in the political electoral system) but rather in its civic dimension, especially with regard to the practice of respect as an element of mediation in social relationships. Citizenship in this broader sense also refers to institutional participation (representation of Brazilians in schools, the health care system, NGOs, and so forth) and to access to basic public services (especially schools, health care, and housing).

Next, I will analyze the internal divisions among Brazilians to show that the cultural memory of an immigrant group may vary in terms of its degree of homogeneity and association. Finally, I will analyze the possibility of ethnic identification among Brazilian immigrants to show that it has an instrumental nature and is related to a system of open incentives in the host society.

How Should We Approach the Topic of Cultural Memory?

When I began my study of Brazilian immigrants residing in Massachusetts in 1994, I was surprised by the positive way in which Brazilians perceived and evaluated various aspects of their experiences in the United States, even though the great majority were in the uncomfortable position of being undocumented aliens and were engaged in occupations valued little by the locals and completely devoid of prestige. Despite finding themselves in such an adverse situation, I rarely obtained from a Brazilian an account of an experience in which he or she had been the victim of discrimination.

It would be hasty, however, to characterize this perception of American society as naïve, idealized, or superficial. In fact, few Brazilians have mastered the English language or, more importantly, were educated in Brazil to recognize other cultural codes, including those of discrimination and exclusion. But the opinions given with regard to the United States gain a new significance if they are related to the way Brazilians themselves construct them, that is, by contrast. They evaluate American society by looking to Brazil. Not coincidentally, some aspects considered positive in the United States are considered negative in Brazil, and vice versa.

Brazil is not only alive in memories or in letters; videotapes of major Brazilian news programs are easily obtained, Brazilian programs are transmitted on community channels on cable TV (Rede Globo de

Televisão, the Globo Television Network), and Brazilian newspapers can be purchased in Greater Boston.[2] And almost anyone with Internet access can communicate with friends and relatives anywhere and receive news any time.[3] Thus, stating that immigrants evaluate the destination country by looking at the country of origin does not mean they are only looking back. Right in front of them, television sets, telephones, and newspapers are at their disposal.[4] The increase in access to means of communication and new technologies also brings new elements to the discussion of cultural baggage.

Recent anthropological approaches have adopted a transnational perspective in studies of immigrants and migratory movements, conferring a different treatment to the question of cultural memory than that used by Portes. Transnationalism is a "process by which immigrants construct social spheres that connect the country of origin to the destination country" (Schiller et al. 1992). Feldman-Bianco and Huse (1995) have observed that the cultural memory of an immigrant group is permanently reconstructed over succeeding generations,[5] and precisely in the process of reconstruction the groups become communities of meaning, institute values, and promote collective actions. It is not a matter, then, of a set of life experiences and reminiscences brought from the country of origin, preserved intact, and suspended in time. On the contrary, in order to be understood, cultural memory must be contextualized, taking into account not only the bonds permanently developed in the destination country but also in the country of origin. Brazilians should not be included in the category of "transmigrants," since there has been no evidence among them of the creation of significant bonds connecting the two poles of the migratory flow;[6] but I think this type of approach is more interesting because it incorporates dynamism into the notion of cultural baggage by grappling with memory as a process that encompasses different contexts and times.

I argue that the manner in which memory is considered in the transnational approach and the notion of culture underlying it permit the concept of culture as an inventory of values, features, and patterns to be abandoned in favor of a more flexible notion that allows culture to be understood like language, that is, as a form of communication capable of expressing and interpreting new situations by referring to past situations. In the end, understanding cultural baggage as a set of reminiscences omits from the notion of culture its characteristic dynamism.

Yet another observation can be made about the more formal content of cultural baggage. Above all, the immigrants bring with them axes that structure the reference points from which they will position themselves, identify themselves, and differentiate themselves internally and externally. I want to call attention to the possible contents of this baggage as not necessarily homogeneous and associative. This characteristic is especially relevant in a country formed by various races and ethnicities and that has the continental dimensions of Brazil. My research revealed a set of divisions based on references to Brazilians' regional origins, levels of education, and rural or urban roots. Such divisions separate identities and are essential to understanding the internal dynamics of the group as a whole. These significant cleavages have as their point of reference divisions that already exist in Brazil and that are reinforced in the course of the migratory experience. The divisions show that having Brazilian nationality is not always enough for people to identify, associate, and socialize with each other. But analyzing the internal dynamic of the group, taking differences as the subject of that analysis, is as important as incorporating the cultural memory that is "common to all." Stuart Hall (2001) argues that social scientists should not consider national cultures as unified but rather as constituting a "discursive apparatus" that represents difference, or heterogeneity, as unity or identity.

Thus, despite internal heterogeneity, which it is my aim to highlight, notions and values that tend to be more uniform also constitute the cultural baggage of Brazilian immigrants; these notions and values constitute the discursive apparatus of the group. I want to call particular attention to the current notion of solidarity. In Brazil the word "solidarity" tends to have a religious, Christian, and more precisely, Catholic connotation. In terms of the "common sense" of a body of relatively organized thoughts within a cultural system (Geertz 1983: 75), in Brazil having solidarity means above all helping those who need help. Nevertheless, the one who receives help generally finds himself in a position of "inferiority," which means that recognizing that someone helped him connotes affirming the superiority of the benefactor and simultaneously his own inferiority relative to that person. It is a matter of a moral act, but helping or practicing solidarity rarely appears as connected to the exercise of a "civic moral conscience" or to the exercise of citizenship. The moral act is one of religious origin that tends to connect solidarity to compassion and charity. In other words, being the object of solidarity implies personal benevolence or piety and not the recognition of a right. Compassion, more than citizenship, is expressed through solidarity.

In the context of the tradition of a civic conscience, the notion of solidarity does not necessarily generate the expectation of the duty to personally acknowledge assistance nor the expectation of receiving treatment or consideration of any kind in exchange (Cardoso de Oliveira 1996), for it is more properly an activity that occurs between peers. In this case, compassion does not structure the basis of solidarity and reciprocal duties, but rather a contract does. A contract is a central document for stipulating reciprocal duties and obligations between "individuals" and not between "people."

According to the *Little Encyclopedia of Church Social Doctrine* (Ávila 1991), in the religious doctrine of the Catholic Church the term "solidarism" employed in Brazil originated with the German thinker Heinrich Pesch as a "doctrine based on the principle of real solidarity between person and community, and of a social, political, and economic system that is an intermediary between the atomizing decentralization of individualism and the monolithic centralization of collectivism" (413). As a doctrine, solidarism "is an effort to systematize the social implications of the Christian biblical message, which is centered on the nature of the human person and offers him ultimate discretion over his choices and structure" (ibid.). Having solidarity means denying self-interested egotism and elevating the other.

If solidarity in Brazil is more immediately related to help between people, in the United States this notion is particularly related to association, self-organization, and the creation of communities. If in Brazil saying that someone practices solidarity means saying the person generally helps others, in the United States it more precisely means taking an active part in the process of association in order to advance common interests. The essential point is that respect is an acknowledgement of status and citizenship is the recognition of rights. We are referring to a "discursive apparatus" that establishes the predominance of some elements over others in both countries. Thus the dimension of civic participation is not absent from manifestations of solidarity in Brazil, nor is "helping whoever needs help" absent in the United States.

In the most egalitarian of modern capitalist societies, Richard Sennett reminds us (2004), there is little room for charity (solidarity as helping others) because the welfare state occupies this place and carries out this function. These societies, however, may lack any kind of social assistance of an emotional or subjective nature: "A gift is no longer a personal donation, [as] it would be necessary to thank the treasury department's computers; welfare is aid without compassion" (166). The contrast between the two countries is again evident here because I believe that being emotional is the characteristic feature of solidarity in Brazil. Sérgio Buarque de Holanda contends that "solidarity exists where there is an emotional connection more than a relationship based on self-interest—in the sanctuary of the home or among friends" (1973: 182–83). This is one of the cultural legacies of the Iberian colonial past that profoundly marked the formation of the Brazilian people. Roberto da Matta (2000) follows another path to a similar conclusion. Refusing to conduct an analysis of Brazil's history that points to the current characteristic features of Brazilian culture, da Matta analyzes situations in contemporary Brazil to show the structure that can reveal the coexistence "in the scheme of ideals adopted as important values, of equality and the hierarchy of individualism and personalism, of individual autonomy and the primacy of relationships in a country that, despite wanting to be modern, is hierarchical and unequal" (94). As such, the Brazilian challenge or dilemma is that of maintaining ties of affection characterized by respect and citizenship and that consequently cease to be transformed into "areas of privilege."

I believe it has already been made clear that the supposition that immigrants perceive the environment of the receiving country as hostile is not always true. In fact, the Brazilian immigrants residing in Massachusetts stated that they were surprised in an agreeable way by American society. Despite not having actual citizenship in this country, they recognized that they had rights in their daily lives. In Massachusetts, they experienced a dimension of citizenship that they had not known or did not practice in Brazil. It is not only through the right to vote that individuals recognize themselves as citizens. Receiving good service in a government office, being respected by a police officer, and not feeling disdained when entering a banking agency—despite not being very well dressed—are examples of how someone may feel himself or herself to be a member of a "polis." This generally positive opinion of American civic life becomes even more surprising if we consider that most Brazilians are undocumented. Feeling oneself to be a "citizen" in this case is linked to another factor as well: the ability to be a consumer. However, it is not merely a matter of purchasing luxury goods to which they did not have access in Brazil (athletic shoes, leather jackets, big cars) but also the ability to make use of public or collective goods such as schools and health care.

Ideas Regarding Respect and Citizenship

> *America is neither a dream nor a reality: it is a hyper-reality . . . a utopia that from the beginning has been lived as accomplished. Everything here is real, pragmatic, and everything makes us dreamers.*
>
> Jean Baudrillard, *América*

The literature stresses the perception of the host society as full of discrimination and hostility. In this section, I will analyze why, instead of this negative opinion, Brazilians tend to value the respect and citizenship they perceive to exist in American society.[7]

When I began my research, I envisioned a set of difficulties that I would face, including being able to locate and interview Brazilians because most of them were clandestine immigrants. Perhaps because the idea of what it meant to be clandestine was impressed on me during the period of the Brazilian military dictatorship, I imagined my interviewees living in hiding and fleeing from the police. However, it was not only that. The United States is known worldwide for its endless racial and ethnic conflicts, which suggested another connotation of being clandestine: besides being fugitives from the police, Brazilians would have to defend themselves from American society itself. Setting aside the exaggerations of my imagination and my ignorance, I needed little time to discover that my expectations were mistaken. Being clandestine in the United States was different. Because in the early stages of my research the Brazilians I interviewed rarely spontaneously defined themselves as immigrants, although considering their common expectation of returning to Brazil, they saw their circumstance as immigrants as temporary and transitory. The interviews revealed an ambiguous stance that is on one hand elitist and on the other one of shame. Nevertheless, my initial expectations were reversed after I had conducted a series of interviews. The data began to indicate that the undocumented, poor Brazilian immigrants felt more respected in the United States than in Brazil.

It is difficult to understand the meaning of the data without considering that such judgments and life experiences were invariably established by contrast and that it was therefore necessary to reinterpret them in light of the mediations that the interviewees themselves made about the two countries, Brazil and the United States. Thus, I began with the key word explicitly contained in the interviews themselves: respect. Respect as a mediator of social relationships, as a form of communication, as a habit, or even as a practice incorporated into daily interpersonal relationships and as an institutionalized practice, in these ways respect is the key to understanding the perception and the feeling of citizenship to which the Brazilians referred. The meaning attributed to respect in the United States stands in contrast to the inequality of relationships (and of daily treatment) among different segments of Brazilian society and workers' occupational status, as well as the treatment dispensed by the Brazilian bureaucracy.

Meanwhile, this does not mean that the immigrants perceive and experience American society as a realm of democracy and equality, much less that there is no discrimination in the United States. In the 1996 survey of 300 Brazilian immigrants, 23% indicated that discrimination was one of the problems that Brazilians confronted in the USA, while 75% of the interviewees cited "lack of documentation," the most frequent response, followed by "loneliness" for 56%.[8] What the data indicate is that given the economic and social inequalities in Brazil, its tradition of inheritance, the violation of citizens' rights and human rights, and the impossibility of attaining a life of dignity because of the low wages, Brazilian immigrants attributed importance to the degree (or the absence) of such characteristics in American society. Thus, it was not a question of idealization but rather of an interpretation anchored in the perceptions and the contrast in life experience in the two countries. And why do Brazilian immigrants attribute importance to these differences? It is particularly because the arrival of Brazilians in Massachusetts is recent. They are first-generation immigrants for whom the past in Brazil is still very recent and loaded with resentment of that country.[9] To cite but a few examples, several interviewees stated that when they emigrated they were disillusioned with the "Brazilian government," with "Brazilian politicians," with corruption, and with "social injustice." In this context, a view of America as the land of opportunities occurs—opportunities that were denied them in Brazil.

In the early 2000s, there was an important change in the references used by the interviewees to describe Brazil and define the contrasts with American society. Violence and political corruption came to be stressed as much as the lack of opportunities and economic problems. Following the daily Brazilian news via cable TV networks, which enabled them to follow the accusations of corruption in the executive and legislative branches, led them to make comments like "This country is really hopeless" and "Brazil is never going to turn out right." The violence reported in the media caused them to state even more stridently that they bet right when they exchanged Brazil for the United States, albeit temporarily for some. Brazil continues to deny its citizens opportunities to work and to buy things, as it did in the 1980s and 1990s, and violence in Brazil is reaching such an alarming level that it has come to be used to justify not only staying in the United States but also to encourage more emigration from Brazil: "I came to Boston because I couldn't stand the violence any more. I was growing afraid of everything; I didn't want to go out any more; my children were afraid of being kidnapped; here I feel very safe." Statements such as this by a 32-year-old woman who arrived in 2005 have become more and more common.

These perceptions about the United States have their origin in a belief in the superiority of the United States over Brazil. American patterns of consumption and the influence of the American cultural industry are predominant in Brazil. To deduce that this influence was already present in the country of origin and that it is part of the "cultural capital" that Brazilians bring with them to the United States, one need only count the number of signs on commercial establishments in the city of São Paulo and of Brazilian products whose names are written in English in order to gain greater acceptance in the Brazilian market. This does not mean that Brazilians do not criticize various aspects of American society. Americans are invariably characterized in the interviews as being "cold," "hard," "very serious," "distant," "excessively formal," "only thinking of money," and so on. The interviewees counter these descriptors with Brazilians' "happiness," "warmth," "friendship," "informality," and not infrequently, *jeitinho*.[10] Therefore, the favorable opinion of the United States appears more evident when limited to the arena of civic relationships, that is, of U.S. society as a nation.[11]

The following passages from interviews conducted between 1994 and 1996 contain references that Brazilians made to the notions of respect and citizenship and call attention to the ambiguities present in the interviewees' discourse. These are not isolated opinions but rather are representative of the accounts collected from the whole group of interviewees.

Joel was a teller in a private bank in the city of Rio de Janeiro, and he arrived in Boston in 1992. The son of small-business owners earned a degree in business administration at the Faculdade Gama Filho, a private university in Rio de Janeiro, two years earlier. Joel did not have any prospect of getting a job that would compensate him according to his expectations. His only brother already had emigrated to Boston, was working as a cook, and encouraged him to take a chance. Joel was then 29 years old and earned $3,000 a month cleaning houses. He is white with curly black hair. A self-declared homosexual,[12] Joel lived with an American man and interacted very little with Brazilians:

> I have been lucky here; I have never suffered discrimination . . . I live among excellent professionals; I go to chic restaurants . . .
> Q: Are you afraid of the INS [Immigration and Naturalization Service]?
> A: No, why? I'm not doing anything wrong.
> Q: Do you feel valued here professionally, even though you are a housecleaner and in Brazil you were a banker?
> A: I think I am more valued now because I have recognition and return.
> Q: Financial return?
> A: Yes! And I am not ashamed of being a housecleaner. Everyone can see my effort; I already have an apartment; I am not mistreated in anyone's house or by my bosses. In Brazil, the poor are discriminated against. There, I never greeted the doorman of my building because I thought: "I don't have anything to do with riffraff." But here, there is a law that works against discrimination.
> Q: What have you learned in this country?
> A: To respect people, laws . . . I can get on the train, and no one bumps into me or curses me, and they ask to be excused. Here corruption also exists, but when it's discovered, it's punished. In Brazil, no one who is honest succeeds in life, and that is what most catches my attention when I hear news from Brazil.
> Q: Have you ever used American welfare?

A: Never. Only once, when I went to the hospital. I said I didn't have any money, and I was enrolled in Free Care . . .
Q: Do you intend to legalize your situation?
A: . . . It doesn't bother me to be illegal. I have everything: an apartment, a credit card, a financed car, a bank account.

In this interview, discrimination in the United States is associated with ignorance: it is the ignorant who discriminate. Joel indicated that this is different from Brazil, a country where the rich routinely discriminate and the poor are the victims of discrimination. Thus, while in Brazil there is a greater risk of being discriminated against by a rich person, in the United States there is a greater risk of being discriminated against by someone who is ignorant, irrespective of social class. In fact, the interview takes on an elitist tone when Joel says that he belongs to a quality circle (he lives among "excellent professionals"), and he understands that, precisely by avoiding living among ignorant people, he can construct a personal space that is safe from discrimination. In a hierarchical society like Brazil's,[13] discrimination occurs against anyone who is perceived to occupy an inferior level, be it economic, professional, or social, and it is practiced with a certain naturalness because those who discriminate do not question themselves, nor is their conduct questioned by others and rarely is it punished. In this interview, as in the others, racial discrimination against blacks in Brazil is hardly mentioned. The emphasis is on the poor and the unskilled worker, not because Joel identifies himself with these workers in that he is engaged in the same type of work or in the same condition of migration but because he identifies with American society. It is American society that "does not discriminate," and this is why Joel, who identifies with it, no longer does, either.

Because it is a social practice, discrimination can only be recognized as such by those who identify certain actions as discriminatory. That is, as a social practice, the forms of discrimination may manifest differently in each society, and for this reason, for a certain action to be recognized as discriminatory that previously was not seen as such, it must be contextualized and recodified.

Thus, being clandestine is not a problem for Joel, given that if American society's rules of good behavior are obeyed, the illegal immigrant does not run a risk of being deported. The interviewee indicated that in the United States there are still opportunities for those who are prepared to work tenaciously and earn a living honestly. Initially he declared that he had never used a welfare program, but soon he confessed to having exercised the "right" to Free Care. He made a point of emphasizing that it was only in an occasional situation. Generally, the interviews corroborated the perception that illegal immigration status is a grave problem for Brazilians, but it is an issue for federal authorities and not local police, which considerably reduces its gravity. Not having legal residency puts immigrants in a difficult situation in the labor market: those who do not have papers are limited to the informal market. Worse yet, they cannot visit Brazil and later return to the United States.

Rose is the daughter of a military man and was born in Juiz de Fora in the state of Minas Gerais. She was 32 years old at the time of the interview. As a teacher, she could not earn a good salary in Brasília, her last place of residence, and worked as a housecleaner in Boston with her husband, who is also Brazilian. Rose is blond and of Italian descent.

> Q: Have you ever heard Brazilians complaining of discrimination?
> A: In Cape Cod, yes; here, no, because the Brazilians here have light skin . . . but Naninha [a Brazilian acquaintance], for example, married an American, and his family never discriminated against her. She was received with open arms . . . she's a little dark, but she doesn't have kinky hair . . . she isn't white according to American standards. I didn't marry a Jew; I didn't marry an American, and in this society, if you enter in that way, that's when there's discrimination. In that regard I'm completely out of it; I didn't make any ties like that . . . in the homes where I work I don't feel the least bit of discrimination . . . they know I have attended college . . . I think they treat me differently because of that.

According to Rose, remaining isolated from American society may be a way to protect oneself from discrimination. Thus, isolation itself is not perceived as discrimination, which more likely occurs in the process of integration into American society. Yet the example she cites of the friend who married an American denies the occurrence of discrimination precisely in the same situation in which Rose said discrimination occurs. Another relevant point in her statement is Rose's non-identification with other immigrant workers who, like her, do housecleaning. She says she is different in that she has a college degree, and she makes a point of letting the women for whom she works know about her peculiar circumstance;

because of this difference, she believes she has received good treatment. Her college education is the difference she uses as a shield in the attempt to avoid discrimination.

As can be observed in the two interviews cited above, formal education plays a central role in defining who is the agent and who is the victim of discrimination. Yet level of education does not seem to carry the same weight when the interviewee lacks a college degree. According to the survey of 300 Brazilians for this study, only 15% of the interviewees said they had college degrees. The following interview illustrates this point.

Alberto was 32 years old and came from Rio de Janeiro; he wore orthodontic braces and a ponytail. In the United States, his appearance is readily identified as Latino due to his dark skin and indigenous features. He married a Brazilian woman and worked as a produce manager for a large supermarket chain:

> I have heard people saying on *Fantástico* that their dream is to eat at a good restaurant . . . I don't have formal education, but I have educated myself about daily life in America.
> Q: What have you learned here?
> A: Respect for human beings, not for what they have, but for the person they are. In Brazil, the rich don't respect the poor. It's shameful . . . Americans may discriminate on the basis of race. Because you're from another country, you're an intruder, and even so, they respect immigrants as people.
> Q: Do you feel respected by the authorities here?
> A: More than in Brazil . . . the majority of Brazilian people don't know their rights. Discrimination here is sometimes indirect, subtle. For example, my boss comes to do inspections without me being present, and this doesn't happen to the Americans . . . if you don't speak English well, you're discriminated against. This type [of discrimination] is even legitimate. Other types [are] not listening, not helping . . . if you try to be equal to them, you're discriminated against. But, if you work autonomously, there is no discrimination.
> Q: Where is life better?
> A: It's better here because opportunities always come up and in Brazil they don't.

Once again, open discrimination against the poor in Brazil is mentioned, and the feeling of being respected as a person in the United States, independent of occupational status and, in this case, level of education. This interview calls attention to three quite relevant points: the degree of discrimination is proportional to the level of competition in the hierarchy of positions in American firms, positions that are reserved for locals; immigrants recognize that in the United States there are other forms of discrimination, not necessarily verbalized and open as in Brazil, because in the United States those who discriminate tend to be punished with relative frequency; and discrimination can be legitimate, as the example the interviewee cites of the immigrant ("intruder") who does not speak English well.

As in the cases analyzed here, all the in-depth interviews record a generic identification by the interviewees with American society and, concomitantly, a disparagement of Brazilian society. To counterbalance this disequilibrium, Brazilians reject the identity of immigrant and do not identify with workers in the service sector (housecleaners, dishwashers, and so on), emphasizing their differences and denying their identification with Hispanics.[14] And while some interviewees said most Brazilian immigrants have at least finished high school, others stated that they only met "uneducated" Brazilians, and they established distinctions between themselves and the "other Brazilians" who were uneducated, "farmhands," and "hicks." By way of illustrating this point, no immigrant admitted in the interviews to being from a working-class family. They preferred to say only, "My father works in the Vale do Rio Doce." After some insistence, one of them admitted that his father worked "in carpentry." Another example involves the distortion of information with respect to work in America. A young man who worked for a supermarket chain in Boston as a salesclerk and was known in his hometown in the countryside of Minas Gerais as the "manager" of the chain bears mention. It is not always the immigrant who invents for himself a more elevated status but rather the immigrant's family in Brazil. Some families consider it chic to have one of their family members living in the United States. Especially in smaller towns, the immigrant's status rises in the opinion of family and neighbors simply because he or she has gone to America.

These considerations are important in understanding the more obscure details of the process of reestablishing the value of respect and citizenship. Nonetheless, they do not invalidate perceptions and life experiences in the two contexts. In the end, if for first-generation Brazilian immigrants America is the country where they believe they can attain the opportunities they were denied in Brazil, it would be very difficult for them to question the inequality of the structure of opportunities in American society simply based on a comparison of their life experiences in the two countries.

Taking as reference points not only the interviews mentioned above but rather the whole set of interviews from the field research conducted between 1994 and 1996, the notions of respect and citizenship can be summarized in two categories. The first refers to the civic dimension of the term "citizenship" and the second to the effective access to public or collective goods and services.

Respect as a dimension of civic life includes respect in personal relationships; respect on the part of local authorities in the guarantee of civil and human rights; respect on the part of civil servants at public agencies in the form of courteous treatment, professionalism, and security; and respect from employers, especially in housecleaning, as demonstrated by a relatively satisfactory level of pay, politeness in personal treatment, and acknowledgement of the worker's professionalism.

Access to public or collective goods and services includes access to niche services especially oriented toward Brazilians, Portuguese-language speakers, or Hispanics in a number of areas. These areas include health care (Saint Elizabeth Hospital's services for Portuguese speakers),[15] housing (through the Ecumenical Committee of East Boston for Hispanics and Brazilians), and basic education (bilingual education programs for Portuguese-speaking students). There is also access to public resources or nongovernmental entities to finance community development through representative entities (Massachusetts Alliance of Portuguese Speakers, Brazilian Immigrant Center); access to health care programs, especially to Free Care; and access to employee benefits such as holidays, paid sick leave, and overtime, provided that the businesses are unionized.

Respect appears as an element of mediation in social relationships and is not limited to the public sphere. On the other hand, citizenship is anchored in a guarantee of access to social programs and to the quality of service rendered. The stress on quality goes back to the notion of respect. That is, receiving a service considered satisfactory means having taken appropriate advantage of the right to the service.

Therefore, the perceptions regarding respect and citizenship refer to a set of public services that do not depend on the limitations imposed by the condition of citizenship in the formal sense of the term precisely because these services favor minority groups. That is, access is facilitated because the services are intended to serve specific ethnic categories. Thus, this type of service leads to and encourages ethnic identification.[16]

These notions of citizenship draw attention to the changes that have been occurring in its meaning in various countries. Soysal (1994), while researching guest worker programs in Western Europe (Germany, France, Switzerland, and England), stressed the emergence of a "more universal" concept of citizenship that is legitimized by principles centered on personhood and not on national belonging. Although the guest workers do not have formal citizenship, they participate in various sectors of the institutional life of the places where they reside, such as the educational system, welfare programs, the labor market, associations, unions, collective-bargaining processes, and in some cases they participate in local disputes by voting. Such forms of participation challenge the traditional model of citizenship based on fixed criteria of territorialization and cultural and national belonging in favor of a notion of citizenship that has as its legitimizing and normative principle the politics of human rights. The means of incorporation, Soysal finds, are delineated by the institutional system of the receiving society: "The variations in the model of incorporation in each state affect the strategies of the immigrant groups and their participation in the receiving society" (5).

Keeping in mind the differences, my research indicates that in the United States, Brazilian immigrants have certain rights and feel that they have these rights. The limits and extent of these rights are determined by the U.S. institutional system, which is based on principles shaped on a policy of human rights and social rights. In other words, the Brazilian immigrants feel that they are respected as people and have access to basic social programs of a quality superior to those available in Brazil.

The concept of citizenship here is taken in its broadest sense, embracing aspects of the economic, sociological, and institutional spheres. Citizenship in the economic sphere is equivalent to access to consumption not only of private goods but also of public and collective goods. Citizenship in the sociological sphere refers to the practice of respect as the principal element of mediation between social sectors and to the treatment extended by the public bureaucracy (the police, the justice system, and public departments and services). Finally, although Brazilian immigrants do not have political citizenship in a formal, legal sense, they have institutional participation (Brazilian representation in education, health care,

NGOs, and so on) independent of the formal limits imposed by their clandestine status.

When Brazilians look toward the United States and contrast this country with Brazil, they tend to converge on common ground: they value the respect and citizenship that they perceive in American society.[17] The cultural memory brought from the country of origin can reinforce their perceptions about the host society in a positive way, contrary to what the literature emphasizes.

Post–September 11

The slums in Brazil are no less dangerous than the Mexican border.

Tuco, 22 years old, 2005

Overall, the events of September 11, 2001, did not affect the general notions about rights and citizenship expressed above, but important considerations should be made. Fear of deportation, apprehensiveness about finding employment, difficulties in getting a driver's license, and entry into the United States through Mexico began to become a frequent part of the accounts about the lives of Brazilians. Besides this, the discourse of the NGOs and evangelical churches became more political and the leadership more alert. Nonetheless, the favorable opinion of American society has remained, and the two previously highlighted elements—respect and citizenship—continue to lend support to that opinion. In 2005 an immigrant named Cida expressed feeling less apprehension in the United States than in Brazil:

> Here people are afraid, it's true; anyone can be deported if they don't have documentation. But I also feel afraid in Brazil. I lived in Rio de Janeiro, and I couldn't stand it any more. I saw a little boy die right in front of me; he was hit by a stray bullet. Which is worse? I don't want to return. I prefer to see my children growing up here.

Cida, age 55, said she was going to appear on *The Oprah Winfrey Show*. Cida arrived in Boston in 2000 and was close to getting her green card:

> My American employers are marvelous, and I was very lucky to end up working for them as my very first job. I never left there . . . Now I have brought my son through Mexico, and I am going to help him

> open a pet shop. Can you see how I have succeeded in America in five years?!

I spoke with a Brazilian man who was about to be deported. He had been detained during a police raid by mistake, but as he was undocumented, he ended up being arrested. He arrived a year earlier through Mexico, and he told me that in Brazil he earned 350 *reais* a month. It is surprising that the financing plan for human trafficking allows a Brazilian who earns the equivalent of one minimum wage in Brazil (not even $200) to emigrate. This is because the whole trip, costing $10,000 to $16,000, is financed in monthly installments that can be paid off within a year or two of working in the United States. This means that whoever accepts this arrangement will do nothing else but work for one to two years to pay his or her passage. My interviewee told me that if he were lucky, he would try to return: "I like life here. I work a lot, but I know that here I can manage to live well, with more money . . . even working in a restaurant or as a painter, I can get everything I want." I asked him how he was feeling and how he had been treated by the local authorities responsible for his deportation. He responded:

> They treated me politely, and they told me what my rights are. Here the police don't go around hitting people, beating them up. I already knew that being deported was something that could happen to anyone who didn't have documents. It happened to me; it was the luck of the draw.

Five months after September 11, the resilience of those living in the area was amazing in the face of the attacks in which Boston was one of the perpetrators' tactical points.[18] However, there were consequences for the Brazilian immigrants residing in the area. In the airport itself, 400 Brazilians employed by a cleaning company were arrested. A Brazilian community leader named Paulo said in 2005, "The community is now more visible and the authorities know where to look for them."

Everything indicates that the measures taken after September 11 have not prevented Brazilians from continuing to arrive in large numbers, although it has made the return to Brazil and entry with a tourist visa more difficult. But after crossing the border, the difficulties inside the United States have increased. Getting a driver's license can make any immigrant's life hellish. Margolis (2008b: 7) finds that

> several schemes have surfaced in the Brazilian community to meet the demand for driver's licenses. While a license usually costs about $50, some Brazilian immigrants have paid as much as $800 to get one using counterfeit papers. Organized "tours" also have been arranged to states where it is easier to get a license. Typically Brazilian immigrants in the northeast travel in minivans to states like Delaware, Virginia, and North Carolina, which, unlike New York, Connecticut, and Massachusetts, do not require a green card or valid social security card to obtain a driver's license. Such excursions can cost up to $3000. . . . But in some cases this does not solve the problem . . . [and] the issuance of driver's licenses to undocumented immigrants also emerged as a political issue in the United States after 9/11. . . .
> Undocumented Brazilians have been on the receiving end of many petty (and not so petty) annoyances since 9/11. Police in some communities began randomly asking for passports and visas, while schools began checking residency documents and denying school registration for the children of immigrants if they could not prove residency in a particular school district.

Fear, not surprisingly, has entered into the routine of the daily conversations between Brazilians. Obviously, fear begins with the border crossing through Mexico. Of the Brazilians interviewed in 2005, 29% were not granted tourist visas and entered undocumented through Mexico; they represent almost all of those who entered after September 2001.[19]

The accounts of crossing through Mexico are full of adventure, fear, and dramatic situations in which the very lives of the immigrants are put at risk. Jorge is another Brazilian who attempted the crossing twice. At age 33, he left the city of Inhumas in the Brazilian state of Goiais and was caught at the U.S. border by Mexican police. A month after returning to Brazil, he attempted to cross again. He had finished college, and when I interviewed him, he had been living in the United States for eight months.

> I came through Mexico, and I knew about the risks, but I didn't know that the risks would be so big. During the crossing, the border guards demanded $100 to let us cross. No one had that much money; but there was no negotiating, and all of us who were on the bus were deported. There were twenty-two of us. As soon as I

returned to Brazil, I went to the same agency because I had already paid half the cost, $4,000. They had told us that if one of us were left behind, the agency would arrange the trip again. So, about forty days after having been stopped in Mexico, I returned to the United States. This time everything worked out. We were caught by the American immigration [agents], but it was all worked out, so after they detained us, we were released. The risk that I hadn't counted on when I accepted this challenge was the risk to life itself. The crossing is long; you have to run more than four kilometers and cross rivers, swamps, and filthy places. But in the end it was worth it because, for me, my biggest dream was to get to know this country.

The crossing through Mexico and immigration into the United States itself were the subject of a Brazilian *novela* called *América* that was shown in 2005 on the Brazilian national network and broadcast at the same time on cable TV in the United States.[20] If at first Brazilians were ecstatic over the possibility of seeing themselves portrayed in the prime-time *novela* that reached the largest free television audience in Brazil, as the plot developed, they began to show frustration and disappointment: "The *novela* is very unrealistic. Sol [the protagonist] cries all the time, [and] the owner of the Mexican boardinghouse has parties every day for the Brazilians. The Hispanics get along so well with the Brazilians that they seem to be one people," commented a Brazilian waitress in a *churrascaria* restaurant where the TV was tuned to that channel all day.[21]

In fact, by victimizing the immigrant protagonist, the *novela* was unable to portray the complex reality in which Brazilians find themselves, its ambiguities, and the system of rewards that leads them to relativize their circumstance as undocumented immigrants. The statements collected in 2005 definitively refuted the representation of the Brazilian immigrant as a victim:

I worked in the countryside; I was going to turn 50, and I was very beat up because it was hard work, using a hatchet, a scythe, thugs in the woods, and everything . . . My region there, Bico do Papagaio [in the Brazilian state of Pará] is violent. An American nun died there because she was defending the farmworkers[22] . . . Some people from my town were here, and I came. I came through Mexico, risking my life, risking rape, etc., but the only problem was that they only gave us enough bread to last four days . . . The rest was normal, like

> any other trip. Here I work in housecleaning. For me it's easy work; I'm used to it. The Americans are polite, my employers are good to me, and I'm never going to go back there. In Brazil, I don't even have a pension. I'm really going to work until I die. I'm not afraid of Americans, but I don't trust Brazilians; some don't keep their word, they don't respect agreements, but they're not all like that, see? I keep staying . . . being undocumented doesn't make any difference to me.

This female interviewee, who said she did not know how to read or write Portuguese, made a point of showing me that her hands were very rough and marked by calluses and scars. Her hands gave testimony to part of a story that she did not wish to hide but that she would rather leave behind.

Cleavages in the Cultural Memory and the Internal Dynamics of the Group

In the stories that Brazilians tell about themselves, distinct divisions appear. They are divisions that check the artificially homogeneous treatment given by the U.S. literature to immigrant groups in the country. Due to the focus on "ethnic groups"—and it is important to note that ethnicity is conceived in the literature as a broader category than national or racial groups—the more detailed and subdivided aspects of the elements that interact in the internal dynamics of each group are lost from view.

The divisions to which I refer are the means that allow the reconstruction and highlighting of differences that the generic category "Brazilian immigrants" tends to erase or cover up. These are not rigid divisions that constitute a classificatory system of clearly structured representations. They merely reveal an attempt to reorder social roles, taking as a reference point a set of experiences, values, and life experiences in Brazil that still preserve some sense because they allow the protagonists and interlocutors to situate themselves in the present.

Such divisions express categories that are often superimposed, constructed on the basis of a simple system of binary opposition used to define "us" and "the others" in situations in which "the others" are "farmhands," "uneducated," "from Governador Valadares," and "from Minas" (when the intent is to attribute a pejorative value to the two latter terms). Returning to the demographic characteristics of the 300 Brazilian immigrants interviewed in the surveys, people from Minas represent a little less than 50% of the total. Immigrants from Governador Valadares represented 17% in 1996 and 13% in 2005, and farmhands, understood as small-scale family farmers, made up to 1% of the interviewees in 1996 and 2% in 2005. This means that the references that Brazilian immigrants make to these categories are not necessarily significant from a quantitative point of view. They can be better understood if they are contextualized in the sphere of the meanings that they represent. That is, such categories become reference points that permit identities and differences to be established in a dynamic way that makes it possible to cut across boundaries and even move them when necessary. Except as regards Catholics and evangelicals, the divisions are not used as criteria to exclude people from or incorporate them into the same group because Brazilians follow the "golden rule" of Brazilian sociability, "different but together," in the words of da Matta (2000).

I use precisely that author as the basis for explaining these divisions because I argue that they express, in another context, a social practice deeply rooted in Brazilian society. I offer as an example the interview with Ana Elisa, a young woman who told me that "in America, what is classic is chic," and this was why she dressed in a way that was a little too matronly for her age. The daughter of local elites from a small town in Minas Gerais, she left the college that she was attending in her second year because "I didn't see any future in it." In the United States she worked as a housecleaner. However, she emphasized that she lived in a house with a swimming pool in a tree-lined Boston suburb.

> A: I don't think I'm better than they are, but it's just that there are people who come here straight from the countryside. They have a very low cultural level; they are not educated . . .
>
> Q: But what harm does that do?
>
> A: . . . [T]here are cases that have made people lose their jobs . . . The stories here make your hair stand on end. For example, the case of a friend of mine: when we found out that Paulo was going to arrive, we went to find him a job. We got a job for him, but João [another friend] went there and presented himself as Paulo, and he took the job for himself.
>
> Q: Did you use that example because João came from the countryside?

> A: No. It's everyone; the damage they do with credit cards! They buy a bunch of things and leave without paying . . . This is common . . . they only make a mess of things!

This statement is representative of the way Brazilians speak among themselves about their compatriots. She began explaining the difference: they come from rural areas and are uneducated, and thus they do not know how to follow basic social rules like not stealing a friend's job. However, the person given as an example was not from a rural background and had the same level of education that Ana Lisa did. When questioned, she reacted by saying that "everyone" is like that—except her. The way out, then, is to transpose "farmhands are uneducated" to a moral plane by concluding her argument by mentioning the malfeasance that ends up on the police blotter.

The passage from this interview illustrates how Brazilians speak about themselves in an ambiguous and exaggerated manner: "the majority of Brazilians are uneducated; they come from the countryside," an assertion that appears to be untrue; the speaker attempts in a dramatic way to find some means of giving meaning to what is perceived as a "mess." In this context the complaints about the "lack of solidarity" among Brazilians can consolidate meanings that demand a reordering in the immigrants' minds. The chaos generated by the move from one country to another and by the absence of reference points in pre-established roles in the new society presents itself as a drama. The more egalitarian situation in which they find themselves (an equality accorded by the common condition of being Brazilian immigrants) encompasses a set of ambiguities, conflicts, and competition, including competition for employment. The divisions are responses to the short circuit that permit a repositioning—of themselves and of "the others"—in a hierarchical alignment capable of ranking "superiors" and "inferiors."[23] The moral tenor that underlies the divisions reveals the attempt to legitimize the "superior" before the "inferior." The "mess" is an explicit reference to the absence of mechanisms of social control within the Brazilian immigrant population.

Divisions likewise are fundamental in the construction of the other who, in conflict situations, is blamed for the breakdown of the relationships of solidarity in the community. Such assignment of responsibility surfaced in an interview with Elisa:

A: My good friend is from Governador Valadares, a city that is looked down on here because the people arrive here without any idea of anything. They are people who came from the sticks . . . they never saw a big city before. So, they don't have any scruples about taking someone's job . . . Perhaps because of the lifestyle they had in Brazil . . .
Q: Do they have this reputation only among Brazilians?
A: I know of restaurants where people from Valadares don't get work. They are of a very inferior type.

Those who violate the norms of good social relations are classified as inferior, reinforcing the roles characteristic of a hierarchical society like that of Brazil. The divisions represent a desire and the result of an effort to reorder roles, putting "each one in his place" in the unfamiliar context brought about by immigration in which the farmhand and the cowhand are in the same situation as the child of the *carioca* middle class and of the rural elite.[24]

I argue that the reasoning that underlies the discourse about the lack of solidarity has to do with demarcating differences: "I am not like them." It is a symbolic discourse and therefore ambiguous by definition, and it exaggerates critical aspects of the relationships between Brazilians in order to sort out a reality that is new and uncomfortable. Thus, the recontextualization of past practices occurs according to which social roles should obey a hierarchy that determines inferiors and superiors.

Nevertheless, constructing divisions by taking as a reference point the values and practices of a hierarchical society does not prevent Brazilians from valuing the greater degree of equality they say they are experiencing in American society. On the contrary, it is precisely by establishing a contrast between the two experiences that Brazilians can stress the equality that marks the American ethos. On the other hand, this does not occur without ambiguities because, as I sought to show, part of this valorization stems precisely from a belief in the superiority of American society, a belief anchored in hierarchical values.

Only by looking at it from the inside is it possible to understand the cultural memory that orients the internal dynamic of the group, to perceive how the culture of (national) origin affects that dynamic. It is further necessary to look from the inside when working with the culture, solidarity, and identity of an immigrant group. The U.S. ethnic system, like the ideology of ethnicity, should be examined from a certain critical distance so that the so-called ethnic groups also can be understood as part of a political construct in order to avoid essentialist approaches to culture.

Community Organizations

The identity of "Brazilian immigrant" is constructed in a particular way and a specific context. This context involves the associative organizations that in some way seek to represent immigrants, to speak in their name, or to protect their interests before public authorities or other immigrant groups. I am not going to refer to social identity itself here but rather to collective identities made explicit by Brazilians who join organizations that seek to represent or work for Brazilian immigrants. The operation of community organizations will not be analyzed either, rather only how the leadership struggles with ethnic identification.

In her pioneering book *Little Brazil* (1994) about Brazilians in New York in the early 1990s, Maxine Margolis notes the absence of community associations as "one of the most marked features of the panorama of Brazilian immigration" (304). Yet this statement is not applicable to Massachusetts.[25] In that state, between 1994 and 1996, when my research was conducted, seven of the ten entities that existed up to 1997 were created. It is easy to conclude that this picture of association differs from that presented by Margolis of Brazilians who lived in New York during earlier years.

Margolis found Brazilians disorganized because they did not have a tradition of association and gave preference to family ties to the detriment of community actions. This premise is quite questionable, but it is noteworthy that in the data collected in New York, the family as an institution is absent. On the other hand, Margolis emphasizes the lack of motivation to organize since Brazilians did not intend to remain in the United States but rather to return to Brazil. She indicates a reason of a temporal nature, too: the migratory flow was still recent, and Brazilians had not had sufficient time to organize.

Yet other factors can be used to explain the greater degree of organization among Brazilians in Massachusetts. The Boston metropolitan area is composed of several smaller cities, which, perhaps because they are small, are less disperse than New York and facilitate greater sociability and association. In the Boston area, for example, stores that sell Brazilian products and function as gathering points are located in the same neighborhoods where Brazilians reside. The situation is different in New York City, where the stores are concentrated on Forty-sixth Street in Manhattan, while many Brazilians live in Astoria in the borough of Queens or even in Newark. It is probable that the immigrants do not organize in the places where they work but rather where they have community life, where they live, go to church, get together to eat, and so on.

The profile of the Brazilian immigrant residing in Greater Boston differs from the occupational and family profile presented by Margolis. That is, more Brazilians live with their nuclear families in Boston than in New York, and there are differences in occupational profiles as well. To be more specific, in New York it is common to find Brazilians working as taxi drivers or in shoe repair. In Greater Boston, men work in cleaning, landscaping, home delivery, building construction, dishwashing, and even the kitchens of bars and restaurants. Brazilian women work in the kitchens of bars and restaurants and for housecleaning services.

By mid-1996, ten groups had been organized exclusively by Brazilians or relied exclusively on their participation: Massachusetts Alliance of Portuguese Speakers (MAPS), Brazilian Immigrant Center (BIC), Grupo Mulher Brasileira (GMB, Brazilian Women's Group), Brazilian Community Center (BCC), Portuguese Speaking Providers Network (PSPN), Brazilian Boston Network (BBN), Rio Maria Committee (RMC), Associação dos Brasileiros de Cape Cod (ABCC, Association of Brazilians of Cape Cod), Brazilian Children's Foundation (BCF), and American Brazilian Association (ABA).

Of the ten organizations created in the 1990s, only four managed to remain active for more than five years: GMB, MAPS, CIB, and BCF. According to Sales (2006), the Brazilian entities found it difficult to arrange political representation for their base and to oversee the organizations' administrative services. As a result, although they showed that they were capable of political mobilization, they faced problems in getting the financial resources necessary to maintain their activities. To compensate for this, other NGOs were created (or were being created) in or after 2000: Centro do Trabalhador Brasileiro (Brazilian Worker's Center), Brazilian American Association (BRAMAS), Associação de Cidades Irmãs Framingham–Governador Valadares (Sister Cities Association

Framingham–Governador Valadares), and three capoeira cultural centers.[26] The celebration of September 7, the anniversary of Brazil's independence from Portugal, is one event that almost all the Brazilian NGOs help organize and carry out.

MAPS, the oldest of these organizations, was founded in 1970. It was originally located only in Somerville and intended to aid Portuguese immigrants with various social assistance services. After the arrival of Brazilian immigrants, MAPS began to help them as well as immigrants from Cape Verde and Portuguese nationals from the Azores. A MAPS leader explained that "more than 50% of the services are oriented toward Brazilians, approximately 27% toward immigrants from Cape Verde, and 22% toward the Portuguese." Meanwhile, on the organization's board of directors, Portuguese immigrants still predominated. Until 2002 MAPS had two offices; three years later it had five (Cambridge, Allston, Dorcherster, Somerville, and Lowell). This expansion seems to have contributed to the organization's stabilization.

The CIB, created in 1995, has a nine-member board, a six-member staff, and a mission to defend the Brazilian community in Massachusetts in the areas of education, workers' rights, and immigrant rights in general. The CIB is involved in several projects. The Partnership Project with the University of Massachusetts at Lowell, the Lowell Heath Care Center, and the Massachusetts Coalition for Occupational Health and Safety aims to improve the health conditions of workers. Civic Participation is a project to raise the consciousness of second-generation Brazilians regarding the importance of exercising citizenship even when outside the country of origin. The Workers' Rights project offers weekly talks at the group's headquarters and at area churches. These talks on workers' rights inform participants, for example, that the minimum wage in Massachusetts is $7.50 and that after working forty hours in a week the employee should receive overtime pay. Speakers talk about immigration to encourage participation in movements working for the reform of U.S. immigration laws. Fausto Rocha, the main leader and founder of the organization, said that in April 2005 the project became engaged in the Do Not Destroy Our Families campaign organized by the National Alliance of Latin American and Caribbean Communities (NALACC).

Among the CIB's accomplishments since its founding was the resolution of 130 documented cases of violations of workers' rights by means of public pressure and direct negotiation with the employers; as a result, more than $500,000 in salaries and overtime was restored to the workers.[27] The Workers' Rights project, in a single class-action suit, helped twelve Brazilians recover $300,000 in wages. The CIB helped train more than 200 construction workers, supported reform of immigration legislation and a law that prevented access to universities by undocumented students, and contributed to the development of print and broadcast media in Portuguese and English. In 2006 the organization got its own AM radio program, *The Immigrant Center on the Air.*

The CIB has the support of collaborative organizations, notably Citizens Bank and the Clipper Ship Foundation, Haymarket People's Fund, Hyams Foundation, Lenny Fund, Harvard University, Jewish Fund for Justice, Massachusetts Bar Foundation, Barr Foundations, Boston Bar Foundation, Muller Foundation, Highland Foundation, Boston Department of Public Health, and Massachusetts Department of Industrial Accidents (Centro do Imigrante Brasileiro 2009). The group's director reported that in the early 2000s the CIB redirected its work to serve Latinos and immigrants from the Caribbean as well as Brazilians and therefore no longer had Portuguese speakers as its principal associates:

> The Latino groups with which we cooperate are Salvadorans, Dominicans, and Colombians. For every five immigrants in Boston, one is a Brazilian. Brazilians need to know that it is not necessary for a worker to be documented in order to join a union, and what we want is to unionize the greatest possible number.

The Grupo Mulher Brasileira was created in 1995 by Brazilian immigrant women under the leadership of Heloisa Souza. It is developing a Housecleaners Cooperative project in which it partners with the University of Massachusetts at Lowell, the CIB, and MAPS. The project seeks to "support Brazilian women housecleaners in their professional development [and] promote healthy methods of cleaning in the community that will not harm the environment." The group's mission is "acting politically, providing leisure, and raising awareness, contributing to the development of the Brazilian community in an environment open to all interested women." It works by discussing problems and the role of Brazilian women immigrants, supporting their families, informing the community and helping search for solutions to its problems, and promoting cultural activities. The group has a policy of valuing and respecting cultural differences, cooperating with other Brazilian NGOs, fostering political awareness and awareness of immigrants' human rights, promoting community organizing and its leadership, and fostering Brazilians' adaptation to U.S. society and cooperation with other immigrant groups (Brazilian Women's Group 2009).

The Brazilian Children's Foundation was founded in Framingham in 1996. From the beginning, the group had the support of Brazilian and American citizens in collecting donations of medical supplies and equipment, clothing, and toys that are sent to Brazil. The group's mission is to help street children and other poor children in Brazil. The programs developed by the group aim at prevention of health and social problems, providing for basic needs, and occupational training to offer the children a higher quality of life in the present and preparation for a better future (Brazilian Children's Foundation 2009).

Among the groups created beginning in 2000,[28] the Brazilian Worker's Center merits highlighting. It was founded in 2000 by a Brazilian immigrant woman, Maria da Hora, and is headquartered in a building belonging to the Catholic Church in East Boston. It came about with support from the Ecumenical Council of the East Boston Community to assist Brazilians in that area. Its projects extend to English classes, responding to workers' disputes, immigrants' rights campaigns, and talks of interest to the community.

The Brazilian American Association was founded in 2000 in Framingham with initial support from the city's Brazilian small-business owners who had formed an association, the Brazilian Business Network. BRAMAS is oriented toward Brazilians who have become American citizens or hold green cards and are in a position to apply for American citizenship, as well as Americans who are directly involved with the Brazilian community or who sympathize with the immigrants. It has been led by Frank Kavanagh since 2007, and one of its main projects involves sensitizing politicians and the community to demands such as the passage of the law that permits application for a driver's license and reform of immigration laws. In 2005 the group organized a cultural fair called Spring into Arts with the support of the mayor's office and the Start Framingham Partnership (Brazilian American Association 2009).

Initially the networks like MAPS and other NGOs that supported many of these groups were formed by Brazilian professionals who worked in local public and private institutions. These professionals varied in their command of the English language, legal status, and level of education.

They belonged to public education and health care networks and often were contracted to aid Brazilians. They acted as intermediaries for and representatives of the community, organizing activities and support groups. Among them, women occupied a prominent place in numbers and level of participation.

Among the ten groups, MAPS was formed before Brazilians arrived in Massachusetts in large numbers,[29] and three (RMC, BBN, and CIB) relied on the support of non-Brazilians in their formation. In the 1990s Brazilians learned how NGOs and U.S. institutions operate. They also were beginning to learn that in the United States, belonging to a national group (or an ethnicity) could be transformed into a means of obtaining benefits, articulating interests, and expressing solidarity. Another characteristic that is no less important is that some of these groups were trying to make connections with certain places in Brazil in order to serve as links for binational cultural, commercial, and philanthropic activities, following the example of other immigrant groups in the region.[30]

An important point to note is that Brazilian businesspeople do not actively participate in these groups. Several sociologists have called attention to the meaning and role of businesspeople in active community life (whether the activities are religious, athletic, cultural, or political in nature) in the acquisition and advancement of social capital of the most varied groups and particularly of immigrants (Putnam 1996, Merton 1968, Portes 1995). In the Brazilian case, however, a large majority of businesspeople have scant community life, to judge by the number of associations or groups in which they formally participate. In a study of fifty Brazilian businesspeople conducted in 2001, only 12% were engaged in this type of community activity.[31] Few engaged in community activities, and at the same time all complained that the Brazilian community was "not united." But in 2003 the Overseas Chamber of Commerce was created. The participation of businesspeople in this organization was restricted to highly institutionalized businesses, leaving out Brazilian citizens who migrated as unskilled workers and set up small businesses to serve the consumer needs of Brazilians overseas. The only exception is this chamber's Boston affiliate, which includes some small businesses as members.

The main problems Brazilian businesspeople face have to do with the lack of associative articulation among them and the lack of start-up capital, working capital, and credit. The establishment of the Overseas Chamber of Commerce tentatively answered the problem, but it depended on the consulate's decisive involvement. Indications are that the members of the Brazilian American Chamber of Commerce of New England were sensitive to and interested in these issues because, as can be seen in its business plan, the BACCNE proposed to offer information regarding resources for "financial and skill development, awareness of available resources, and developing networks" and to identify and provide resources "such as business-to-business contacts, resources within the local community, statewide, and the federal government (such as the Small Business Administration)."

This group's formation could have contributed to an increase in the volume and density of the social capital of Brazilians in Boston, but not in a way limited to small-business owners, as the entire community may benefit from the development of social and commercial networks. To accomplish this kind of development, the Brazilian consulate in Boston maintained an active presence, as Brazilian government representatives have with similar groups in other American cities and regions. Despite the efforts of the consulate and some Brazilian businesspeople, the Overseas Chamber of Commerce did not survive. Some said it lacked leadership and confidence.

The Instrumental Nature of Ethnic Identification

In the 1990s the tendency of Brazilians not to identify with Hispanics was clear. In fact, there seemed to be few affinities between the two groups: Brazilians did not live in the same neighborhoods and enjoyed a relatively better economic status than the rest of the Latino population in Boston, which was considered the poorest in Massachusetts (Osterman 1989). Few Brazilians participated in Hispanic organizations.[32] The most significant tendency seen throughout the forty interviews was that of identification with the Portuguese. Up to the time this study was completed, Brazilians were more likely to join an organization that consisted of Portuguese speakers including Portuguese, Azorean, and Cape Verdean members.[33]

Brazilians in general tended to justify their rejection of Hispanic identity in the 1990s because Brazilians do not speak Spanish or see themselves as part of Spanish culture. Like other Latino groups, a large percentage of Brazilians wanted to assert their own identity, and they struggled to do so. Nevertheless, this rejection also was associated with disadvantages that the label "Hispanic" could cause because of the discrimination against the group in the United States and on the part of many Brazilians. The attitude of these Brazilians reinforced the prejudice against Latinos and consequently against Brazilians themselves, who tend to be seen as Hispanic by non-Brazilians.

Saying that Brazilians tend to reject their inclusion in the category "Hispanic" does not mean that this rejection is complete. Belonging to an officially recognized ethnicity can lead to advantages, as well, such as participation in affirmative-action quotas, and it is obviously an important factor when Brazilians seek to defend or expand the scope of their civil rights. Some community leaders show that they are conscious of this situation, and they seek to associate either with Portuguese-language speakers or with Hispanics. Parallel to occupying these two alternative spaces, some Brazilian community leaders have the short-term objective of forming groups through which Brazilians can express themselves autonomously. Comments of one community leader illustrate this point:

> The Brazilian community has been facing problems with the Portuguese, which is an older community here . . . When I arrived, I had a problem where I worked with the supervisor, who was Brazilian. He placed me under the manager, who was Portuguese. This Portuguese man sent me to another, worse type of work, and I went to an organization that provides legal assistance to immigrants, especially to Latinos. They helped me, and one of the directors of that organization invited me to participate. I joined and later was elected as an officer, representing Latinos. The idea was to have a Brazilian representing the community in the future . . . There was already an organization of Portuguese-language speakers, but despite the fact that the language was the same, their opinions were different, and they are the majority. So, we planned to form an organization that we would lead ourselves . . . And, so as not to compete with them, we opted to act in an area in which the community has no support: the area of labor . . . Here any worker can join a union, even an undocumented worker . . . Forming an NGO is not difficult; it's just a matter of proving that it's serious and that it will be able to get financing from American institutions.

This interview shows that once in the United States, immigrants tend to identify and organize themselves as ethnic groups. Brazilians see themselves as having the option of choosing from the categories of Hispanic,

Portuguese speakers, and Brazilians.[34] As this interviewee indicates, Brazilian community leaders are conscious of the importance of ethnic affiliation. Thus the Hispanic identity has a special appeal for some.

Among the Brazilian immigrants interviewed, community leaders or not, identification with the Portuguese was held as being most natural. The common language has great appeal, but the relationship with the Portuguese is not so easy, and the disputes that arise in the organizations of Portuguese-language speakers reveal misunderstandings. The Portuguese, in turn, fear that Brazilians will gain autonomy and distance themselves from the organization, which could affect its budget. It is not surprising that Brazilian leaders complained when the organization opened an office in front of the CIB in Allston, a city with more Brazilians than Portuguese. This initiative was interpreted as a way of "suffocating" the Brazilian organization to prevent immigrants from having their own voice. Any such intentions were denied by the Portuguese.

Although associations of Portuguese speakers by definition are meant to unite those who speak the same language, Portuguese immigrants began to arrive in Massachusetts in the nineteenth century, and many can hardly speak Portuguese. This is true for the majority of second-generation Portuguese who make up the leadership of the society. The Cape Verdeans who also participate in the organization speak Creole Portuguese that is unintelligible to a Brazilian. It is significant that the group's board meetings are invariably conducted in English. Thus, despite being considered more natural, the unity between Brazilians and Portuguese seems to be quite forced.

"It is difficult for them to understand what we are trying to say, where we want to get to," commented a Brazilian leader. "We are always thinking of the movement, of the broader organization. They are more concerned with organizing the soup dinners offered to senior citizens on Thursday nights and with the society's bureaucracy." Others commented that the Portuguese of Boston came from the Azores and are therefore "more backward." Distinctions appear even outside the context of the association, especially differences in behavior that invariably are expressed as stereotypes. An opinion prevalent among the Portuguese suggests that Brazilians are promiscuous and Brazilian women "are easy." Brazilians react to this by saying that the Portuguese are authoritarian and conservative. Some say Brazilian women are frequently sexually molested by Portuguese men, especially in the workplace, and so it goes.

Brazilians perceive that the Portuguese leadership exhibits a paternalistic attitude toward them that conceals a desired position of superiority that is more advantageous. According to some of the Brazilian community leaders, the Portuguese act as if they wished to inhibit the Brazilians' emancipation, making it difficult for them to assert their own identity and gain a majority in political and association representation. This gives them the impression that history is repeating itself centuries later and in a foreign land. Once again, old actors meet: Cape Verdeans, whose country only gained its freedom from Portugal in 1975, ally themselves with Brazilians, whose homeland also was colonized by the Portuguese; they say they identify more with Brazilians than with the Portuguese. These alliances, like the ethnic identities, are dynamic; they include some and exclude others, depending on the circumstances and interests involved. In the face of the domination that the Portuguese exercise over the society of Portuguese-language speakers and the composition of its leadership, the Cape Verdeans find in the Brazilians convenient allies with whom they can confront the minority position of both groups. In this context, centuries-old cultural references still echo because they give meaning to the current situation for the purpose of articulating interests.

Brazilian immigrants find themselves in the midst of a society that emphasizes ethnicity and their specific cultural identification. Brazilian community leaders know that in order to have a voice, visibility, and access to resources—including financial resources—their organizations will have to find a place in the official spectrum of ethnic labels. However, ethnicity also involves ideological positioning. Ethnic groups differentiate themselves by contrast with other groups or immigrants. In other words, a group defines itself as ethnic not only because its members share a common culture but also because it relates to other groups as such. Roberto Oliveira (1976) argues that ethnicity is a classifier in an interethnic system in which collective representations are established in circumstances of manifest or latent opposition. Contrast with other identities expresses the essential nature of the ethnic identity.

I argue that so-called ethnic communities have an important place in the self-image of the "American nation" because they reinforce the communitarian and pluralistic nature that this society desires to perpetuate and idealize for itself. Used to incorporate some and exclude others, ethnic categories are constructed to define spheres of political struggle based on the interplay of exclusion and inclusion. Thus, these categories force the reinvention of citizenship to the extent that they define the terms of the debate about the rights and duties of the various social sectors.

This organizational logic orients (and is oriented by) the institutional system. In other words, the U.S. ethnic system establishes a matrix of institutional organization (forms of community participation, of distribution of resources, and of forms of association and institutional participation). In this sense, the term "ethnicity," or "ethnic group," expresses more a form of organization than cultural content, and this makes it possible for ethnic identification to become an object of manipulation and negotiation.

There is, of course, a connection between ethnic group and culture. But if the ethnic identity results from self-designation and from the recognition of this designation by other groups, then it is an identification adopted due to social interaction among groups. Barth (1969) notes, however, that it is not the cultural elements—institutions, customs, and technology—that define the parameters of an ethnic group but rather its social organization, its self-designation, and the social recognition of that designation. Ethnic identity is a process of group identification. An ethnic group is not a cultural unit but rather a type of organization. The shared culture, meanwhile, results from organizational involvement. The cultural characteristics associated with ethnic groups are more symbolic than authentically based in the culture of origin (Gans 1979, Steinberg 1989).

Incentives for and Constraints on Identification

The immigrants' process of establishment is also a process of "community institutional building" (Silver 2001) and learning. The institutional learning that for Brazilians includes some kind of insertion into local institutions (schools, NGOs) with support from the Brazilian consulate and churches is particularly strong in situations that involve the recognition of ethnic and racial rights and gender equality. Furthermore, access to better-quality public services than those available in Brazil (public schools, health care, mortgage plans, and so on) reinforces a "feeling of citizenship." When they receive fair treatment under the law and social benefits, immigrants have a stronger perception of being respected and recognized as "people who have rights," and this suggests that somehow they do not define citizenship as the classic legal and formal category usually employed.

In this chapter I have shown that Brazilian immigrants find themselves in a situation in which they have to define their ethnicity to be able to find some space, even if it lies at the margins of the U.S. social structure. The U.S. ethnic system provides the basic structure for social relationships and the way groups organize themselves. There is no evidence that Brazilians desire or strive to construct an ethnic identity, but it is true that they want a reference point from which they can defend their interests. The organization of the groups with which Brazilians identify have resulted from pressures and incentives from the host society. American society discriminates and classifies people based on their ethnicity, and Brazilians attempt to take advantage of the positive aspects of this system. In doing so, Brazilians play with different categories: Latino, Hispanic, Portuguese-speaking, and Brazilian. They change their ethnic emphasis depending on the context and the situations generated by the groups with which they are associated. In other words, they define an ethnic identity for instrumental reasons.[35]

Maintaining this ethnic identity can bring personal or collective advantages—or reduce disadvantages—because it enables the use of alternative identities that permit "house rules" to be followed. At the same time, Brazilian community leaders have made efforts to construct a collective identity that allows some degree of insertion into the U.S. institutional system. Articulations based on collective identities can increase the group's opportunities for success because the U.S. system values this type of organization.

Lawrence-Lightfoot calls attention to two different notions connected to the word "respect" (2000: 9):

> Although our views are no doubt both fluid and hybrid, traditional conceptions of respect still have a potent influence on the ways we judge our society. Respect is commonly seen as deference to status and hierarchy; as driven by duty, honor, and a desire to avoid punishment, shame, or embarrassment. Often our view does not involve individuals, as in "respect for propriety," for the law, the flag, or institutions. In many contemporary cultural views—calls for more respectful relationships in health care, urban planning, education, or the more strident calls for civil society—we do not hear the voices of individuals; neither do we see any recognition of the

> painstaking work involved in nourishing respectful relationships. The traditional view of respect, though rarely expressed in its pure form, tends to be relatively static and impersonal. The remnants of this view survive today and shape our expectations, our apprehensions, and our disappointments.

In summary, while the traditional notion of respect expresses a duty owed to another due to his or her position, age, class, professional status, and so on, the more contemporary notion does not imply a hierarchy but rather symmetry, empathy, and connection in relationships, even in bureaucratic or official situations. Curiously, the loci of this author's study are some hospitals, classrooms, and other institutions in Boston and Cambridge; even more curiously, in many of the situations described, the people to whom Lawrence-Lightfoot refers as being treated with respect (empowerment, healing, dialogue, curiosity, self-respect, and attention) are immigrants, including Hispanics (Dominicans, Puerto Ricans, and others from the Caribbean). It is on this point, I believe, that respect and citizenship converge into a common meaning by demanding symmetry in the relationships formed in the most varied institutional spaces.

It is interesting to observe, however, that seeking and valuing symmetrical social relationships is stressed in relationships between Brazilians and Americans but not necessarily asserted in internal relationships among the members of the group. In this vein, the importance of the operation of institutions, including state institutions, should not be underestimated. First, institutions encourage the identification of immigrant groups as ethnic groups, especially through incentive programs for the organization and distribution of resources. Second, public institutions delimit the rights of citizenship (in its broadest sense) to the extent that they provide access to a set of basic public goods and services, many of them directed at ethnic minorities regardless of their condition as illegal immigrants.

Public goods and services like the health care system, schools, parks, libraries, museums, and financing programs for homebuyers were either unavailable to them in Brazil or of lower quality. Thus, although the U.S. welfare system is considered quite limited when compared to those of European social-democratic countries and has been the object of much criticism for deficiencies and poor quality (especially in education), it is more comprehensive and tends to offer services of a quality superior to

Table 5.1. Health Care Expenditures in Brazil and the United States, 2003

Measure of Expenditures	Brazil	United States
Percent of GDP	7.6%	15.2%
Percent of public resources	45.3%	44.6%
Per capita	$597	$5,711

Source: World Health Organization 2006.

those of the Brazilian system. Although it may seem ironic, in the midst of the 1990s—a decade marked by a polarized debate involving restrictions on the social services that should be offered to immigrants—immigrant groups still felt respected and satisfied when they took advantage of the public services to which they had access.

The difference between the health care services offered in each of the two countries jumps out when, for example, expenditures are compared. In 2003 Brazil applied $597 per capita to health care, or 7.6% of the GDP (Table 5.1). In the same year, the United States spent twice that, 15.2% of the GDP, and nearly ten times more per capita, while U.S. per capita income is five times greater than Brazil's (Ocké-Reis 2006).

In relative terms the Brazilian public expenditure on health care represents a rate of 45.3%, a level of investment similar to that observed in the U.S. system (44.6%). The Brazilian constitution guarantees universal access to the public health system. In per capita terms, including the amount of private expenditures, Brazil's $597 was a little less than the average for Latin American countries ($622) and approximately five times less than the average among select countries of the Organization for Economic Cooperation and Development (World Bank cited in Ocké-Reis 2006).

Although Brazilians in Massachusetts do not enjoy unrestricted access to health care, they do have a kind of access that, although limited, permits them to take advantage of programs that they say are of higher quality than those provided by the Brazilian public health service. In addition to the issue of quality, as we have seen, the way they are treated by health care workers is considered part of the comparatively positive appraisal.

The Analytical Implications of the Findings Regarding Respect, Citizenship, and Solidarity

Cultural memory has a dynamic content. That content is neither necessarily homogeneous nor associative, even when it refers to only one national group. In the internal dynamics of the group (in the relationships of Brazilians among themselves and the ways they speak about themselves and fellow Brazilians), the reference points and life experiences (cultural memory) are structuring axes in the sense that Brazilians appeal to them to position themselves (identify or differentiate themselves) internally and externally. Within the group, what is striking are the divisions that are nothing more than attempts to order the "chaos." On arriving in the United States, many Brazilians find themselves perceived as the equals of fellow immigrants from whom they wish to be distinguished. To counter this perception, Brazilians attempt to position themselves as being different and apart from farmhands, uneducated people, and other such fellow immigrants. Thus, it is by taking an internal view and observing the internal dynamics of the group that the differences, ambiguities, and conflicts can be perceived.

In the daily lives of immigrants in a new country, a contrast becomes evident in the perception of U.S. society as more egalitarian and Brazilian society more hierarchical. The United States as a nation provides Brazilian immigrants with the experience of a different civic culture that reinforces the notion of respect as the element of mediation in social relationships and citizenship rights. On this point, the host society is valued. Within this comparative perspective in which notions of respect and citizenship become relative, Brazilians feel that they have more rights in the United States than in Brazil, although they may be undocumented immigrants in the destination country and citizens in a formal sense in the country of origin.

It would be worthwhile to study whether the positive perceptions related to respect and citizenship are restricted either to certain immigrant groups or to certain U.S. states as a consequence of the differences stemming from the American federative system. Such a study might ascertain whether the identities and formation of ethnic groups take as their point of reference the type of institutional operation of the receiving society. I suggest that the research give greater emphasis to the incentive structure in American society and to the possible federative differences that affect the process of identification and organization of immigrant groups.

A large part of the literature addresses the idea that the affirmation of ethnic identity, ethnic solidarity, and the ethnic community increases proportionally to the degree of discrimination and hostility with which immigrants are treated in the host society. I contend that this is only partially true. The results of the present study suggest that affirming identity, solidarity, and the ethnic community are not necessarily part of a process of antagonism toward the host society (a negative reaction). The affirmation of these three concepts also may be motivated by the U.S. institutional system itself and encouraged by the American ideology of ethnicity. The Brazilian case shows that the assertion of a collective and necessarily contrasting identity can adopt another ethnic group, and not necessarily the host society, as its point of reference for the purpose of contrast. This is what we will see in the next chapter as individual choices in the identification of ethnicity are analyzed: the onset of friction between Brazilians and Hispanics.

6

Nationality, Ethnicity, and Hybridization

Dilemmas of Racial-Ethnic Identification

Every immigrant lives in a singular condition of displacement, as suggested by Abdelmalek Sayad (1998). The immigrant, this "displaced object," is a human being alienated from every stable, uniform classification. If he or she lives on the border, both material and symbolic, it is because the conditions of the immigrant's existence are characterized by constant binary oppositions: absence/presence, mobility/stability, presence/absence, and so forth. Social identities are critical points in this process, as we will see in the case presented here. The U.S. category "nonwhite," for example, could be interpreted as a kind of symbolic violence from the perspective of a Brazilian immigrant, since in Brazil apology for racial miscegenation is the norm. Emigrating from a country where the "whitening of the race" is part of the country's history and arriving in another where the category "nonwhite" replaces the category *mulato* constitutes a reversal in the expectation of identity.

Generally speaking, the majority of Brazilian immigrants see themselves as white. However, in the United States, they quickly perceive that the natives are not classifying them in the same way. There, they will be seen as Hispanic or Latino, nonwhite, or "other," according to the social pattern in the United States. These categories, which are fraught with ambiguities, insinuate a condition of nonbeing. The category "other" in particular seems to represent something that does not fit in and suggests the idea of being left over, and it thus reinforces the condition of displacement.

First we will see how Brazilians tend to self-identify ethnically and racially, using for this purpose cultural references brought from Brazil. Next, I intend to show that Latino and Hispanic can be two categories that are different in content and scope (Oboler 1995; Cashmore 1996; Margolis 1994, 2002, 2009; Marrow 2002), but they also appear as mutually exclusive options when subordinated to national affiliation. More specifically, affiliation with the category "Hispanic" excludes the possibility of claiming Brazilian identity, and often, being Brazilian means precisely stressing the negation: "I am not Hispanic."[1] In the same way that they do not self-identify as Hispanic, most consider themselves white, even though they clearly understand that they are taken as Hispanics or Latinos and nonwhite by the members of the receiving society.[2]

In the second part of the chapter, I will deal not with Brazilians in general, but specifically with black Brazilians who categorized themselves as black before migrating from Brazil.[3] Over the fifteen years during which I have been studying the Brazilian communities in Massachusetts, the presence of so many black Brazilians in that region was not seen previous to 2000. I say "black" in reference to the color of their skin, which is the criterion used in Brazil and which does not include mixed-race (*mulato*) or light-skinned blacks. I will focus on two questions: How do they compare being black in Brazil with being black in the United States? And how does the condition of displacement that is characteristic of every ethnic group affect their notions of race and discrimination from the same comparative perspective?

I am concerned throughout this chapter with understanding how Brazilians deal with the differences between Brazilian and American categories when they seek to define themselves. Such differences will be not resolved by choosing what should be kept and what should not, by deciding if Brazilian categories should be replaced by American categories, thus eliminating ambiguities, euphemisms, and the like. The most important point is to recognize that Brazilian immigrants are trying to preserve the possibility of manipulating the category or categories to which they belong in order to survive in a social structure that condemns them to the uncomfortable condition of displacement.

From the researcher's perspective, perhaps the main question is how to manipulate the categories to which the immigrants belong and their very heterogeneous identities so that it is possible for the immigrants to proceed further along the path to success in adapting to a new culture. A good answer could be one that makes it possible for everyone to categorize himself or herself based on the principle of self-determination.

Nevertheless, this would be very difficult given the inflexibility of American racial categories. But since people can find their own human richness in the way they confront differences and diversity, perhaps the tendency toward sycretism present in Brazilian culture might offer ways to avoid the limitations of existing categories and ultimately enhance the value of difference itself.

In this context, I seek to demonstrate that ceasing to be a national group in order to present it as an ethnic group is a step in the direction of cultural assimilation. Quite paradoxically, the justification used to substitute racial categories for ethnic categories has been the desire to preserve and maintain the immigrants' cultural roots. Multicultural discourse and ideology have taken the place of the ideal of assimilation, but the current official ethnic categories make it difficult for the multi-ethnic populations of the same nation to be able to express their belonging by simultaneously drawing on their national and racial-ethnic origins. This seems to constitute a true dilemma for the first generations of recent immigrant groups and is also true for Brazilians.

When White Is Hybridization Instead of Purity

Data obtained in this study, conducted in the first three months of 2002,[4] indicate that when asked to self-identify, Brazilian immigrants in Massachusetts tend to follow certain patterns. For one, they declare their national identity as being the primary social identity of the group.[5] However, they are seen as Hispanic or Latino, and they suffer from a kind of social pressure in this sense. Next, they reject the label "Hispanic" and voluntarily accept the term "Latino." But they understand that they are Latinos (more precisely Latin Americans) according to the meaning this term has in Brazilian culture and not in U.S. culture. Finally, from a racial perspective, they tend to self-identify as white, which means "not black" in Brazil. Yet many are seen in the United States as black or nonwhite.

When questioned about the way they classify themselves ethnically and racially, the majority of Brazilians tend to choose the categories "other" and "white." In the survey mentioned above, which was conducted in 2002 among 200 Brazilians,[6] 34% of those interviewed declared that they classified themselves as "other" and 32.5% as "white."[7] Both responses, which total 66.5% of the interviewees, are compatible with the parallel assertion of the national identity of the group: "white and Brazilian" or "other, but specifically Brazilian."

Meanwhile, the option "Hispanic" excludes the possibility of the assertion of Brazilian identity, and, as noted above, being Brazilian means the assertion: "I am not Hispanic."[8] In this sense, Brazilians perceive the categories "white" and "other" as inclusive. They are complementary to the national identity of the group, while the category "Hispanic," chosen by 7.5% of the interviewees, is interpreted as exclusive; to a large extent, the friction arising from the notion of "Brazilians versus Hispanics" is an important element in the construction of the identity of the Brazilian community in Boston.[9]

Among the rest of the interviewees, none identified himself or herself as Native Indian, and only 0.5% identified themselves as Asian. Meanwhile, 7.5% declared themselves to be Hispanic, and 1% of the interviewees said they were black. The justification given by one of the two interviewees to choose "black" was, "In Brazil, I am dark, a *mulata*, but as this does not exist here, I put down 'black.' Here I became more black; I am a black Brazilian."

Cultural Assimilation Versus Hybridization

For the Brazilians interviewed, national identity joins with racial identity to the extent that they attempt to portray Brazil as "a mixture of all races." Brazilian immigrants in the United States could affiliate themselves with various racial categories because Brazil is (or was) a country of immigrants, and its population has African, European, indigenous, and even Asian origins. Besides this, Brazil has a high rate of interethnic marriages, which makes the Brazilian phenotype quite diverse,[10] with some more homogeneous regional tendencies.[11]

As no uniform, global, and hegemonic discourse is capable of defining what race is, we must take into account the manner in which codes of racial identification are established and put into practice in Brazil and to note how they are used in the process of incorporation. Because they are mostly first-generation immigrants, Brazilians tend to identify themselves in Boston the same way they identified themselves in Brazil.[12] And since the systems are very different, if future generations come to adopt the U.S. system, I believe this will indicate a kind of cultural assimilation for three reasons.

1) In Brazil, color is the principal characteristic used for racial identification,[13] while in the United States, color is an important characteristic but secondary because the idea of race is strongly linked to the culture of origin. Thus, the superimposition of ethnicity over race makes sense when it is understood that ethnicity is a more comprehensive category in the United States and, inversely, more restricted in Brazil. In summary, in Brazil racial categories are more closely linked to phenotype, especially to color.[14]
2) Brazil does not follow the U.S. "one-drop rule," that is, the categories "black" and "white" are not necessarily mutually exclusive. For this reason, in the 1990 Brazilian census the category "brown" (or whatever in the United States could be equivalent to the term "multiracial") included 42% of the Brazilian population who self-identified as such (IBGE 2010).
   In what some call "hybridization," people of mixed race in Brazil more frequently are assigned to the category "white" than the category "black"; in the United States, people of mixed race historically have been more frequently assigned to the category "black," which can carry a lower social status in the United States than the category "white."
3) Therefore, 52% of the Brazilian population self-identifies as white (IBGE 2010).

If in the Brazilian multiracial context white supersedes black, upon their arrival in Boston, Brazilians become "more black" as noted in the interview cited above. That is, they perceive that they are classified as black in the receiving society, and they come to reinterpret characteristics based on the color of their skin. In the face of the black/white polarization of the U.S. classification, many reaffirm the criteria used previously and continue to consider themselves white. The fact that only two Brazilians classified themselves as black in this survey proves the rule and shows that becoming "more black" is part of the process of assimilation into American culture.

Analyzing racism in Brazil is beyond the scope of this chapter.[15] The objective here is to emphasize the reasoning that underlies each of the two systems of classification. In Brazil the emphasis is on mixture,[16] taking into account color, and in the United States "purity" is maintained.[17] It is not coincidental that the imputation of a relatively harmonious relationship among the races in Brazil is part of a myth constructed in opposition (or contrast) to the perception of race relations in the United States. Since World War II, U.S. researchers like Donald Pierson and Charles Wagley have contributed much to the creation of this myth, as Guimarães contends (1999: 41):[18] "Anglo-American anti-racism, however, did not constitute a less active element in the mystification and idealization of Brazil as a 'racial paradise.' Hellwing (1992), gathers impressions about Brazil from black U.S. travelers and social scientists from between 1910 and 1940, without a single record of racial discrimination in the country." Despite the differences, U.S. relationships and models of racial classification have had a great deal of influence in Brazil, whether in the form of a game of reverse mirroring or in black Brazilian movements that began in the 1970s to discuss discrimination and to adopt classificatory and other points of reference from the various U.S. black and civil rights movements.

The majority of the interviewees who self-identified as white justified their choice based on the color of their skin and, to a lesser degree, on their European—especially Italian, Portuguese, and German—descent. However, six interviewees mentioned directly that "white" is the most generic category, one that represents the mixture of all colors: "I am brown, but more white than black, so I classify myself as white," or "white because we are a mixed race, neither black nor white," or even "because I consider myself brown, but here this category does not exist," or "In Brazil there are mostly people of my same color, but here I have seen people of color who think I am dark, that I'm of the black race, even though they don't know that my mother is white and my father was light brown just like me." These statements illustrate that not all of those who self-identify as white could, in effect, pass as white in the United States.[19] But this choice reveals their desire to highlight their whiteness and thus to avoid being targets of the prejudice against blacks in the United States. Likewise in Brazil, whiteness and "European" features are valued and are associated with the higher social classes.[20]

According to the same reasoning behind racial classification, in Brazil the category "white" is not mutually exclusive with the category "other" because there is no category like "nonwhite" that encompasses the category "other." Racial mixture or a multiracial category is not defined as "nonwhite" but rather as a category that includes white, brown, mixed-race (or *mulato*), and dark and therefore can only exclude the "nonmixed" black, that is, the "pure" black. This is because, while in the United States "mixed-race" ("mulatto") is considered a subgroup of "black," I believe that in Brazil *mulato* tends to be seen as a subgroup of "white" or as another, separate category.[21]

But the category "other" most closely approximates the idea that Brazilians are "a mixture of all the races." Interviewees who opted for this category largely justified their choice in this way: "other, because I am a Brazilian." The exceptions were four interviewees who chose Other because they called themselves Brazilian Americans even though they were first-generation immigrants. On one hand, "other" is perceived as a multiracial category, and on the other, it offers the opportunity to escape the label "Hispanic."

In Boston, Brazilians reproduce the same discourse of valuing the Brazilian people as a racial mixture, which demonstrates their difficulty and discomfort in attempting to fit into American patterns of racial classification: "Brazil is a country with a mixture of races; I don't fit here." Thus, in the survey as well as the interviews, the idea emerges that "Brazilians are simply Brazilians" and that they therefore do not fit the "classic" racial categories, as Gilberto Freyre claimed (cited in Nobles 2000: 117). Several of them stated, "My race is Brazilian" when referring to racial miscegenation. In this sense, the variable of race—referring to hybridization—cannot explain the rejection of affiliation with the label "Hispanic" since the interviewees recognized that Latinos or Hispanics are, in general, multiracial, *mulato*, or mestizo, as they themselves are.

Defining the Brazilian as a mixture of races allows subordination of racial identity to national identity. On the other hand, the options "white" and "other" are compatible with being Brazilian to the extent that being white means not being "black with no racial mixture" and "other" presupposes a racial mix. In the same way, the self-classification of Brazilians follows a hierarchical order: first Brazilian, then Latin American.[22]

However, in Boston they experience the inversion of this order: first Latino or Hispanic, then Brazilian. We will next see the reasons this inversion favors not an approximation but on the contrary an antagonism that results in the emphasis on national origin.

Hispanic/Latino and the Strength of the Pressure to Assimilate

In the past decade, the replacement of the term "Latino" by the term "Hispanic" has been successful in the academy and among civil rights activists.[23] However, the empirical point of reference is the same for both labels: a group organized as a minority and that includes immigrants from Central and South America and the Caribbean. The term "Hispanic," as defined by the U.S. government—notably by the U.S. Census Bureau—in the 1970s,[24] tends to "mask the diversity that exists between Latinos and to over-emphasize the Spanish and European aspect of South Americans" (Hero 1992).

The U.S. literature on immigration has noted that Hispanics and Latinos do not constitute a homogeneous group but a pan-ethnic group.[25] Therefore, I believe that beyond reaffirming the heterogeneity of the group Latino/Hispanic (Klor de Alva 1988), the wider scope of the term "Latino" (Oboler 1995, Margolis 2009), or even that the two terms are not interchangeable (Marrow 2002), the data from my research reveal that Brazilian immigrants construct an antagonism between the two terms to the extent that for them being Brazilian and Latin American also means not being Hispanic. In other words, Brazilian identity is of a contrasting type because it establishes a friction with Hispanic identity. When referring to other immigrants from Latin America, Brazilians use the term *hispano*, which refers to Hispanic and never to Latino.[26]

The 7.5% of Brazilians who self-identify as Hispanic justify this option as linguistic, because Brazilians do not speak Spanish,[27] and geographic because Hispanic means immigrants from the Caribbean, Central America, and Mexico, and Brazil does not have ties or points of identification with those countries.[28] That is, the stronger geographic point of reference is South America and not Central America.[29]

The allusion to these three elements—linguistic, geographic, and historic—to define the meaning of the term "Latino" is plain in Brazil.[30] The elements are part of the official cartography and of the curriculum of history courses offered as early as primary school, and they are found in dictionary entries.[31] For the interviewees, the basic point of reference for Hispanic is that of language (Spanish), and the basic point of reference for Latino is geographic location (South America).

The term *hispano*" is used routinely by Brazilian immigrants for the purpose of forming collective identities. They perceive a kind of pressure—at times direct, at times indirect—to include themselves in the category "Hispanic." They react to this perceived pressure by refusing Hispanic identity and affirming their national origin. Meanwhile, being Latino does not have the same connotation for Brazilians. The term "Latino" fills the gaps imposed by the label "Hispanic" when it is associated with Latin America;[32] that is, Portuguese is a Latin language, and Brazil is in Latin America. Other studies call attention Brazilians' tendency to reject affiliation with the category "Hispanic" but not with the category "Latino" (Margolis 1994, Gustavo Ribeiro 1998b, Martes 2000a, Penha 2001, Marrow 2002, and Fleischer 2002).

Meanwhile, for some Brazilians, being Latino is not exactly a choice but a historical and geographic reality, objectively given and imposed. The interviewees who said they preferred to be categorized as Latinos claimed that they are Latinos because Brazil is in South America.[33] Those who rejected the label "Latino" justified their choice because although they considered themselves Latinos when they lived in Brazil, in the United States they found no difference between the terms "Latino" and "Hispanic."

But the preference for the term "Latino" is not due to its being broader than "Hispanic"; rather it is because Brazilians as well as Hispanics are considered subgroups of the category "Latino." That is, the term "Latino" can affirm the differences between Brazilians and Hispanics. It would be a mistake, though, to suppose that affiliation with the category "Latino" is interpreted by Brazilians as equivalent to "other Hispanic" because, independent of the reasoning underlying U.S. ethnic classifications, Brazilians have developed their own idea that Hispanic a subgroup of Latino and not the reverse. Therefore, when Brazilians identify the terms "Hispanic" and "Latino" as equivalent, they tend to reject them both.

That rejection can be explained by differences but also by similarities and proximities, which appear greater the further one moves away from Brazilian culture. The Portuguese language can be confused with the Spanish language—but not by a Brazilian.[34] Brazilians tend, like other Latino immigrants, to be multiracial. Yet Brazilians have much in common with Spanish America: a colonial past linked to the Iberian Peninsula, an economy based on slavery and monoculture, the predominance of the Catholic religion and of religious syncretism, a native Amerindian population, and a high rate of interethnic marriages. Along with this legacy, in Boston they share niches of the informal labor market and equal deficiencies in their levels of education (Martes 2000a).

Brazilians who self-identify as Hispanic say they have assimilated certain U.S. criteria. That may be because it is something of an "imposition of the condition of being an immigrant" or because they wish to benefit from the advantages provided by the institutional system, as one interviewee explained: "When I fill out a form, and I see that it is going to make my life easier, I put down Hispanic." The calculation used to affiliate with this category is the result of a cost-benefit analysis. When the cost of being Hispanic is reduced, references to national culture lose force, be they linguistic, geographic, or historical; they are relativized or resignified by emphasizing the similarities among the groups. Finally, being Hispanic ceases to be a straightjacket and is transformed into a competitive advantage.

To the extent that ethnic nomenclatures are rejected or embraced by generations, social classes, or national or political groups, they are resignified. Thus what might be called the hard nucleus of the concept of ethnicity (cultural traits) appears in empirical reality as vague references (although loaded with symbolism and affection) that take on meaning when historicized and contextualized. This is why an essentialist notion of culture cannot explain the dynamic. Abandoning the essentialist position opens the way to enabling us to understand ethnicity as a phenomenon of an instrumental nature. Beyond defining content (the hard nucleus), it is also essential to understand the manner in which such content is negotiated or imposed, rejected or embraced, as a function of personal and collective interests and advantages and of the structure of opportunities and the very social meanings that the content may acquire. Therefore, the fundamental cultural question that the concept of ethnicity entails is of a symbolic nature and does not merely refer to the intrinsic content of specific ethnic taxonomies.

It is true that geographical, linguistic, and historical references mark the borders of the taxonomy Hispanic/Latino, but the symbolic dimension of the representations (with the whole burden of ambiguity that the symbols inherently possess) permits that such borders be amplified, that differences be resignified or omitted, and that history be "used in pieces." Because they are flexible, the symbols enable their own manipulation. If, in using the classification to distinguish between groups, ethnic categories are employed to establish who is inferior and who is superior, as Hollinger states (2000), perhaps therein lies the most relevant symbolic question, for social hierarchies are immediately perceptible, and the definition of who we are and what our place is on a scale of values mobilizes feelings and memories and leads to rankings.

The Black Brazilian Immigrant

Black Brazilian immigrants live a double condition of exclusion: black and immigrant. Thus, it is to be expected that their accounts would bring anecdotes and reflections about discrimination and exclusion. But this is not exactly the content gathered from their interviews. The interviewees rarely made spontaneous reference to their racial situation in the destination society or in their society of origin because self-reference is asserted in their general situation as immigrants.

Black Brazilians, upon emigrating, reinforce their use of a "practical strategy of dissimulation," brought when they emigrated and incorporated as a "fact of life" due to having lived in a society marked by inequality (Fazito and Martes 2005). Recourse to dissimulation is characteristic of the immigrant's circumstances generally, according to Sayad, but in the case of blacks, this process is particularly intensified. In other words, dissimulation is exercised by black Brazilian immigrants in a more immediate way than by white Brazilian immigrants. For the latter, the experience of displacement can be an uncomfortable "novelty" due to having become foreigners, a discovery that they had not yet experienced fully.

Six interviews that may help us understand this process are analyzed below.[35] One of the most evident points in these interviews is a generally positive valorization of American society, which, as we have seen, is also found in the narratives of Brazilian immigrants in general independently of their racial or ethnic classification. However, there are obviously exceptions, and the most significant among those interviewed is Giba's account. He expressed the most critical and far-reaching vision with regard to American society and was able to integrate the United States into the capitalist system and at the same time distinguish specific characteristics of the two:

> I am in a Puritan area [New Hampshire]; it is very conservative, and therefore, I think that there is greater hypocrisy. But American society is hypocritical. It wants to take advantage of people in need, the very nature of the economic system in which they live, capitalism, because it colonized to maintain power, has to exploit other peoples, like Latin Americans, those from Asia, Indians, those from Kuwait. Here you can have a car, more security, but this is a normal part of the system, it isn't from the American.

At the age of 27, Giba was the father of two children and married to an American woman, "a blonde with blue eyes." He is an atheist; he was never a member of a political party, but he said he liked the Workers' Party (Partido dos Trabalhadores, PT) in Brazil, explaining, "I was born in Rio de Janeiro; I am from the common people." Giba is a musician as his father was, and he considered himself a citizen of the world because his migratory experience provided him with "a greater facility to live in different situations." Being married to an American woman and having children who attended a public school permitted Giba to perceive and experience situations in which his situation as black and as an immigrant emerged in a significant way.

> My children are *mulatos*, but for American society they are black. They have suffered from racism in school. There they don't even celebrate Martin Luther King Day. One of the other children pointed at him [a son] and said, "Look at his skin." My wife went crazy . . . she talked to the teacher because he's a child, and this could cause him some greater psychological problem. The school was very supportive of us.

Despite the institutional support, the sensitivity and attitudes of the principal and the teacher, Giba said this experience revealed to him that "racism exists even among children. When you are among Americans, you see that white is white, Latino is Latino, and black is black . . . each one has his or her place. But I am a black Latino."

From Giba's perspective, in the United States, discrimination is principally related to social class, level of education, and race:

> They have more respect for Europeans because they are educated. Latinos, Asians, and Africans are seen more negatively. They respect the Japanese the most. I have had various experiences with racism and discrimination. Once I was driving slowly, and a police officer stopped me and asked me if I knew why I was being stopped. I was polite because I wasn't going to challenge a police officer. I answered that it was because I was driving slowly. He answered that it was for exactly that reason, but I am sure that, because the car was old . . . it was in front of Harvard . . . and there you are supposed to drive slowly like I was driving, and therefore, I wasn't wrong . . . Another time I was working in the Brazilian Cultural Center with some

> carpenters, and one of them called me a monkey; he was white but suburban, and he said, "Why don't you go back to Brazil?" He said this ironically, with an air of superiority. I didn't answer because it was just those guys' ignorance. White Americans, well, you just have to look at them, you can't explain it. You can feel it when a person is open or when that person has his nose in the air. You can feel it . . . they are racist here, it doesn't matter if you're black, if you don't fit in their place, they discriminate against you.

In the narrative concerning discrimination, the prevalence of social class in Brazil is notable:

> Pelé is respected; he's accepted by all social classes. Not here. The history of blacks from here is much more perverse . . . In Brazil, they mixed in, here they were totally separated—families, children . . . Today's generation still feels this. I have a number of black American friends; their grandparents experienced this; they are racist due to the fact of having been excluded. In Boston in the 1930s, blacks couldn't use Prudention Street. This is a segregated country, but it has many civil rights, strong laws. I have had problems with the police in Brazil. One day when I was returning from work, on the Copacabana sidewalk an officer came toward me and began to investigate me . . . he ordered me to take off my shoes, he looked for marijuana, but he didn't find anything, then he ordered me to leave. I was so embarrassed, I was about eleven years old, and I didn't have any papers. Here racism is more structured . . . but blacks are more untouchable, each one has his profession, his work, and he knows that these professions are important. Here a housecleaner is respected, independent of the profession, there is respect for the work. This doesn't exist in Brazil.

It is noteworthy that although even in Brazil he self-identified as black, Giba did not feel comfortable having to struggle with the racial-ethnic categories in the United States: "Sometimes I don't put anything down; sometimes I put Brazilian, sometimes 'other.' But, I think I am Latino and black, sometimes only black. I became a Latino here."

The second interviewee, Cilene, already had changed her religion and color (racial choice) while in Brazil after she connected with her Afro-Brazilian roots through dance. This was greatly reinforced after she immigrated to the United States. Because she was a woman and black and knew *candomblé* (a religion of African origin practiced mainly in Brazil), Celine was able to seek a specific professional niche, different from the kinds of work done by other Brazilians. She said that by being part of the black Brazilian community, she possessed an attribute valued in a context of multiculturalism:

> I came looking for a project for my professional life, something that can make me grow, grow as a human being. I think that the black communitarian movement in Bahia [state in northeastern Brazil] is very beautiful; the music market shows very well what is coming from this work . . . I decided that, as a black woman, I have the social duty to invest as a professional, and I would be contributing to that movement.

Cilene said she brought this consciousness with her from Brazil but that in the United States it was reinforced:

> Here I am a black woman, there I am a *mulata*; when I was very young I identified myself as a *mulata*, but at the moment I felt that I was participating in a black cultural movement and that I am a part of that history, I began to consider myself a black woman, even in Salvador [Bahia].

In comparing Brazil and the United States, Cilene highlighted the specific characteristics of each without putting one above the other: "In Brazil there is a distinction between blacks and whites, but there is also assimilation, an encounter that is hard to find here . . . I think that people mix a lot more in Brazil, and that is very good." In fact, Cilene carries with her a vision of syncretism rooted not merely in the values that she verbalizes, but also in her life experiences. Syncretism seems to permeate everything she does:

> All of the experiences that I bring from my life I put into dance. When, for example, we do the seventh *chacra*, which in *candomblé* we call Ourim's *chacra*, the moment when we offer the herbs, the foods, and communication to the *orixás* [deities or spirits of *candomblé*]. For Catholics, it is the moment when the godparents wet the baby's head with holy water. So, it's the same point, so that the cultures are not separated.

Although blacks and whites tend to live together in the same communities more frequently in Brazil, which Cilene identified as an asset,

> racism is stronger [there] . . . When I finished primary school, my teacher gave me a hairbrush as a present. At that time, I didn't like my hair. I have indigenous blood too, I am conscious of my indigenous roots. My hair was very similar to my grandmother's hair: long, very wavy, gypsy-like. My teacher was a *mulata*, [and] she had worse hair than mine.[36] I was a bit of a rebel; I didn't let anyone untangle it. At the end of the year, she gave me a comb as a gift. There were things that I did just to be aggressive. I think she did that to motivate me, I think she was unaware.

Cilene and Giba were the two black Brazilians interviewed who demonstrated that they sought support and a foundation for their insertion into American society based on their Afro-Brazilian roots. Because they are both artists (a dancer and a musician), they have in their professional activities a direct connection with black African culture (samba and African dance). They have additional incentives for this in the United States because that connection permits them to maintain their artistic activities and to be valued expressly because they divulge their cultural roots, as Cilene found:

> In this country of differences, this becomes very strong in you. When I left Salvador, I was very disappointed with the labor market, and I was beginning to be disappointed with some groups . . . the Afro blocks had created marvelous things . . . but I prefer hearing their earlier compositions—Ile Aye, Olodum—to hearing the current ones . . . here I was sponsored by MIT, which is not an art school but a technology school. They put everything into it . . . five rehearsals on the stage, three nights in the theater . . . a seminar; I received a contract for one semester; they liked it.

On this point, she differed from Giba. Without ambiguity or euphemisms, Cilene did not vacillate when she was asked to identify her ethnic-racial affiliation: "I am a black woman."

In contrast, Nico, a 26-year-old construction worker who arrived in Boston in 1999, exhibited a discourse full of ambiguities. He said he classified himself as Brazilian and, when that option was not available, as Hispanic: "Because we are close to Argentina and Colombia, we are of that race of beautiful people." In Brazil he considered himself more mixed-race (*mulato*) than black. After thinking for a few seconds, he struggled, then finished:

> Black, because my grandmother is black, my mother is black; she's a little darker than I am . . . In Brazilians there is a lot of mixing of black with white. My father was Italian, my mother, black, not black, well, yes black, she is black. There are Brazilians who are ashamed; I don't hide it; they say that they are brown. I think that it's because of the racism in Brazil; it's very strong there. When a black and a white are competing for a job opening, it's the white who gets it.

Then I asked if life was better for blacks in the United States. Nico answered: "Here the blacks have fought a lot, that's why black Americans don't like black Brazilians. They think that Brazilians are weak. I really believe that now that they are beginning to react, this is yet going to change; next to the Americans, we are nothing."

I asked if his wife, who is the daughter of Portuguese parents and has blond hair and blue eyes, helped him claim his identity. As if he was looking for a piece that could be used to put together some kind of figure, Nico answered: "Yes, she points out to me those who are really black, who have those large lips, kinky hair. Black for them is not a color like mine; for them, I'm a little brown, and for me, I am black." What should really be gleaned from this discourse full of "comings and goings" is that Nico showed that his circumstance as a black Brazilian immigrant did not bother him. His evasive attitude was similar to that of Gina, the next interviewee. She said she had not had any racial problems in the United States and did not even worry about that.

At 37 years old and having lived in Somerville for seven years, Gina was dating a black Brazilian. She was the only interviewee in this situation, since the rest of the interviewees were married to or dating whites. Gina said that in Boston, "it's getting much better. I have never had racial problems. In Brazil, I was raised by a family of very light-skinned Italians, and I was black. I arrive here, and I don't see this difference." Although she initially attempted to make a comparison favorable to the United States, she concluded that there is no difference in the two countries because ethnic-racial factors did not interfere in social relationships in either. But soon afterward, she pondered:

> In general, here they are more respectful, not that they really respect; I think that Americans are also a little bit fake. In Brazil, they play games, they mock you. A domestic worker can't go beyond the kitchen door; here she can sit at the table with her employers. I think that this difference is better here.

Gina let slip a critical perspective of the Portuguese as "rude; the men are cruel. I worked with them in a factory; they are very rude among themselves and with others." Her American friends "are better, normal; they're more like in Brazil. I dated a Cape Verdean; he was nice." She said she did not like "people from the Caribbean. They are extravagant, have no manners. I've worked with a lot of Haitians." She had no contact with black Americans: "I have never gone to one of their clubs, associations, parties; I didn't have friends to go with to those places."

At the end of the interview I again asked her to compare her experiences in the two countries: "There is no way of comparing the customs here with those in Brazil. There it is very good; it is our country; there are beautiful, happy women." However, after thinking it over a little bit longer, she concluded: "I have left behind that phase of liberty that we have in Brazil; I like the laws here better. If these laws didn't exist, what would become of this place?" But, she added, "it's not a paradise, as I used to think. That was an illusion." Gina said she had not become Americanized, and then I asked her about the little braids in her hair. She answered:

> I also used hair extensions in Brazil; here I saw a lot of people doing it, and I decided to do it also . . . I have always had good taste; I do everything I can to acquire material goods. It's what I do most. With the situation that you have here, you don't need to spend a lot of money to look nice . . . Here there is no problem of race. People say that I look like that woman who is the host of a TV program or channel, Oprah. I think that's great. A woman like that, how is she not going to be respected?

Gina did not remember how she responded to the 2000 U.S. Census but said, "I think I responded 'black.'" Her Brazilian birth certificate says "brown."

> I see myself as being of the black race, although a little lighter-skinned. Isn't there that business of "before six" and "after six"? I am

> 6:15, 6:20 P.M. In Brazil, I always speak of the black race, sometimes brown. I see black Haitians. They can be almost blue, their skin looks like it's stained; not even Africans are like that. Black Americans also have a prettier tone. I don't know if it's that their skin is better cared for. You see that difference between black Americans, Haitians, Africans; it looks like they're [Haitians are] dirty.

After making a few observations about the tonalities of black skin, she concluded,

> Here there is more respect; people don't worry about skin color, about the house they live in. In Brazil, those farmers who come into a store all dirty to do their shopping, they aren't served well; then someone else comes, in a suit and tie, all dressed up, and he gets VIP service. He could write a bad check. The people are very much like that, they go by appearance.

Vivian, a spirited 25-year-old woman with a degree in journalism from the city of Recife, where she also lived, did not miss Brazil much. On the contrary, she said, "I feel more and more distant." She observed values like respect and honesty in American society:

> Being honest in the situation we are in isn't really OK, [and] being dishonest is worse yet. That's what matters. Brazilians understood that message, and they are much more honest here than in Brazil. Respect is stopping at the crosswalk, helping another person cross the street, not having that social difference . . . a person goes to the bank with dirty clothes on, and he's treated just like a rich person. That respect exists more in the United States than in Brazil . . . safety, being able to go out, it is so great to go around here without having to worry about pickpockets, your car being stolen, walking with your purse behind you. When I'm wearing jewelry here, I'm not afraid of coming home late.

But I insisted and asked if her opinion of the United States changed after she emigrated: "I see that in Brazil there are stronger family connections." I asked if the idea of community associations was stronger here or there:

> In Brazil I didn't even pay attention to that. An aunt of mine worked for an NGO, but I never paid attention. It was when I arrived here

> that I found out that one worked with Indians, and another aunt with needy children. It was after I came here that I began to help by giving information, about doctors, etc.

Vivian said that in the United States she had only felt discriminated against "by a Brazilian. When I was here on vacation. I needed to go to the hospital. It was a Brazilian who attended me. He was very rude to me; he asked me who I was living with, and I said: with my boyfriend. He said that I was lying." I asked if she thought Americans discriminated.

> I can't say that, but I think that the idea of neighborhoods only for blacks is bad. It's more likely that a black person will be a thief than a white person. Many Brazilians say that Americans are cold, but they don't interact with them. The Americans who I know are great.

Like the two previous interviewees, she did not know how to define her ethnic-racial affiliation:

> When I was going to get married . . . I said: "I'm none of those," and I didn't have the option "other." In Brazil, I wasn't sure, black, brown? People here see it like this: black or white. I feel fine with that; that never bothered me; I never stopped to think about it.

Because she repeated an invariably optimistic account with regard to American society, I asked Vivian if it was possible for an immigrant to succeed in this country. She answered:

> For me, success in this country is getting a green card. It means that I can go to Brazil to alleviate my homesickness, and I can return without being afraid to start a business, and if it doesn't work out, I can return [to Brazil]. My husband's American boss is going to request a green card for him . . . My husband wants to dye his hair a lighter blonde to look more American.

Returning to Brazil after having lived a few months in Boston made Vivian begin to question things that she had previously appreciated about her native country:

> I no longer liked the music or television. In Brazil, everything is very dirty, in the airport, garbage in the streets. I became very aware of that, that chaos, visual filth. I am very satisfied here, and I still don't

> have a job because soon after I arrived I became pregnant, and my husband, at that time my boyfriend, always paid for everything. The day that I get a job, I will be completely happy.

In contrast to Vivian, Tatiana could not wait to return to Brazil. Tatiana came to the United States with her parents. Tatiana, 26 years old at the time of our interview, worked and attended college: "If I had this money there, I wouldn't have had to come here. Here you work and pay a lot to survive. You live better there because you have incredible freedom. . . ." She missed Brazil, but said,

> Brazil is here, in the supermarket where you see Brazilian things that Americans have adapted. The children, the stores, the shopping malls are different . . . for example, the children are treated in a special way, mothers are always there for their children. I always say that people here make lists, everything just so. Either you adapt to their way of doing things, or you stay the same; I can't go into the store because . . . I go into the store looking at everything . . . only I don't throw paper on the ground.

Tatiana said American society discriminates against immigrants because they are foreigners and not specifically against blacks: "Here I have to stay in my place; there is a lot of discrimination; yes, they are right; they are right, but I'm not here to destroy their world. They don't see us as people who are here to help, they see us as invaders. I see that, there's a lot of difference." Finally, I asked her if at the hospital or in the school they ever asked her about her ethnicity. She responded: "I say that I am Brazilian." I asked if she ever thought about her ethnic heritage, her father, her mother, where they came from, if they were black, indigenous, or Portuguese:

> My mother comes from a very strong race, from the time when they were cutting down the forests. She is a brown-skinned woman, the color of coffee with milk. My father is white. I got my color from my mother. I never had a conversation like that to find out . . . but they come from the time of the discovery of Brazil. So, they are as black as white . . . Italian, my son also has Italian blood. It is a racial mixture, indigenous people . . . from the way they lived . . . are a very strong race.

To close the interview, I asked Tatiana if she ever thought about race, color, in Brazil: "I felt myself to be free with regard to that."

Returning to Sayad (1998), the migration process presents universal characteristics as well as unique local features in the same sui generis relational context. Physical displacement is also a displacement of power—in other words, the ability to give significance to the event within the social structure. In the case analyzed here, it is the ability to establish racial-ethnic labels capable of structuring social relationships and cultural meanings. In Sayad's words, the dualities that constitute the immigrant's situation represent a profound disruption at the individual level, so that dissimulation emerges as a way to deal with these dualities as a kind of survival strategy. The characteristic of ambiguity is present in the immigrants' migration narratives and in their unspoken attitudes as well.

Types of Origin and Insertion

The U.S. institutional framework encourages immigrant groups to present themselves in that country as bearers of attributes that involve ethnicity. It is, therefore, a very different situation from the one Brazilians knew in Brazil. Luis Cardoso de Oliveira finds that the concept of ethnicity presupposes "relationships between collectivities within surrounding societies that are dominant and culturally hegemonic and where such collectivities live in the condition of ethnic minorities, or even as nationalities inserted into the space of a Nation State" (2001b: 23).[37] The possibility of the ethnicization of the national identities of immigrants in host societies leads to the formation of ethnicized racial identities, the fruit of the institutional configuration of the host society.

Research has emphasized that in the Unites States, immigrants must decide on their ethnic and racial origin, a question that was not always clearly raised for them in their country of origin, or at least not in the same way. Despite this, little attention has been given to the local and regional institutional arrangements of the host society, which tend to encourage the formation of social identities and community organization based on ethnic classification and identification. In this sense, some questions might be raised: When they are compared, do collective identities and forms of community organization vary within the same ethnic group according to local institutions? Is there a differentiated structure of incentives on a state-by-state basis?

Corroborating Sayad's conclusions, Cardoso de Oliveira stresses the ambiguity that characterizes the immigrant's process of self-identification and raises the following question: Why don't Brazilians from the poorest and least-prepared sectors of the immigrant community assume the Hispanic ethnic identity as a personal identity strategy when it can mean, for example, eventual participation in affirmative-action quotas? I understand that second-generation Brazilians will tend to assume the identity Hispanic in a less ambiguous way. More than their parents were, second-generation Brazilians are forced to self-identify according the U.S. classification system since the institutional insertion of the second generation tends to be greater. To begin with, they are enrolled in school, a place where their national, ethnic, and racial origins will certainly become evident. Besides going to school, second-generation Brazilians speak English and have friends and contacts outside the Brazilian community.

Subsequent generations of Brazilians may be more likely to make use of the advantages that the U.S. ethnic system can offer them. In fact, self-identifying as Hispanic can be more profitable in some contexts, such as access to quotas. Mariana, a second-generation Brazilian woman, stated that when she took a civil service examination, the fact that she is Brazilian helped her pass by allowing her to enter under the Hispanic quota. However, Mariana hardly knew how to speak Portuguese, was not familiar with Brazilian music, and had no friends from Brazil. In fact, she had only very recently come to consider herself Brazilian because her work was connected to the Brazilian community.

In summary, the identification process of Brazilian immigrants tends to be affected by aspects of their native culture but also by sociodemographic characteristics (questions of generation, social class, and origin in Brazil) on one hand and by the structure of local institutional incentives (including the history of the institutional insertion of immigrants in the context of incorporation) on the other. This, consequently, reduces the potential for an explanation of identification based essentially on a common cultural origin. Thus posited, not all Brazilians self-identify in the same way. National identity includes the manipulation of various possible contents. Processes of identification produce a certain uniformity but not a predetermined and requisite unity over the way people and groups adapt it.

As Capuano demonstrates (2002), poor Brazilians in Miami associate with Latinos due to the political presence of Cubans/Cuban Americans. However, this is not true for Brazilian businesspeople who "want to be

Americans" and therefore do not opt for the strategy of joining a minority group; on the contrary, they seek to incorporate themselves into the social mainstream of Miami. They want their children to become "legitimate Americans," and they try to cover up their national origin, which they perceive as a stigma. Such businesspeople hold capital (human and financial), and this facilitates their institutional insertion. Capuano's research in Miami shows that there, unlike their counterparts in Boston, Brazilian workers in the informal market participate in Hispanic/Latino communities, including religious communities.[38]

Meanwhile, wealthy Brazilians (businesspeople and successful professionals) do not organize themselves in the same way; they do not even have points of contact with poor Brazilians, much less with the Hispanic/Latino community.[39] This is because nationality without the mediation of social class does not always become the primary identity for defining belonging (Oboler 1995). In New York, Margolis (1994) found a similar situation, in which social class was more important than national origin for Brazilians. The case of Brazilians, like that of other immigrants, shows that identity, or more appropriately ethnic affiliation, is a social process that can be understood only when contextualized and that the culture of the group studied cannot be considered an inventory of traits and values that repeat themselves systematically. More specifically, the process of identification of Brazilian immigrants will depend both on sociodemographic characteristics (especially those of generation and social class) and on the means of institutional insertion that are available in the host society, which, consequently, reduces the potential for explaining identification based essentially on a common cultural origin (Martes 2000a, 2007).

Being Hispanic/Latino in Miami increases social capital for those who have no other kind of capital. Being Hispanic in Massachusetts means, above all, entering into a universe of discrimination. In Miami the affiliation is advantageous; in Massachusetts, with a few exceptions (among them the ability to participate in the system of quotas reserved for Latinos), being Hispanic means losing visibility. In search of an integration strategy, the wealthy and/or professionally successful seek to assimilate into the mainstream by Americanizing. The poor who desire to achieve some type of integration participate in minority groups in a process similar to what Portes (1995) called "segmented assimilation."

Multiculturalism, based on the binomial of ethnicity and diversity as replacements for race and assimilation, respectively, is also part of the U.S. culture that immigrants must absorb; there is a set of constraints and incentives—including economic incentives—so that this may occur. Marcelo Suárez-Orozco states (2000: 13): "The cultural models and social practices that we call multiculturalism mould the immigrants' experiences, perceptions, and repertoire of behaviors . . . In that ethos, racial and ethnic categories become instrumental and expressive vectors." For Brazilians, coming to value ethnicity is part of the U.S. migratory experience. Specifically in Massachusetts, if second-generation Brazilians eventually follow in their parents' footsteps, they will probably identify themselves as Brazilian Americans, that is, not as Hispanics, Latinos, or blacks.[40] There seems to be nothing to prevent them, in the future, from adopting the category "multiracial" as they seek an equivalent to the terms "brown" and "mestizo" without excluding "black" and "white." In the event that such a tendency occurs in this region, it will permit them to keep the reference to national identity strong, an identity that currently constitutes the most fundamental aspect of the group's identity.

Conclusion

Brazilians are also "birds of passage," to use the expression that designates the desire of first-generation immigrants to return. For most Brazilian immigrants, if the United States is a good country to work in, Brazil is a better place to live. Life is not reduced to work, and any other dimension of life outside the strictly economic sphere or what cannot be grabbed up by it remains in suspense, latent, but even so acts as a force that draws the immigrant back to his or her native land. The ideal situation would be to be able to stay in the United States until they manage to obtain a green card, because with this document they could more freely move between the two countries. It is as if a U.S. visa could provide the best of both worlds: working here and living there, taking advantage of Brazilian forms of sociability without losing the opportunities that the United States can provide.

The interviews collected during this study reveal that first-generation Brazilian immigrants feel attached to several aspects of their lives in Brazil, especially to what is familiar in all senses of the word: "I don't feel at home," "I don't feel at ease," "This isn't my place." The general feeling is one of displacement, lack of familiarity, and not belonging. It is upon hearing them talk about returning that the dimension of displacement becomes evident as the central piece in the flow of their narratives. This is why they make a point of emphasizing that the main problem they are forced to confront in Massachusetts is the feeling of "loneliness and longing." Since the beginning of the migratory movement, this dimension has been emphasized in the experiences they have related and remains consistent over time, expressed in a very moving way, as if it were something that cannot be contained.

Although the subjective dimension, particularly of family ties and other bonds of affection, is increasingly evident in the narratives about returning, the situation that precedes a return is analogous to an "accountant's balance sheet" on which the calculation is not exclusively economic. Reasoning that is not reducible to the economic sphere was evident in all of the interviews. The interviewees revealed an extensive and complex interplay of compensations and preferences, what is lost and what is gained by staying and by returning. Departing for the destination country can even be veiled in a sense of adventure, but returning seems to demand more pragmatic behavior. More than when they left Brazil, their considerations about returning are motivated by feelings. However, returning demands facing a brutal reality. Since the beginning of this migratory movement, Brazil as well as the United States has undergone changes significant enough to affect plans, expectations, and behaviors.

If in the United States today the situation of the undocumented immigrant has become more critical since September 11 and the crisis in the housing market that began in 2007, various aspects that led immigrants to leave Brazil still remain or have gotten even worse. Security—or the lack of it—is the most important of the new variables. Economic uncertainty adds to the problems of public safety and violence, especially in the large urban centers that previously were able to absorb internal migrants. More than the restrictions on illegal immigrants, the two factors that really appear to be leading Brazilians to return to Brazil permanently are the exchange rate and the crisis in the housing sector. We have seen in this book that the principal occupation of male Brazilian immigrants is manual labor in the construction sector, which crashed when the mortgage lending bubble burst in 2008.

The idea of possibly returning to Brazil remains strong. In the plans to return, a series of obstacles are anticipated and enter into the equation particularly when many Brazilians find themselves in a certain stage of life. They are older and probably married with children. This situation generates inertia toward undertaking the return to Brazil, and many of them tend to stay in the United States instead. Although it is not possible to determine exactly how many immigrants will in fact return or stay, there are many expectations around these decisions. The majority of first-generation Brazilians still plan to return to Brazil. This tendency was found in the 1990s and did not change in the 2000s. In the survey conducted in 1995, 36% not only wished to return but already determined the time frame within which they would return; rarely was that more than five years. In the 2005 survey, 40% said they wished to return and already had a date in mind or had set goals, generally economic ones, that they wished to achieve, after which they would return.

However, the 15% (in 1996) and 21% (in 2005) of Brazilians who stated that they did not wish to return contrast with the general perception that "they all want to return." For these immigrants, returning is an option they have rejected definitively. Among those who did not know when they would return (7% in 1996 and 8% in 2005), some had not yet decided if they would stay or return to Brazil. It is possible that the interviewees who did not intend to return were generally satisfied with life in Massachusetts: "I like life here. If I am able to become legal, I will only return to Brazil to visit"; and "Brazil has become very violent, and my children will have a better life here." Again, Brazilians tend to value their migratory experiences and American society positively. In short, they stay because they want to stay.

This conclusion is far from being obvious or trivial, since returning to the country of origin is an arduous process, and the difficulties it involves can be a determining factor in the decision to stay in the United States. The experience they have obtained during the whole migratory process allows the immigrants to have greater clarity about the problems they must face in the event they return to Brazil: financial difficulties, problems in adapting to the previous lifestyle, (re)socialization in their cities of origin, and perhaps most complicated of all, helping their children readapt in school and to their new life. Nevertheless, many stay because they wish to stay and not because they think it will be difficult to return. Both factors can be complementary, but these immigrants assert that they stay by choice. In other words, some stay not because of socioeconomic, structural, or financial constraints but because they in fact choose to stay: "I prefer to live here."

Affirmation of the "American lifestyle," the desire to maintain consumer power, and access to public schools that they consider to be of higher quality than those available in Brazil all appear as incentives for many Brazilians living in Massachusetts to stay in the United States. Those Brazilians who have created strong enough bonds in Massachusetts, either because relatives and friends have emigrated or because they have married Americans, are also in this situation. The following response seems to be paradigmatic: "I don't want to return. I married an American here. I have a good job now. I was a cleaning lady, too, but now I'm an interpreter.

Why return?" This reasoning was expressed by Nilda, a 29-year-old from the Brazilian state of Minas Gerais who had been in the United States for more than three years.

Nina's interview calls attention to an important factor: she worked as an interpreter in a hospital serving the Brazilian population. Like dozens of other Brazilians who do not wish to return, she received better employment prospects and remuneration in Massachusetts than in Brazil. In Brazil, Nina was a seamstress, but in the United States she was an interpreter. Generally, Brazilians who, like her, get jobs providing services to other Brazilians have a greater incentive to stay. The existence of a Brazilian population in the state generates employment opportunities in the area of social services (interpreters, psychologists, nurses) and in education. These people in a sense speak "in the name of the community" before various local public agencies and often participate actively in Brazilian community associations. Given the institutional integration of these professionals, it would be less beneficial for them to return to Brazil. For them, this is one of the opportunities stemming from the ethnic system in the United States.

This choice is even more evident among Brazilians who have opened small businesses in Massachusetts. From 2002 to 2003, sixty-six such businesspeople in Somerville, Allston, East Boston, and Cambridge were interviewed. Of this number, fifty-one said they had decided to live permanently in the United States, regardless of whether they had the required legal documents.

Brazilians are investing in real estate in Brazil as well as in the United States. This means they are leaving the decision to return or to stay for the future. Investing in the two countries is also a way of dealing with their current situation of staying. By far most of their investments are made in Brazil, and the remittances sent reveal this. A study conducted in 2004 in Massachusetts found that of all those interviewed, 78% were sending remittances to Brazil with some frequency, 8% had sent remittances but were no longer sending them, 13% had never sent them, and 1% did not respond (Martes and Soares 2004, Martes 2008a). The purpose of these remittances, however, was not principally investment but rather to help the immigrants' families in Brazil. This was the case for 75% of the interviewees. The qualitative interviews conducted in the same year with the families in Governador Valadares underscored the importance of the money the immigrants sent, especially to supplement pensions, pay school expenses, and to augment monthly incomes. Of the rest of the remittances, 25% was used to purchase or maintain real estate, 5% was sent to establish or maintain businesses, 16% was used for financial investments (especially savings), 6% was used to pay debts, and 4% was sent to help nongovernmental entities.[1]

In any event, the factors that influence the decision to return or to stay are different from those that immigrants faced at the beginning of the twentieth century. Air travel and eventually competitive airfares, the comparative ease of transportation in general, and the speed of transmission of information and communications have made returning easier, thus favoring "yo-yo" immigration (Margolis 1994), that is, leaving and returning with some regularity. However, the choice depends on the immigrant having appropriate documents, on having obtained his or her green card.[2] The green card represents a step toward returning to Brazil, paradoxical as that may seem, because receiving the official document that permits the immigrant to stay permanently is the only resource capable of both encouraging a return to Brazil and leaving the entry door to the United States open. Thus, the document that allows the immigrant to come and go ends up being the only instrument capable of giving a secure feeling about returning to Brazil.

Post–September 11

During the field research in 2005, I was in fact able to see the effort that many Brazilians were dedicating to getting green cards, the surprising number of people who said that they already had gotten that document, and the great importance that they attributed to it. The explanation for this lies in part in the obstacles that the post–September 11 period added for those who were undocumented. Yet the green card, a document that permits immigrants to stay in the United States, also makes it easier for them to come and go. In addition, Brazilian law allows dual citizenship, which can favor transnationalism, the maintenance of ties with the country of origin, and at the same time, a greater degree of incorporation into U.S. society.

If the advantages attained by getting legal documents are so clear, why has the number of legalized Brazilians remained so low? In the survey conducted in 2005, 52% had no type of document, 13% had green cards, 11% said they had begun the legalization process, 2% said they were U.S.

Table 7.1. Passports and Authorizations in Boston for Return to Brazil, 2000–2004

Year	Number of Passports and Authorizations Issued by Boston Consulate
2000	2,953
2001	6,991
2002	7,964
2003	12,905
2004	15,489

Source: Information provided to the author by the Brazilian consulate in Boston, 2005.

citizens, and the rest did not respond. For Brazilians who really wish to return to Brazil as quickly as possible, "the green card is very expensive. It's not worth it. It's of no use, not even for my children to go to school." Still, many applied for the green card under an immigration law passed in 1998 because it is a document that makes permanent residence in the United States easier, as it allows holders to visit Brazil and return. The president of the Centro do Imigrante Brasileiro said in 2005 that 20,000 Brazilians already owned homes in Massachusetts, which indicates that they wished to remain in the United States and to acquire legal documents. The data supplied by the Brazilian Consulate in Boston, on the other hand, show a tendency toward an increase in the number of those who returned, although no data are available on the total number of immigrants per year, which limits the interpretation of the numbers.

When they return, their accounts of the whole process stress emigration as an experience and a training period. Like other immigrants, when Brazilians return to their country of origin they take with them material goods and savings, social contacts, and important life experiences (Levitt 2000). Having been exposed to new knowledge, they see before them the possibility of increasing their cultural and social capital. Living in another country and getting to know other societies is part of the individual motivation generally linked to the middle class and the social imagery of "living in another country." How do the returnees employ not only physical capital but also the profits arising from the rich life experiences that emigration has provided them? The literature tends to emphasize the monetary remittances more than the use of skills they have acquired. For Brazilians, such skills include those learned in formal education and on-the-job training, a type of learning that comes from practice and that can be related to the ways of running a business, relating to employees, or simply giving greater value to work. Therefore, it says less about techniques and more about a kind of involvement in, attitude toward, and resignification of work. Returning with money is not everything. Emigration gave them priceless life experience. Returning more mature, with a new mentality, with more tenacity to fight for what they want, all are subjective factors that in and of themselves reaffirm and give value to the migratory experience, according to the interviewees.[3]

Conceiving of immigration as a training period means reaffirming emigration positively because it allows one the experience of daily living in a different culture with values capable of reorienting economic behavior: will power and aggressiveness in the day-to-day operations of business; and reconsideration of the value of work, whatever it may be, and of family. At least part of this long process—that part during which one is an immigrant—is lived as a completely solitary experience. Understandably, emigrants say that to be an immigrant is to learn to "become alone." Because most of the returnees interviewed were very young when they left Brazil, emigration generated a more specific training in their daily lives. Being there forced people to learn to no longer count on family support for day-to-day necessities and to compensate for the role previously played by familiar, domestic figures that were typically female: mother, wife, and domestic employee.

What do they wish to take home with them when they return? Money. Yet this is not always what they do take. Conceiving of emigration as an experience allows the interviewees above all to value whatever work they do in a manner similar to the valorization of work as a vocation analyzed by Max Weber, although in this case there is not a religious connotation, and work does not correspond to a divine calling. For some of the interviewees, working hard is part of American culture; for others, it is part of the very condition of being an immigrant no matter what the destination country. In any event, the experience of having lived as an immigrant worker in another country reinforces their desire to be self-employed. Yet we need to avoid hasty conclusions in this regard. The specific knowledge necessary for opening a business—such as having to face the risks that are typical in Brazil—is not gained from emigration. Neither does being successful depend solely on having money. The start-up capital brought from the United States is merely a push; it is a necessary element but not sufficient in and of itself. Brazilians who save some money in the United

States have many difficulties using it well in Brazil. Their businesses rarely last due to oscillations in the Brazilian economy and even more so to the lack of knowledge about the specific type of business that the returned emigrant chooses to open.

The Advantages (and Disadvantages) Available in the Destination Country

In this study I have sought to call attention to the concept of emigration as a kind of investment. Once they become immigrants, people begin to add up the advantages (and disadvantages) of living in the destination country. This is not merely a matter of counting economic advantages because, as I analyzed in Chapter 5, many aspects of American society are positively valued. The English skills these immigrants acquire can constitute a form of cultural capital in Brazil. Those who plan to make use of their English or other skills acquired in the United States when they return to Brazil are those who already have higher levels of education. They represent a specific type of immigrant: one who emigrates in order to add value to his or her individual human capital.

Many Brazilians with whom I was able to converse and interact over the course of these almost fifteen years did not know exactly when they would return to Brazil, and neither did they know what they would do in that country in the event that they did return. As I sought to emphasize in Chapter 1, push/pull theory views the immigrant as a rational individual, as one who calculates costs and benefits to make choices about emigration. The Brazilians interviewed showed that they had made financial calculations prior to their departure when, along with their families (and not just individually), they chose to emigrate. However, for some the economic factor did not predominate either in the decision to emigrate or in the decision to return to Brazil. And economic plans for the return to Brazil often are vague and imprecise. Finally, the interviews highlight another dimension. In devising their plans to emigrate, Brazilians make selections (choose variables) in order to decide (the cognitive dimension) by calculating the cost-benefit relationship of the decision. They are modern emigrants: they make economic calculations to convince themselves that it is more worthwhile to go than to stay, and thus they bet on the new situation. In this calculus, the dimension of self-deception recurs frequently in the interviews. They select from the "imposed reality" whatever helps them strengthen their own personal conviction that it is worthwhile to emigrate.

In effect, what do they select? Often it is the concrete dimension of remuneration: How much can I earn? How much can I work and save? They stress whatever they would earn in economic terms, added to a new life experience and an increase in cultural capital. However, a kind of self-deception occurs at this point: the cost of being uprooted is not calculated because it is immeasurable. At the moment of emigration, the social and affective dimensions are suppressed. Once the crossing is accomplished, however, even if they attain a relative degree of economic and material satisfaction fairly quickly, they see the clearer outline of economic motivation fade. Thus, we return to a classic question of sociology that has been considered for a long time: the dilemmas (including moral dilemmas) that arise from social and spatial mobility in modern societies.

Although Brazilian immigrants are very far from being the typical "economic man," they likewise are not "solidary man." Why is solidarity, or the lack thereof, such a cherished topic for Brazilian immigrants? Their complaints about the lack of solidarity are in themselves significant since they signal that solidarity is highly valued by Brazilian immigrants. Thus, it is only possible to understand its significance if the internal context of the group or the community in which it acquires significance is considered.

Recently arrived Brazilian immigrants are in a circumstance of extreme vulnerability and dependence stemming from their scant knowledge of the workings of American society and of the English language. This makes them susceptible to various kinds of exploitation and opportunistic behavior, as well as in need of seeking help from other Brazilians who, because they arrived earlier, know how to approach communication, lodging, and especially employment problems. The interviewees revealed that they arrived in the United States with great expectations regarding the possibility of raising their income and how Brazilians who were already in the United States would welcome them. The expectations are translated into a kind of conviction that they will be able to count on the support of friends and relatives. Still, such expectations are accompanied by the fear that support will be denied them in some way at some time, a dimension of solidarity that is expressed in day-to-day interpersonal relationships.

The other dimension, the associative dimension, is much less valued and much more difficult to accomplish.

Emigration is a highly selective process from the individual perspective. It requires courage and a willingness to face new risks coming from an unknown situation.[4] While Brazilian immigrants show sufficient courage to face adversity, they also experience, perhaps in equal measure, an unfamiliar personal situation: a feeling of fragility imposed by having become a foreigner. This sense comes from the perception that they will have to face situations they have not yet deciphered and in which they see themselves as lacking, emotionally and otherwise. The Brazilians lose much of their previous ability to handle a whole set of basic information relative to daily life involving both written and oral communication—reading a simple street sign, knowing how they should do their jobs, or how to handle a new currency—at the same time that they experience the absence of friends, of family, of their hometowns, of a place where people are "of another sort." Almost everything has to be learned again.

This sense of fragility intensifies over the course of the first years in the United States, which are marked by instability: changing jobs and places of residence, separating from or reuniting with old friends, and incorporating into new social relations. As they described the process of arriving in the United States as having been difficult, complicated, and full of suffering, not all of the Brazilians interviewed sounded overly emotional, but it is not surprising that churches try to offer safer places of sociability, familiarity, and solidarity, a topic I addressed in Chapter 3.

The Regulation of Social Life

Churches are perceived as more trustworthy than NGOs or any other type of organization that may represent Brazilians. The churches are restricted communities in which social control mechanisms are more clearly defined, to the point of making their members feel some assurance that they are joining a network of beneficial reciprocity. It is in this regard that the churches were used here as examples of safe spaces for sociability. The position taken by the churches toward job selling was analyzed as an attempt to implement social control mechanisms. We saw that the commercialization of jobs does not constitute an open market but rather one that is restricted to Brazilians, especially through friendship, kinship, and religious networks. Priests and nuns attempted to discourage this trade in the name of community solidarity. Evangelical pastors, although they did not condemn this trade, directed it so that the selling would take place among members of the church and for a fair price. Now the idea of a fair price involves the idea of community. For an orthodox liberal economic thinker like Hayek, for example, prices are neither fair nor unfair, but rather, they are what is established (negotiated) among the agents of the exchange (Hayek 1985: 2:101).

Brazilians do not stop selling jobs in the name of community, but in its name a fair price is established. In this way, job selling within restricted communities (and not in the Brazilian population of Massachusetts as a whole) requires a minimum degree of trust between the seller and the buyer, but it may reject solidarity. The ethnic solidarity that is presumed in the act of proposing the next Brazilian housecleaner to the homemaker is an artifice. As an individual or collective construct, solidarity is also susceptible to manipulation because it is part of a dynamic process that contains (de)constructions.

Ethnic solidarity is a specific type of solidarity that can be better understood if it is framed in the political sphere. However, solidarity also may be of another sort. Brazilians express solidarity in churches, among friends, and in their family units. This is a solidarity that permeates small, local networks in which they anticipate reciprocity and trust. Thus Brazilians participate in churches because they want to accumulate social capital. As Robert Putnam says (1996), no one acquires social capital on the street but rather where he or she believes that trust and reciprocity can be expected. I showed that Brazilians seek out churches because they wish to socialize and that the clergy appeal to the Brazilians' loneliness as a way to attract them. They participate in the churches not simply because they "want to make friends" but because such participation is motivated by the expectation that in the churches they will be able to enjoy everything that the networks and institutions provide: social capital, affirmation of values, promotion of interests—and friendship.

Taken together, the state of vulnerability along with the desire to earn money, the courage and fear that accompany the decision to emigrate, conviction and at the same time distrust in the face of expectations generated by dependence, the longing for reciprocity combined with the lack of trust coming from a highly unstable situation, and the desire and obligation to help that accompany the fear of not receiving merited recognition for the effort extended in giving help are all factors that constitute the universe and the myth of the "Brazilian community" in Massachusetts.

All of these factors fuel the persistent complaints about the lack of solidarity and willingness to engage in community participation among Brazilians that also constitute part of this universe. The extensive list of complaints I heard from the majority of the interviewees—the repeated stories of misdeeds and opportunistic behavior involving large sums of money and theft of telephone and credit cards—created an almost folkloric panorama of the Brazilians in Massachusetts. Nevertheless, such complaints, frequently expressed in a tone of moral reprehension, gained special meaning and new vigor by serving as elements of reinforcement for a discourse in which the image of Brazil was generally poor, particularly in terms of the country's politics and economy. After all, the interviewees alleged that they would not have left for Massachusetts if everything had been going well in the country that they still considered theirs. They complained about its flaws in much the same way that one complains about an imperfect family. But despite the complaints about the lack of solidarity, over the years that I have been researching Brazilians in Massachusetts, several Brazilian community organizations have been formed, and Brazilians continue to arrive in the state relying on the help of friends and relatives. Fund-raising campaigns to help Brazilians in need have been organized as well.

What approach should be taken to explain these situations that are so strongly marked by the ambiguity of being a Brazilian and yet expressing an adverse view of Brazil, of stating a feeling of "liking being a Brazilian" while making serious moral judgments regarding the Brazilians who reside in the United States? Such ambiguity places a kind of trap in front of those who experience it as well as those who observe it that becomes evident when they attempt to respond "yes" or "no" to the question Is there solidarity among Brazilian immigrants?

In this study, I have sought to show that solidarity is expressed in different ways and with varying levels of intensity according to the context. Manifestations of solidarity are more visible in smaller networks (principally churches and family units) than in the larger Brazilian population because solidarity involves the idea of community. Mota observes (2004: 12) that

> when talking with a 7-year-old boy who insisted during the whole interview on responding in English to the questions asked in Portuguese, I noticed that when he began to talk about the church, he immediately switched to Portuguese. Seeing my surprise, he explained to me: " . . . praying? Only in Portuguese." That was yet further evidence that the church, identified in the research as the social dominion whose linguistic choice appears clearly defined as "exclusively Portuguese," constitutes the greatest bastion for the preservation of the mother tongue, where ethnic tradition manifests itself as a symbol of the group's spirit of solidarity. Parents as well as children state categorically: "there in the church, everyone has to be Brazilian."

Understanding solidarity as a dynamic process presumes that its practical manifestations constitute a variable geometry. Thus, it is possible to understand that the situation of vulnerability that characterizes the moment of arrival in Massachusetts exacerbates the expectations surrounding the Brazilian community. At that moment, speaking the same language and feeling oneself to be part of a group with which one can share a "common past" and a "culture of origin" acquire great importance. But does this feeling continue with the same intensity in other circumstances? I do not believe so. Compared to the first generation, second-generation Brazilians in Massachusetts construct their relationships with Brazil, with Brazilians, and with their national identity in a different way.

The Future Generations

For the second generation, the contrast that their parents establish between Brazil and the United States, analyzed in the last chapter, loses its essential form. What is most noteworthy among second-generation Brazilians is the extremely superficial knowledge of Brazil that they demonstrate. As the majority of their parents are undocumented, it is rare that second-generation Brazilians can return to visit Brazil (in the event that they emigrated as young children). The second generation receives information about Brazil through parents and family members or else from television (programs recorded on videotape, especially *novelas* and *Fantástico*) or via the Internet.[5] In school as well, they hear about or learn about Brazil because many of them are enrolled in bilingual (English-Portuguese) programs offered in public schools.[6] A statement by Carolina, a

12-year-old who had lived in the United States for nine years, reveals an almost dramatic reality: "I thought that Brazil was a country with slaves and black women with baskets of fruit on their heads. I don't know why . . . I think that it was because of a book that a guy from the bilingual program brought that had [a picture of] a Latin American woman."

In the interviews, the adolescents tended to associate Brazil with police violence and political corruption, and they expressed the idea that it is a good place to live if one is rich. For poor people like them, the United States offers more opportunities. The positive factors that came up were connected with easy sociability, *carnaval*, soccer, and Brazilian geography. Second-generation Brazilian immigrants have a perspective of Brazil that is close to that of foreigners. Júlia, for example, was an 11-year-old who had never been to Brazil. I asked her how she imagined the country. She answered, "Brazil is a place like Florida. Why? Because of the sun and the beaches."

More so than their parents' generation, second-generation Brazilian immigrants are forced to identify themselves according to the U.S. classificatory system. This is because the institutional incorporation of the second generation tends to be greater. To begin with, they are enrolled in school, a place where their national origin will certainly be evident. The pressure for identification is so marked that one of the adolescents interviewed complained that her teacher was pressuring her to associate with her Hispanic classmates. However, the girl's best friend was an "American." The teacher's insistence had gotten to the point that she was thinking of switching schools.

Besides going to school, second-generation Brazilian immigrants speak English and have friends and contacts outside the Brazilian community.[7] This generation tends to have greater connections with the Hispanic population than their parents do. In the interviews, many stated that they had Latino friends. On the other hand, nothing indicates that this generation has been building bonds with "Portuguese-language speakers" (especially the Portuguese).

Because it is dynamic, the concept of ethnicity presumes (re)arrangements. In fact, compared with the first generation, those of the second generation prove more prone to avail themselves of the advantages that the U.S. ethnic system can afford them, manipulating their identification in a different way. We saw that first-generation Brazilians tend to reject the label "Hispanic," some of them preferring to be identified as

Portuguese-language speakers or as Brazilians. But for the second generation, self-identifying as Hispanic can be more profitable in some contexts, as in the case of Mariana presented in Chapter 6.

According to Roberto Cardoso Oliveira (1976), the frictional nature of ethnic identity implies a confrontation with other identities included in a system of representations of ideological content. In this sense, the ethnic identity of one group is asserted to the exact degree that it rejects another identity, in an ethnocentric way. I do not believe that Brazilians of any generation express this ideology. In other words, except for those who participate in groups representing Brazilian immigrants, Brazilians do not convey the desire to construct and express a strong national identity in Massachusetts. They are more likely to allow themselves to be passed over than to collectively assert their identity of origin.

This tendency does not mean they cannot express themselves in such a way under certain circumstances. I believe that the concept of "rejected identity" (R. Oliveira 1976) aids in understanding the way Brazilians tend to struggle with their national origin in Massachusetts. It involves a latent identity that can be expressed and mobilized at certain moments. Precisely because ethnic identity is an ideologically valued category, it encompasses the possibility of choosing criteria that can render results that are more positive.

Throughout this book, I have sought to show that ethnic solidarity is also solidarity of interests. In this respect, a group's cultural identity is one of the requirements for the formation of an ethnic group, but such an identity alone is not enough to turn a given immigrant population into an ethnic group. If we attribute political content that can incorporate differences to the notion of solidarity, then we can treat ethnic groups as heterogeneous. The degree of heterogeneity of a group or of a population also depends on the perspective from which we look at it and the situations in which we choose to study it. If we agree that ethnic identity is contrastive (R. Oliveira 1976, Cunha 1985), the very establishment of the contrast (the assertion of difference) causes an increase in the level of internal identity.

I would suggest that researchers who are beginning their study of Brazilian immigrants in the United States reflect on and keep in mind the following passage written by Pierre Bourdieu in *The Economy of Linguistic Exchanges* (1996: 81):

> Social science works with realities that are already named and classified, that are bearers of proper names and common names, of titles, signs, and shorthands. Given the risk that social science itself will, without realizing it, transform constitutive acts of whose logic and whose necessity it is ignorant, social science should take as its subject social operations of naming and the institutional rites through which they are accomplished. Although at an even deeper level, social science needs to examine the role that words play in the construction of social objects, as well as the contribution that the struggle between classifications, a dimension of all class struggles, brings to the constitution of classes: age classes, social classes, clans, tribes, ethnicities, or nations.

Reconsidering the beginning of this book, I believe that in a sociological approach to the relationship between solidarity and ethnicity, this inside view cannot be lacking and that this is the anthropological view. However, an outside view is also necessary when working with culture, solidarity, and identity. I mean that the ethnic system in the United States should be incorporated into the analysis with a certain critical distance and that the so-called ethnic groups be understood as part of a political construct so as to avoid essentialist interpretations of culture. In this way, studies like those of Hollinger (2000) and Steinberg (1989) are fundamental in order that a foreigner like me, who lives in a country in which race and ethnicity have other meanings and are supported by other (and diverse) social practices and interests, can manage to understand the research data in light of the context of interviewees' reception. In return, my hope is that this book will contribute to enabling non-Brazilians to come to understand this small portion of recent immigrants that consists of Brazilians, remembering that they, too, help give continuity to the American dream, and, therefore, they make their contribution to maintaining the characteristics of a diverse, open, affluent, and cosmopolitan society in this country.

Notes

Introduction

1. According to Smelser and Swedberg (1994), Economic Sociology is "the application of the frames of reference, variables, and explanatory models of sociology to that complex of activities concerned with the production, distribution, exchange, and consumption of scarce goods and services" (3). They add: "Given recent developments in sociology as a whole and economic sociology in particular, we would specify that the particular perspectives for social networks, gender, and cultural context have also become central in economic sociology" (ibid.).

2. Fundamental characteristics of Brazilian emigrants include that they are first-generation immigrants; they are undocumented; they belong to the Brazilian middle class, which is threatened with impoverishment; and they have low human capital.

3. With regard to the networks of intermediaries in Brazilian emigration see Fazito 2005.

4. Only two studies question, although generically, this "romantic bias": Mahler 1995 and Pessar 1995. Both criticize the emphasis given by other authors to the solidarity within immigrant groups. Cecilia Menjivar's book (2000) is also dedicated to explaining the fragmentation of social bonds, this time among Salvadoran immigrants. Other than these studies, few make solidarity an object of empirical inquiry. Generally, ethnic solidarity is taken for granted.

5. In 2009 I was in London investigating Brazilian immigration, and I found very similar research results between the two locations. In London, Brazilian immigrants sell housecleaning jobs in the same way as in Massachusetts and for similar prices.

6. Part of this work was presented in the book *Brasileiros nos Estados Unidos* (Martes 2000a).

7. With regard to the advantages and disadvantages of surveys with random samples see King 1994.

8. This presupposition is based on the concentration of commercial establishments and services in these communities that are oriented toward the Brazilian population. The establishments selected were stores selling Brazilian products, airline-ticket and money-remittance agencies, unisex hair salons, and Brazilian restaurants.

9. That work relied on the following research collaborators: Weber Soares, who was responsible for carrying out the field research in Governador Valadares and in Boston

(second phase); Tania Christopoulos, who was responsible for the tabulation and statistical analysis of the survey; and Pedro Lins, who was responsible for administering the questionnaires in Boston (first phase). Leonardo Barone and Fernando Oshima worked as monitors. Daniel Valente assisted with the final edition.

Chapter 1. Economic Sociology and Brazilian Immigration

1. Swedberg (1992) presents an interesting "synthesis" of this interdisciplinary debate.

2. I do not intend to synthesize the various models but rather to provoke a debate. For this reason, I do not refer to models that propose to explain compulsory migratory movements. The tendency called the "political approach" relates the emergence of migratory flows to a series of political restrictions and incentives defined within the so-called nation-states. It stresses the high degree of induction in migratory movements by considering that the nations, through legislation and government policies, mold the patterns of immigration. The Bracero Accord that permitted thousands of Mexicans went to work in the United States in the mid-twentieth century is given as an example of this case. In contrast to the "push/pull" model, this does not relate displacement of populations to individual choices; on the contrary, it considers such displacements the result of governmental policies and international relations established between nations.

3. George Borjas is one of the most important representatives of this push/pull tendency.

4. For a critical view of the neoclassical perspective in migratory studies see Davis 1989 and Fazito 2005.

5. I will not broach the topic of "network analysis" or research based on graph theory. With regard to that see Soares 2002 and Fazito and Martes 2005.

6. In the same vein, Da Vanzo (1981) finds that the long-term nature of the cost-benefit considerations explains why migration and age are inversely related: "For older potential migrants, the length of the payoff period is not long enough to guarantee a positive net return from migration. This model is not restricted to economic costs and benefits but applies to other important goods, such as friends and relatives" (Myers 2000).

7. See especially Sassen 1988.

8. Sales notes (1999) that the EPZs in Brazil, principal beginning points for the migratory flows from Asia and the Caribbean to the United States, do not represent the places of origin of Brazilian immigrants.

9. It is important to note that characterizing solidarity in Brazil as guided primarily by religious values or doctrine and in the United States by civic culture reflects broad generalizations regarding the two cultures. In a communication with me, Cassandra White noted that solidarity also manifests in Brazil through paternalistic ties and through economic and social obligations and connections formed in relationships such as employer/employee, landowner/tenant farmer (although some might argue that these relationships do not constitute "solidarity"), and so on.

Chapter 2. Betting on the Future

1. For detailed information about Italian immigrants in Brazil see Silvera Beraldo 2000.

2. José C. Moya, *Cousins and Strangers* (1998: 46); L. S. Stavrianos, "The Global Redistribution of Man" (1968: 174); Maria Silvia Bassanezi, "Imigrações internacionais no Brasil" (1995: 8).

3. Brazil is not, however, a country of emigration because these are spontaneous movements and not induced by government emigration policies. It should not be forgotten that Brazil is still a destination country for documented and undocumented immigrants of Latin American origin (especially Bolivians and Paraguayans) and Asian origin (Chinese and Koreans).

4. See www.brazil.com/content/view/9718/78.

5. In Germany and France, respectively, 7,000 and 10,000 Brazilians have the status of undocumented immigrants (Patarra 1995). The Western European countries that have granted the greatest number of visas to Brazilian immigrants are Italy and Portugal, which respectively issued 15,000 and 21,000. In Portugal, Brazilians are among those with the highest professional and educational qualifications in the total population of recent immigrants. According to data from the Brazilian consulate in Lisbon, among those who entered the country legally from 1988 to 1992, 19.4% were professionals, 22.3% were self-employed, and 27.3% were students. With regard to age distribution, 80.1% of these immigrants were between the ages of 15 and 34 (Patarra 1995).

6. The term *dekasseguis* is derived from two Japanese words: *deru*, meaning "to leave," and *kasegu*, meaning "in order to work" or "to earn money by working." In combination, they communicate the idea of "working far from home," and the term *dekasseguis* thus is used to designate anyone who leaves his or her native land temporarily to work in another place.

7. I wish to thank Cassandra White for bringing this information to my attention. Although most estimates are very informal at this point, an idea of the number of Brazilians currently in the Atlanta area can be found in Greear 2009.

8. In absolute terms, the state falls to seventh place.

9. City of Somerville, "Minority and Immigrant Needs and Agencies," 1992.

10. The countries of origin of the immigrants in Massachusetts in 1990 were Puerto Rico (70,652); Dominican Republic (19,212); Haiti (18,553); Jamaica, Trinidad Tobago, and Virgin Islands (11,228); Cambodia (11,137); Russia (10,770); and Greece (8,891) (1990 U.S. Census cited in Halter 1995).

11. East Boston is a neighborhood of Boston; Somerville and Cambridge are considered cities; Allston, Brighton, and Framingham are administratively designated as towns. Here I refer to all of these places as cities for simplicity's sake since Brazilian administrative divisions are different.

12. In a study conducted in 1997 in the Brazilian city of Governador Valadares, Minas Gerais, Fusco found (2002) returned emigrants who had left for this region as early as 1967.

13. It is beyond the scope of this book to present a historical reconstruction of the beginnings of the migratory movement with regard to how and why Brazilians, particularly those from Governador Valadares, began to emigrate for Massachusetts. Here I present some data that may help in future studies about the beginning of the flow.

14. Regarding the role of networks in migratory movements see Boyd 1989, Massey et al. 1987, Reichert 1979, Portes and Rumbaut 1990, and Tilly 1990.

15. See Sales 1994, Soares 1995, and Assis 1995.

16. According to Sales (1999), only 6.7% of the inhabitants of Valadares emigrated and either stayed or returned, and 18% of domiciles included at least one person who emigrated and either stayed or returned.

17. The agents advised that interviewees should appear well dressed and that women should have their hair done professionally and wear jewelry and other accessories that might indicate personal wealth.

18. Cities of the Aço River Valley include Açucena, Antônio Dias, Belo Oriente, Bugre, Coronel Fabriciano, Córrego Novo, Don Cavate, Iapú, Ipabe, Ipatinga, Jaguaraçu, Joanésia, Marlieris, Mesquita, Naquete, Periquito, Santana do Paraíso, São João do Oriente, and Timóteo.

19. Since September 11, 2001, the U.S. government, through its consulates in Brazil, has made the concession of entry visas to Brazilians who live in the state of Minas Gerais more difficult because this is the state in which the flow began. Now to be granted a tourist visa, people from Minas Gerais must present a list of documents at the American consulate to prove that the petitioner has strong employment ties in Brazil. This requirement by the U.S. government is intended to contain the Brazil–United States migratory flow.

20. On networks that provide support for the migratory flow Boston–Governador Valadares see Soares 1995 and Assis 2004.

21. *Veja* is an important Brazilian news magazine similar to *Time* in the United States. It is the most widely circulated magazine in Brazil. *Brazuca* is a slang term used by Brazilians to refer to a Brazilian who is living abroad. The term is not derogatory; if anything, it conveys a light sense of national pride. (Translator's note)

22. For information about the education of engineers, doctors, and lawyers in Brazil see Grun 1992 and *Isto É* 1995.

23. The Federal District and the nation's capital, Brasilia, were created from a small part of the south central Brazilian state of Goiás. (Translator's note)

24. If birthplace is taken into consideration, an increase is seen in the number of states represented, to nineteen states plus the Federal District. The proportion of emigrants from Minas Gerais state also rises to 53% of the total. The number of respondents born in Valadares becomes 13% of the total; that is, the number of people who lived in Governador Valadares and later emigrated to Massachusetts is greater than the number of people born in Valadares who emigrated from Brazil.

25. It is probable that this state's decline in representation correlates precisely with the decline in representation of Governador Valadares.

26. The role media play in the Brazil–United States migratory flow is highly relevant

with regard to the transmission of information about and perceptions of the United States as well as to the propagation of U.S. models of consumption and various behavioral and cultural patterns. Mainstream media encourage emigration, even if indirectly. This topic as it relates to the press is being investigated by Sales.

27. When former Brazilian president Fernando Henrique Cardoso was minister of finance during the Itamar Franco administration, he directed the Plano Real. The plan was intended to stabilize the Brazilian economy through a number of measures that included daily adjustment of prices based on both price indexes and the exchange rate of Brazilian currency relative to the U.S. dollar. As part of this plan, the former Brazilian currency, the *cruzeiro*, was replaced by the *real*. While the plan initially enjoyed some success, the *real* soon began to depreciate gradually, and in January 1999, there was a currency crisis due to the severe devaluation of the *real*. (Translator's note)

28. As many of the emigrants wish to save money while abroad in order to return and open a business in Brazil, it is very plausible that, if conditions were favorable for those seeking to take out small and medium-size loans, they could obtain in Brazil the sum of money that they went looking for outside the country. In other words, stagnation or slow economic growth can stimulate emigration, but so can high interest rates.

29. For a specific analysis of the social networks in Governador Valadares see Fusco 2002 and Goza 2003; for information on Criciúma see Assis 2004.

30. For Brazilians, the migratory movement also is motivated by a gap between personal aspirations and expectations, such as Portes and Rumbaut posit (1990) for other groups of Latin American immigrants.

31. The Brazilian state of Tocantins in the north-central part of the country is the ninth largest Brazilian state in territory. Tocantins has about 1 million inhabitants; its capital is Palmas. Because Brazil is as large as the continental United States, it may be more expensive for Brazilians to fly from Governador Valadares to Palmas than from Governador Valadares to Boston, where they may find more economic advantages than in Palmas. (Translator's note)

Chapter 3. Organizational Resources in the Salvation Market

1. What I call "Catholic churches" are the three local units of that church that were studied: those in Allston, Somerville, and Framingham.

2. The Christ the King Presbyterian Church in Cambridge is the first Portuguese–English bilingual church in the United States with both Brazilian and American members.

3. Although no statistics were available, the churches named here seemed to me to be the most populated churches. The greater participation of their pastors or priests and nuns in the associative and representative activities of Brazilians in Massachusetts also influenced the selection.

4. According to the pastor of the Presbyterian church, 90% of the Brazilian evangelical churches in Massachusetts are Pentecostal and Charismatic. There are, hence, few traditional Brazilian evangelical churches.

5. In this study, only the Assembly of God is Pentecostal.

6. Brazilian churches are here understood as those whose celebrations are conducted in Portuguese for Brazilians and whose orientation follows the Brazilian religious cultural model and not the U.S. model.

7. See also Assmann 1986.

8. Various authors have noted the growth of Pentecostalism in Brazil among the Brazilian middle classes (Machado and Mariz 1997, César 1974).

9. According to Tilly (1990), immigration is a "networking process." Because migratory movements are formed by social networks, the networks that sustain migratory flows can be formed through churches. It would be interesting to research the role of churches in the advancement of this movement.

10. The survey recorded that 65% of all the Catholics stated that they were practicing.

11. In Boston and Cambridge, 106 nationalities and ethnic groups are represented in Christian congregations. The principal ethnic groups represented are African Americans, Asians (Chinese and Koreans), Haitians, Hispanics (there are approximately 280 Hispanic churches in New England), and Portuguese-language congregations (Portuguese, especially from the Azores, Cape Verdeans, and Brazilians). Portuguese from the continent as well as those from the Azores are more concentrated in New Bedford and Fall River, Massachusetts, and in Rhode Island, while Brazilians are concentrated principally in Somerville, Cambridge, Marlborough, Framingham, and Allston, Massachusetts (Emmanuel Gospel Center 1993).

12. See, for example, "Together a New People: Pastoral Statement on Migrants and Refugees," National Conference of Catholic Bishops (NCCB), November 8, 1986; and "The Hispanic Presence—Challenge and Commitment," NCCB, December 12, 1983.

13. I consider laypeople who volunteer in the churches assisting priests, nuns, or pastors to be religious activists.

14. Carlists, members of the Missionaries of St. Charles congregation, work exclusively with immigrants.

15. In contrast to the Catholic clergy, the evangelical pastors are all Brazilians.

16. While in Catholicism the priest is named by the bishop, the process of choosing a pastor in the Baptist and Presbyterian churches is determined by the assembly of the members of the local congregation. Pentecostal pastors are chosen through a complicated process of "mystical revelation" (R. Fernandes 1996).

17. In 2003 the pastor split from the Assembly of God congregation and changed the church's name to the World Revival Church of the Assembly of God.

18. Registered churches have tax-free status with the U.S. government.

19. The Assembly of God is the largest Pentecostal denomination in the United States and in Brazil.

20. The pastoral work of the Catholic Church with immigrants and migrants in the city of São Paulo is very similar to that in Boston with the Brazilians (Silva 1995).

21. The parishes are supposed to be financially autonomous and pay contributions to the diocese, which in turn should have financial autonomy and pay contributions to the Vatican.

22. The *festas juninas* (June festivals) celebrate several Catholic feast days that occur in June, including the feast of St. John the Baptist. Elements of the June festivals include bonfires and children dressing up as *caipiras* (country folk) in overalls, straw hats, and painted-on freckles. The feast day for Nossa Senhora Aparecida (Our Lady Who Appeared), the patron saint of Brazil, is celebrated on October 12. (Translator's note)

23. Many studies have focused on the relationship between religion and the material conditions of life; they relate religion to the socioeconomic organization of societies. Weber and Marx offer us, each in his way, approaches considered classic with regard to this relationship; see especially Weber 1968, 1982.

24. Although in my analysis I make a distinction between evangelicals and Catholics, both groups demonstrate internal divisions. The way the pastors conduct themselves in the communities, the degree of their presence, and the preaching they do vary according to each one's personality, besides, of course, the theological foundations of each of the churches that they lead. Like the evangelical churches, the Catholic Church also admits important divisions, and the work of each of the Catholic units varies according to the personality of the priest who leads it. For example, the Framingham church has a greater number of activities and more active participation by the faithful.

25. The theology of prosperity encourages an increase in income, redirection of spending, efforts toward saving, and the entrance of women into the labor market (Machado and Mariz 1997).

26. *Carnaval* is the Brazilian Shrove Tuesday celebration, the same Catholic holiday as Mardi Gras. In Brazil, *carnaval* has become a national celebration that begins the Friday before Ash Wednesday and generally continues into the early morning hours of Ash Wednesday. *Carnaval* is celebrated in cities and towns all over Brazil and is famous for its costume balls that take place everywhere from elegant hotels to gay clubs and feature often outrageous costumes. The samba parades in Rio de Janeiro feature samba schools (*escolas de samba*), generally community-based groups that prepare their elaborate costumes, music, and choreography all year in order to compete for awards in several categories. The celebrations and dancing also spill out nightly into the streets and continue until the early morning hours. (Translator's note)

27. According to the pastor in charge, the purchase of the building required $500,000 of financing, offered by the national organization of Presbyterian churches. A bank was financing $50,000, and the rest was collected from members of the church.

28. In the interviews a certain convergence became evident between the perception of this priest and the statements made by a couple who were members of the Jehovah's Witnesses church. During the whole interview, this couple emphasized and questioned the way Brazilian immigrants overvalued the "desire to earn money" and said that in their church this materialist emphasis "was not approved of."

29. Liberation Theology has several ramifications, the most important of which is its stance against social inequalities, expressed as a "preference for the poor." About Liberation Theology see Boff 1978, Gutierrez 1973.

30. With regard to the decline of the CEBs in Brazil see Prandi 1992.

31. See Freire 1979.

32. It is not feasible to compare the performance of evangelical churches among the Brazilian immigrants in other countries because no studies on the subject are available.

33. Salvadoran immigrants, like others from Central America, also brought the CCR with them to the United States (Peterson and Williams 2001).

34. The word *cursillo* means "little course" in Spanish. It consists of a three-day retreat that is designed to teach Catholics more about their faith. During the retreats, participants listen to talks given by priests, deacons, and laypersons. Topics of the talks presented include the Christian ideal, the Catholic faith, and the Christian approach to the world. The retreats offer small-group discussions of the topics as well. After the retreats, participants continue the study and discussions begun during the retreat experience in the post-Cursillo phase by meeting periodically in small groups with others who have participated in a Cursillo retreat.

35. The same type of religious support is verified by Ruben César Fernandes (1996). He found that 55% of the evangelicals in Greater Rio were suffering from serious problems at the time they converted: family problems, problems with alcohol, emotional or spiritual problems, or unemployment.

36. A curious example was that of a young woman I encountered in the residence of a priest. She had sought him out so he could help her fill out the application for legalization. This was in the morning. In the afternoon, I went to attend the worship service in the Presbyterian church, and there she was. "I haven't chosen yet," she explained.

37. I believe that Prandi's explanations (1992) of the reasons people embrace Pentecostalism or Charismatic Catholicism in Brazil constitute a strict analogy to the situation described here because religious adherence in both cases responds to the predominance of a mind set that is self-seeking and against solidarity among members of the larger society. But I believe that the case presented here is not restricted to Pentecostal and Catholic reform movements.

38. In Brazil, churches confront each other and position themselves before an analogous scene. Prandi (1992) attributes the growth of Pentecostal and Charismatic reformation movements in Brazil to the absence of a sociability and a social morality related to the welfare of the other; that absence defines what the author calls a post-ethical society lacking in values capable of giving universality to the world.

Chapter 4. The Social Arena of Employment and Businesses

1. Portes questions the dualist explanations by taking as a reference point his studies about ethnic enclaves, especially the Cuban enclave in Miami. According to Portes (1995), ethnic enclaves constitute an important alternative to the labor market to which the immigrants have access; therefore the division between the primary labor market and the secondary labor market is incapable of encompassing the variety of sectors into which the immigrants may be integrated.

2. For a critique of the concept of "informal economy" see Sanyal 1991.

3. The research methodology of the IBGE uses the same definition of "informal economy" as the ILO. The research branch of the IBGE identified that of the total number of occupations in informal urban businesses, 88% are self-employed, and the remaining

12% consist of small-scale employers, employees with and without legal working papers, and unpaid workers. The main areas of activity of these businesses are mercantile and repair, construction, and the mining and mineral processing industries (IBGE 2005: 25).

4. According to Tienda and Raijman (2000a), the informal economy grew in direct proportion to the decrease in mainstream employment. For example, 38% of Mexican households in Chicago are in the informal economy.

5. It is interesting to note that the vocabulary necessary to communicate with customers is very limited in these jobs since the menu is completely standard and not very diverse.

6. There are two other requirements for entering the field of housecleaning: having a car (because earning a good income requires working in at least two houses a day) and speaking at least a little English (because the homemakers are generally from the United States).

7. When I visited the cities of Governador Valadares and Ipatinga in 1997, it was obvious that the value assigned to living in the United States was directly related to social status. That is, while the local elites showed a certain distain for emigrants, the emigrants' families, who were not generally part of this elite, showed pride in having relatives living in the United States. I am grateful to Gláucia Assis for having called this to my attention.

8. In 1967 there were 218 cleaning companies in Boston with 6,757 employees. In 1991 there were 615 companies with 17,925 employees (Lado 1994).

9. Self-employed workers are distinguished from self-employed professionals in that the former have no profession, but the latter do.

10. Regarding domestic work and globalization see Shelley 2007, Hondagneu-Sotelo 2001, Parreñas 2001, Hanchard 1999, and Ehrenreich and Hochschild 2002.

11. Fleischer (2002) likewise emphasizes that being a housecleaner in Boston is something Brazilians have learned to value. Despite the differences (that housecleaning in Boston is not as heavy as in Brazil, for example), the dimension of domination and oppression still persists. In order to understand this dynamic Fleischer conducted an ethnographic study designed to reconstruct the "strategies" employed by housecleaners to deal with the difficulties arising from the nature of work they do and to seek means to resolve conflict, combat abuse, and deal with bosses or clients who considered themselves superior. In this sense, the "world of housecleaning" can be seen almost as a metaphor for the situation of the immigrant vis-à-vis the host society. This is because deep down, what Brazilian immigrants are trying to face and resolve are problems arising from having become foreigners and having to establish new ties and to construct social relationships in a society in which little is familiar to them.

12. I found only two Brazilian women who, because they married Americans, stopped doing housecleaning at the request of their husbands, as these men did not want to see their wives engaged in work that was not valued socially.

13. According to Portes and Rumbaut (1990), immigrants residing in San Francisco, California, also trade in jobs.

14. U.S. researchers also use Granovetter's book *Getting a Job* (1995) as a reference point in explaining the role of networks in the propagation of available job openings.

15. The *jogo do bicho*, or "animal game," is a lottery game in which the numbers are divided into twenty-five groups, each designated by the name of an animal—ostrich, eagle, butterfly, sheep, horse, snake, rabbit, and so on. The tickets for the *jogo do bicho* are sold by street vendors who have unofficial but nonetheless designated corners or "territories" where they sell their tickets. (Translator's note)

16. The Brazilian term *jeitinho* can be roughly translated as a "little arrangement" and suggests a way of working things out by somewhat unorthodox and perhaps not strictly legitimate means. The *jeitinho* is often possible due to personal relationships or connections between parties that allow flexibility in the normal "rules" for social, governmental, or business transactions, permitting something to be accomplished that might not otherwise be possible. This is similar to a notion in the United States captured by the expression "You scratch my back, and I'll scratch yours." (Translator's note)

17. Among these businesses are: *Jornal dos Esportes* (Sporting News), Cartomante Gina (Fortuneteller Gina), and Minas Jewelry (Cambridge); Main Street Café (Everett); Carioca Travel and Market (East Boston); Car Place Wholesalers (Everett); Salão Brasil (Brazil Salon) and Café Brasil (Allston); Coelho Cine-foto (Coelho's Movies and Photos), Madeira Restaurante Peixinho (Madeira Little Fish Restaurant), Barber Salon, and Gabriel's Exxon (East Providence); Silva's Music Distributors (Fall River); Toys and Gifts (Hyannis); Marcos Mecânica (Marcos Mechanics, Marlborough); Urbano Shop and Super Paulo's Mecânica (Framingham); Brazilian and American Languages Institute, Vigo (airplane tickets and remittances to Brazil), Amazonas Seguros (Amazonas Insurance), USA and Brazil Market, Somerville Video Locadora (Somerville Video Rental), Marifone Studio, and Brazilian Fashion Jewelry (Somerville); Ipanema Restaurant (Southborough); and Brasiltour (remittances to Brazil and airplane tickets, Acton).

18. Officially, the agencies that can send remittances to Brazil are the Bank of Brazil and Western Union (a partnership), the Federal Savings Bank, and Vigo. In 2003 and 2004, some Brazilian banks began to enter into partnerships with U.S. institutions that send remittances, among them Itaú Bank with MoneyGram and Bradesco with Bank of America. The Interamerican Development Bank (IDB) and International Monetary Fund (IMF) have played an important role in Brazil in opening the discussion of ways to encourage the formalization of sending remittances through formal institutions and agencies rather than informal-market dollar sellers and to encourage the participation of additional agencies in order to increase competition and reduce the fees for transferring funds.

19. In 1995 when the initial part of this research was conducted, the following Brazilian newspapers were in print in the United States: *Brazilian Times* (Somerville), *Diario do Brasil* (Boston), *Jornal dos Sports* (Cambridge), *News from Brazil* (Los Angeles), and *Brazilian Voice* (Newark, NJ).

20. There is no evidence of the organization of rotating credit associations among Brazilians, a common practice in other immigrant groups that makes rapid acquisition of start-up capital possible; in the literature these associations are used to show the

importance of trust in trade relationships. About rotating credit among immigrants see Geertz 1962.

21. The entities oriented toward the development of small businesses that were mentioned by the interviewees in Allston were the Community Development Corporation and in Boston the Business Information Center and Working Capital.

22. In fact, Brazilian entrepreneurs can receive, and some even count on, the support of city hall, especially in Somerville.

23. The main business difficulties identified by Brazilian entrepreneurs in Somerville and Allston can be used as another parameter in evaluating the importance of the role that the stakeholders end up playing: a lack of access to information and of knowledge about how local customs work, the inability to speak English well, insufficient working capital and a lack of credit, a low level of involvement and social mobilization by the group, and some distrust in the community.

24. According to Iyer and Shapiro's dynamic model (1999) of the evolution of ethnic businesses, firms evolve from the phase of doing business exclusively with their compatriots to a phase in which they sell to larger, non-ethnic markets, getting to the point of constituting an important segment of the market in trade between the native country and the receiving country. Most Brazilian immigrant businesses are still in the initial stage, which makes the clientele a critical variable in their establishment, expansion, and stability.

25. Sociability, organizational resources and the religious discourse of evangelicals are analyzed in detail in Chapter 3.

26. *Sacoleira* literally means someone who sells something out of a sack. It refers to people who bring quantities of Brazilian clothing from Brazil and resell the clothing to Brazilians in the United States. (Translator's note)

27. This was especially true up to the beginning of the 2000s, before the arrival of the Catholic Charismatic Renewal Movement in Massachusetts, as was seen in Chapter 3. This movement fostered a change in the religious discourse on immigration.

28. The study of this relationship leads back to the very birth of sociology. Therefore, it constitutes a classic theme of the discipline, an outstanding example of which is the Weberian thesis that Protestants are more disposed to capitalism because of their religious doctrine and the daily practice that arises from it. The valorization of any work and of becoming wealthier as a sign of salvation, living daily life in an ascetic and planned way, and encouragement to save and to invest all make up the new normative system that fed the increase of instrumental rationality in human activity, which was essential to the expansion of modern capitalism (Weber 1982).

29. Although in most of these areas the presence of Portuguese speakers (Cape Verdeans and Azoreans) and Hispanics is frequently noted, this is neither a necessary nor sufficient condition to attract Brazilians.

Chapter 5. Respect, Citizenship, and Solidarity: Contrasting Perceptions

1. I appreciate the comments on this chapter made by Susan Eckestein of Boston University and Josiah M. Heyman of Michigan Technological University.

2. Videotapes of television programs such as *Fantástico* (the most popular variety show in Brazil, broadcast on the Globo TV network, featuring news reports, music and other performances, and interviews) and *Jornal Nacional* (the most-watched television news magazine in Brazil) can be rented in more than a dozen Brazilian stores. It is easy to subscribe to Brazilian magazines such as *Veja*, and Brazilian newspapers are also accessible both via subscription and online.

3. In the in-depth interviews in 1995, five of the forty people interviewed reported that they had computers at home.

4. All of the Brazilian homes that I was able to enter had, without exception, a telephone and a television set.

5. See also Bash, Schiller, and Blanc 1992.

6. As will be seen later, organizations of this type are just beginning to be formed.

7. About such perceptions see also Sales 1999.

8. The total is higher than 100% because the interviewee could indicate more than one option.

9. It is important to remember that recently arrived immigrants tend to judge the destination country in a more positive manner than those who belong to the second and subsequent generations (Suárez-Orozco 1995, Suárez-Orozco and Suárez-Orozco 2001).

10. See Chapter 4, note 15.

11. Ribeiro (1998a, b) presents an interesting analysis of these perceptions.

12. In his interview, Joel did not make any kind of connection between his motivation for emigrating and his sexual orientation.

13. A hierarchical society is one in which people occupy defined places in a vertical or pyramidal social structure. This notion is used to contrast an egalitarian society, in which there are no pre-established positions and people establish relationships based on contracts between equals. The classic example of the first type of society for da Matta (1983) is Brazil and of the second, the United States.

14. Hispanics themselves reject this label as being too generic, and it consequently ignores the ethnic, racial, and cultural differences that exist in their countries of origin. They also reject it as being socially disparaging. See Oboler 1995, Dzidzienyo and Oboler 2005.

15. The state of Massachusetts offers free medical attention to pregnant women, independent of their legal status.

16. Leo Chavez, in *Shadowed Lives* (1998), examines long-term illegal immigrants who are "incorporated" into the United States, but the author analyzes personal and household dimensions, not institutional politics.

17. For a political history of citizenship rights in Brazil see José Murilo Carvalho 2002.

18. I spent three months in 2002 and one month in 2005 interviewing Brazilians about how this terrible incident had affected their lives, among other topics.

19. However, 27% of those interviewed in 2005 already had legal documentation in the United States, including practically all who arrived in 1999 or later. These figures make

the general picture more complex: it is becoming more difficult to get documentation, while on the other hand, the number of documented Brazilians is growing.

20. A *novela* or *telenovela* is a serial melodrama for television similar to a U.S. soap opera. However, a Brazilian *novela* focuses on a predetermined story of limited duration and generally last from twenty to twenty-five weeks rather that having the open-ended format of a U.S. soap opera. Brazilian *novelas* can address a wide variety of topics, including more controversial ones such as urban violence and homosexuality. *Novelas* have even portrayed the dramatization of classic works of Brazilian literature. (Translator's note)

21. A *churrascaria* is a type of Brazilian steakhouse or barbecue restaurant. These restaurants, which are becoming increasingly popular in certain regions of the United States, serve a variety of meats cooked rotisserie-style over an open flame. Generally, meals are offered at a fixed price for "all you can eat." Most *churrascarias* also offer extensive salad bars that feature both vegetables and sauces to accompany the meats. (Translator's note)

22. Dorothy Stang, an American nun and a naturalized Brazilian, was assassinated in 2005 at the age of seventy-three, killed by seven gunshots. Stang defended the rights of rural people who inhabit regions of the state of Amazonas, including the right to land. She was assassinated by squatters in the state of Pará.

23. The hierarchical mentality is still predominant in Brazil, especially in rural areas in the Brazilian Northeast, among the population with the lowest level of education and the oldest educational systems (Almeida 2007).

24. *Carioca* is an adjective that refers to something or someone from the Brazilian city of Rio de Janeiro. A *carioca*, used as a noun, means a person from Rio de Janeiro. (Translator's note)

25. In a communication with me, Cassandra White pointed out that because Margolis' book was published in 1994 and much of her work is from the late 1980s and early 1990s, some of the differences in the presence of community organizations in the two areas may be due to the time periods, as the migratory flow was recent at the time of Margolis' writing. Many of the community organizations in Massachusetts did not begin until the mid-1990s.

26. The Catholic service centers in Allston, Everett, Framingham (Good Shepherd), and Lowell were mentioned in Chapter 4 and therefore are not analyzed here. *Capoeira* is a Brazilian martial arts form. (Translator's note)

27. In 2002 alone, more than seventy cases of abuse were resolved by the CIB either through pressure on or direct negotiation with the employers or through the intervention of the Office of the Attorney General of Massachusetts (Siqueira and Lourenço 2007: 197).

28. The Association of Sister Cities Framingham–Governador Valadares and the capoeira groups are also among these. In 2003 a commission from Framingham went to Governador Valadares to begin the process of forming this alliance in the U. S. Sister Cities Program. The following year, a delegation of representatives of local government, trade organizations, and educational institutions from Governador Valadares went to Framingham for the same purpose.

29. MAPS was organized by residents of Portuguese descent, and Brazilians and Cape Verdeans have joined it.

30. See, for example, Levitt's study (1996) of Dominican immigrants in Boston.

31. The organizations mentioned by the businesspeople interviewed were the Association of Parents and Students, the Gaucho Club (Centro Tradicional Gaucho, CTG) in Somerville, MAPS, Community Development in Allston–Brighton Borough Trade, and the Hispanic-American Chamber of Commerce.

32. About the influence of Latinos see Hardy-Fanta 1993.

33. About Portuguese immigrants in the United States see Pap 1981; about Cape Verdean immigrants in Massachusetts see Halter 1995.

34. Truthfully, to me as well as to many of my interviewees, it sounds extravagant, a little exotic, that Brazilians organize themselves collectively as "Portuguese speakers." On the other hand, it sounds somewhat forced to Brazilians to identify themselves as Hispanic. Most appropriate would be to identify themselves as Latin Americans.

35. About the instrumental nature of ethnic identity see also M. Suárez-Orozco 2000.

Chapter 6. Nationality, Ethnicity, and Hybridization: Dilemmas of Racial-Ethnic Identification

1. I will use the word "affiliation" (and not "identity") in the way Hollinger uses it (2000: 6): to suggest greater flexibility in the notion of ethnic belonging and to emphasize belonging as a social process more than a psychological process.

2. A previous version of the first part of this chapter can be found in Martes 2002a.

3. The data in this chapter were collected in 2002. Returning to Brazil, I worked with Dimitri Fazito on a previous version of the second part of this chapter called "Novas tramas, novos dramas" (Martes and Fazito 2004).

4. At the time, I was a visiting scholar at the Institute for Studies of Economic Culture at Boston University (ISEC-BU). I am grateful for the support and collaboration I received from Peter Berger and Brigitte Berger and especially from Marilyn Halter.

5. Siqueira and Lourenço (2007) and Fleischer (2002) also consider that in the Brazilian case, the category "national" supersedes racial and/or ethnic categories.

6. Of the total 200 interviews, 100 were conducted via the Internet and the other 100 in Brazilian stores in Somerville. The selection technique used to choose the interviewees is known as the snowball technique. The initial locations of the network of interviewees were chosen through the local Brazilian leaders and their organizations. Over the Internet, I had a 75% return. On the form, the interviewees were asked to self-identify according to these racial categories: white, black, Native American, Asian American, Latino (or Hispanic), and other. The categories used for my survey were taken from those used by Hollinger (2000: 6).

7. In the results, 19.5% of those interviewed declared that they had never been asked to classify their ethnicity or did not know how to classify themselves. This means that they had not entered into the health care system (of programs and hospitals) or schools, because in either of these circumstances, they necessarily would have completed forms

asking their classification. These data indicate, therefore, the low level of institutional insertion among Brazilians in Boston.

8. I recall Torres-Saillant's view (1998: 165) that "declaring oneself to be Hispanic is to make a statement about the ways in which the Latin American ethnic heritage is specified, according to the parameters of mainstream culture in the United States." That author continues, "Strangely, in the American political vernacular, the Portuguese, Brazilians, and Basques are Hispanic."

9. On friction in the formation of ethnic groups and identities see Barth 1969, R. Oliveira 1976.

10. Regarding Brazilian racial and ethnic composition see the classic works of Freyre (2003), S. Holanda (1973), and D. Ribeiro (1995).

11. Most significant of these is the presence of the descendents of Europeans and Asians in the south and the southeast of Brazil.

12. To see how Brazilians self-identified in racial terms in the U.S. Census see Marrow 2002.

13. Color is a fundamental attribute for racial classification in Latin America generally because its countries were formed by different ethnic-racial groups, especially indigenous peoples, Africans, and Europeans (Guimarães 1999). But Argentina, for example, breaks the rule, as a country considered to have been formed exclusively by white European peoples (G. Ribeiro 2002).

14. As Nobles points out (2000: 84), "In Brazil, color and race are related but have been conceptually distinguished: color refers to appearance, race to origin. In the United States, race trumps color; in Brazil, color trumps race." On differences in race relations, power, and identity between Brazil and the United States see also Hanchard 1999. Regarding racial discrimination in Brazil from an historical perspective see Hasenbalg 2005.

15. For the most far-reaching aspects of the social formation of racism in Brazil, especially assimilationism centered on the notion of color and whitening, see Guimarães 1999. For explanations of a structural nature about racism in Brazil see F. Fernandes 1965, F. Cardoso and Ianni 1959. Regarding the difference between prejudice against blacks in Brazil and in the United States see Nogueira 1985; Nogueira argues that in Brazil prejudice is based on appearance and not on origin as in the United States.

16. Stress on miscegenation is not exclusively Brazilian, for it extends to various Latin American countries (Torres-Saillant and Hernández 1998).

17. In the United States the idea of cultural assimilation (conforming to the idea of Anglo-Saxon supremacy) encompasses only white European immigrants and was never extended to blacks and "mestizos," Asians, or indigenous peoples. In Brazil the idea of mixture, the myth of a nation composed of three races, encompasses whites, indigenous peoples, and blacks; it presupposes mixture, which in turn can be translated as "whitening." This is quite different from the United States, where, in Taguieff's words (1987), a "mixaphobic nationality" was formed.

18. Guimarães (1999) presents a comparison between the U.S. and Brazilian systems of race relations.

19. On the meaning of being white in the United States see Hollinger 2000.

20. The reverse is also true: "black" is a category that is often associated with poverty, and it is avoided by some Brazilians who are *mulato* or *mulata* in Brazil. See Caldwell 2007.

21. Donna Goldstein (2003) presents a very interesting analysis of the figure of the *mulata* in Brazilian history, focusing on race relations, violence, sexuality, and humor.

22. It is interesting to observe that being Latino is today a kind of wave that is arriving in Brazil through the media (TV and radio and especially music). However, this is a type of Latino constructed in the United States and, more specifically, in Miami. In this sense, I dare say that Latino pop music, which in my opinion is as Latin as it is American, has drawn Brazil closer to "Latino-ness."

23. The choice to adopt one term or the other can reveal interesting preferences. As Torres-Saillant and Hernández point out (1998), in Florida the term "Hispanic" is generally used, in California the terms "Latino" and "Chicano" are used, and in New York all are used. There is also a split along political party lines: Democrats use the term "Latino," while Republicans use the term "Hispanic." All of these names and contexts have unique histories and distinct political meanings, and the choice obviously is not a matter of mere terminology.

24. The term "Hispanic" was made official in the 1970s when the federal Office of Management and Budget defined it as "a person of Mexican, Puerto Rican, Cuban or Central American or Other Spanish culture, regardless of race" (Torres-Saillant and Hernández 1998).

25. See, for example, Padilha 1985, Oboler 1995, Jones-Correa 1998, Bonilla et al. 1998, M. Suárez-Orozco 2000. Regarding how Brazilians might contribute to this debate see Marrow 2002.

26. The word *hispano* does not exist in the Portuguese language, but the word *hispânico* does. *Hispânico* means: "1. Of, belonging to, or relative to Hispânia; 2. Of, belonging to, or relative to Spain or Spanish." Interestingly, most Brazilians claim they were not familiar with the word *hispano* before arriving in the United States (A. Holanda 1985).

27. The differentiation between Latino and Hispanic made by Brazilian immigrants based on language also is noted by Margolis (1994, 2009) and by Penha (2001: 381): "The Portuguese distinguish Brazilians from Hispanic and include Brazilians in the category Latino. Although Spanish and Portuguese are different languages, they are close to one another and have similarities that facilitate communication."

28. Margolis (1994) and Oboler (1995) note the geographic variable present in the concept of Latino.

29. Marrow (2002) found linguistic and geographic points in her research with second-generation Brazilian immigrants in Boston. While the linguistic question is obvious, the geographic question is not as simple. Marrow took the division between North America and Latin America as her principal reference. However, I believe that the principal reference adopted by Brazilians is the division between South America and the other Americas, that is, North and Central America.

30. For other Latin Americans as well, language and history are used as fundamental references that give meaning to the term "Latino" (Torres-Saillant and Hernández 1998: 161).

31. It is sufficient to consult *Dicionário Aurélio*, the most popular Portuguese-language dictionary in Brazil, for a definition of "Latino": "1. Relative to Latin; 2. Said or written in Latin; 3. Of or belonging to or referring to peoples of Latin origin: the Latin world, Latin Languages; classical Latin, Latin American" (A. Holanda 1985).

32. Some authors call people of Latin American descent living in the United States "Latinos," and they call those who live in Latin American countries "Latin Americans" (Pastor Jr. 1998 cited in Flores 1993).

33. It should also be noted that from the Brazilian perspective, the terms "United States" and "North America" are used interchangeably. The idea that Canada and Mexico also share the North American continent is completely overlooked in this terminology.

34. This confusion of the two languages in the United States may occur because, just as they do in Brazil, Brazilian immigrants use *portuñol*, the mixture of Portuguese and Spanish, to communicate with Spanish speakers.

35. They were conducted in Boston in 2002, and the interviewees were selected using the snowball technique.

36. The use of the term "worse hair" may indicate the internalization of racist categories about phenotype, as Caldwell observes (2007).

37. Thomas H. Eriksen (1991: 131) argues that first, "ethnicity is a property of social formation *and* an aspect of interaction, both systemic levels can be understood simultaneously. Secondly, ethnic differences involve cultural differences have a comparatively [*cross-culturally*] variable impact . . . on the nature of social relationships."

38. Marrow (2002) also calls attention to this point.

39. Klor de Alva (1988) has found that affluent Latino immigrants in general tend to keep themselves apart from their compatriots who belong to the working class.

40. See the discussion of second-generation Brazilians in the Conclusion.

Conclusion

1. The money was sent from Massachusetts to various Brazilian municipalities, but the greatest amounts are sent to the cities of Governador Valadares (14%), Ipatinga (5%), São Paulo and Goiânia (4%), Vitória and Belo Horizonte (3%), and Criciúma, Curitiba, and Sorocaba (2%). It is possible that the impact of these remittances is not very significant in the economic dynamic of these municipalities with the exception of the cities of Governador Valadares, Ipatinga, Criciúma, and Sorocaba in the state of Minas Gerais. This is because the others are state capitals with high demographic densities. The low percentage of funds may indicate that the effects of the remittances on the local economic dynamic are not very significant (Martes and Soares 2004).

2. Margolis has observed (2008b: 8) something in New York that has also become more pronounced in Massachusetts since the September 11 attacks: "Many Brazilians who have lived in the U.S. for years and have jobs and families in this country are prevented from returning home to visit, to attend family weddings or funerals or other important events. As such, they are caught in a vise. Since it has become so difficult to come and go from the U.S., they are afraid to risk returning to Brazil only to find they cannot get a job or otherwise support themselves there and would then be barred from

reentering the United States. I met one such undocumented Brazilian immigrant in New York City who has been 'trapped' there for eleven years, unwilling to risk a visit to her native Brazil. Her only hope of ever doing so without fear of being barred upon reentry is to marry an American or a documented immigrant, a path that would eventually permit her to get a green card."

3. In addition to my research in Governador Valadares and Ipatinga, I conducted a study in 2005 and 2006 in Poços de Caldas in Minas Gerais about return migration and entrepreneurialism; that study's title translates to English as "Lessons Away from Home: Immigration as a Type of Apprenticeship" (Martes 2005b).

4. Regarding immigration as a selective process see MacLaughlin 1990.

5. I agree with Mota (2004: 6) when she emphasizes "the highly relevant roles of television and the church, which, by occupying a significant space in daily life, offer the most efficacious 'Portuguese classes.'"

6. Mota (2004) finds that it is unknown what the chances are that Brazilian children will preserve Portuguese and reach a stable standard of bilingualism. On the other hand, the existence of social pressure to assimilate English is undeniable. However, many families wish to reconstruct the Brazilian community and make an effort to preserve Brazilian language and culture. Menezes notes (2003: 172) that "the Brazilian adaptation pattern seems to be following a path analogous to that of other immigrants, that is, unstable and transitory bilingualism that has a cycle that lasts no more than three generations." With regard to second-generation Brazilians see also Assis 2004, Sales and Loureiro 2004, Marrow 2004, De Biaggi 2002.

7. Sales and Loureiro (2004) find that the annual growth rate in the number of second-generation Brazilians in Massachusetts was 17% from 1998 to 1999, 29% from 1999 to 2000, and 24% from 2000 to 2001. Although the growth rate declined in 2000 and 2001, it has continued to rise in most subsequent years. The authors further verify an increase in the proportion of children born to Brazilian mothers from 1998 to 2001, both in raw numbers and relative to other national groups. In 1998 these births represented 0.8% of the total 81,406 children born in Massachusetts; in 1999 they represented 1.0% of this total, in 2000 they represented 1.3%, and in 2001 they represented 1.6%.

Bibliography

Abramovay, Ricardo. 2004. "Entre Deus e o diabo: Mercados e interação humana nas ciências sociais." [Between God and the devil: Markets and human interaction in the social sciences] *Tempo Social: Revista de Sociologia da USP* 16, no. 2 (November): 35–64.

Adriance, Madeleine. 1986. *Opting for the Poor*. Kansas City: Sheed and Ward.

Agência Estado. 2008."Deportação de brasileiros aumenta nos Estados Unidos" [Deportation of Brazilians increases in the United States]. http://g1.globo.com/Noticias/Mundo/0,,MUL352482-5602,00-DEPORTACAO+DE+BRASILEIROS+AUMENTA+NOS+ESTADOS+UNIDOS.html, accessed March 16, 2008.

Agência de Informações Religiosas (AGIR). http://www.agirbrasil.org.br, accessed March 15, 2010.

Allen, James P. and Eugene Turner. 2004. "Boston's emerging ethnic quilt: A geographic perspective. Presented at the Annual Meeting of the Population Association of America, Boston, April 1. http://www.csun.edu/~hfgeg005/eturner/gallery/Bostonatlas/B6Brazilian.pdf, accessed August 22, 2009.

Almeida, Alberto C. 2007. *A cabeça do brasileiro* [The Brazilian's head]. Rio de Janeiro: Record.

Amin, Ash, ed. 1994. *Post-Fordism: A Reader*. Oxford, England: Blackwell.

Apostolado Brasileiro nos Estados Unidos da América. n.d. "Comunidades católicas do Apostolado Brasileiro nos Estados Unidos da América." http://www.apostoladobrasileiro.com, accessed June 22, 2009.

Assis, Gláucia. 1995. "Estar aqui, estar lá" [Being here, being there]. Master's thesis, Universidade Federal de Santa Catarina, Florianópolis, Brazil.

———. *2003. "Os novos fluxos de migração internacional da população brasileira e as transformações nas redes familiares e de gêneroô [The new flows of international migration of the Brazilian population and the transformations in family and gender networks]. In Martes and Fleischer, Fronteiras cruzadas.*

———. 2004. "De Criciúma para o mundo: Rearranjos familiares e de gênero nas vivências dos novos migrantes brasileiros" [From Criciúma to the world: Family and gender rearrangements in the lives of the new Brazilian immigrants]. Ph.D. diss., Universidade Estadual de Campinas, Unicamp, Brazil.

Assmann, Hugo. 1986. *A igreja eletrônica e seu impacto na América Latina* [The electronic church and its impact on Latin America]. Petrópolis, Brazil: Editora Vozes.

Ávila, Fernando Bastos. 1991. *Pequena enciclopédia de doutrina social da igreja* [Little encyclopedia of the church's social doctrine]. São Paulo: Editora Loyola.

Azevedo, Tânia Maria Cordeiro de. 2003. "Brinquedos e gênero na educação infantil: um estudo do tipo etnográfico no Estado do Rio de Janeiro" [Toys and gender in childhood education: An ethnographic study in Rio de Janeiro state]. Ph.D. diss., Faculdade de Educação, Universidade de São Paulo, 2003.

Baltar, Paulo, and Cláudio Dedecca. 1997. "O mercado de trabalho no Brasil: O aumento da informalidade nos anos 90" [The labor market in Brazil: The growth of informality in the 90s]. Paper presented at the workshop O Setor Informal Revisitado: Novas Evidências e Perspectivas de Políticas Públicas [The informal sector revisited: New evidence and public policy perspectives]. Instituto de Pesquisa Econômica Aplicada (IPEA), Brasília, July.

Barreto, Luiz Paulo Teles Ferreira. 2001. "Considerações sobre a imigração no Brasil contemporâneo" [Considerations about immigration in contemporary Brazil]. In *Migrações internacionais: Contribuições para políticas* [International migrations: Contributions to policies], ed. Mary Garcia Castro, part 1, 63–72. Brasília: Comissão Nacional de População e Desenvolvimento.

Barros, Sebastião do Rego. 1996–1997. "O Itamaraty e os Brasileiros no exterior" [Itamaraty and Brazilians abroad]. *Revista Política Externa* 5, no. 3 (December/January/February): 106–114.

Barth, Frederick, ed. 1969. *Ethnic Groups and Boundaries: The Social Organization of Cultural Difference*. Boston: Little Brown.

Bash, Linda, Nina Glick Schiller, and Cristina Blanc. 1992. *Towards a Transnational Perspective on Migration: Race, class, ethnicity, and nationalism reconsidered*. Annals of the New York Academy of Science, July, 1–258.

Bassanezi, Maria Silvia Casagrande Beozzo. 1995. "Imigrações internacionais no Brasil: Um panorama histórico" [International immigrations in Brazil: A historical panorama]. In Patarra *Emigração e imigração internacionais*, 1–38.

Baudrillard, Jean. 1986. *América*. Rio de Janeiro: Rocco.

Becker, Gary. 1993. *Human Capital*. Chicago: University of Chicago Press.

Bell, Daniel. 1975. "Ethnicity and Social Change." In *Ethnicity: Theory and Experience*, ed. Nathan Glazer and Daniel P. Moynihan, 141–175. Cambridge: Harvard University Press.

Berger, Peter L., and Robert W. Hefner. 2003. *Spiritual Capital in Comparative Perspective*. Institute for the Study of Economic Culture and Institute on Religion and World Affairs, Boston University. http://www.spiritualcapitalresearchprogram.com/pdf/Berger.pdf, accessed September 13, 2009.

Beserra, Bernadette. 2005. "From Brazilians to Latinos? Racialization and Latinidad in the Making of Brazilian Carnival in Los Angeles." *Latino Studies* 3, no. 1 (April): 53–75.

Bicalho, José V. 1989. *Yes, eu sou brazuka* [Yes, I am a Brazuka]. Governador Valadares, Brazil: Fundação Serviço de Educação e Cultura (FUNSEC).

Boff, Leonardo. 1978. *Jesus Cristo Libertador: A Critical Christology for Our Time*. New York: Orbis Books.

Bonacich, Edna, and John Modell. 1980. *The Economic Basis of Ethnic Solidarity*. Berkeley: University of California Press.

Bonilla, Frank, Edwin Melendez, Rebecca Morales, and Maria de los Angeles Torres. 1998. *Borderless Borders: U.S. Latinos, Latin Americans, and the Paradox of Interdependence*. Philadelphia: Temple University Press.

Borjas, George. 1990. *Friends of Strangers: The Impact of Immigrants on the U.S. Economy*. New York: Basic Books.

Borjas, George, and Marta Tienda, eds. 1985. *Hispanics in the U.S. Economy*. New York: Academic Press.

Boswell, Christina. 2003. *European Migration Policies in Flux: Changing Patterns of Inclusion and Exclusion*. Bognor, England: Wiley-Blackwell.

Bourdieu, Pierre. 1989. *O poder simbólico* [Symbolic power]. Rio de Janeiro: Editora DIFEL.

———. 1996. *A economia das trocas lingüísticas* [The economy of linguistic exchanges]. São Paulo: Editora da Universidade de São Paulo (EDUSP).

Bourdieu, Pierre, and Loïc Wacquant. 2000. "The Organic Ethnologist of Algerian Migration." *Ethnography* 1, no. 2: 173–182.

Boyd, Mônica. 1989. "Family and Personal Networks in International Migration: Recent Developments and New Agendas." *International Migration Review*, no. 23: 638–670.

Brandão, Carlos Rodrigues. 1988. "Ser católico: Dimensões brasileiras" [Being Catholic: Brazilian dimensions]. In *Religião e identidade* [Religion and identity], ed. Viola Sachs. Rio de Janeiro: Graal Editora.

Brazil, Ministério das Relações Exteriores (MRE). 2009. "Brasileiros no mundo: Estimativas" [Brazilians in the world: Estimates]. sistemas.mre.gov.br/kitweb/datafiles/BRMundo/pt-br/file /Brasileiros% 20no%20Mundo%20-%20Estimativas.pdf, accessed June 22, 2009.

Brazilian American Association. 2009. http://www.framingham.com/org/bramas.htm, accessed June 22, 2009.

Brazilian Children's Foundation. 2009. "Brazilian Children's Foundation." *Framingham Online* http://www.framingham.com/org/br_child.htm, accessed June 22, 2009.

Brazilian Women's Group. 2009. www.verdeamarelo.org/home, accessed March 1, 2009.

Brito, Fausto. 1995. "Os povos em movimento: As migrações internacionais no desenvolvimento do capitalismo" [Peoples in movement: International migrations in the development of capitalism]. In Patarra, *Emigração e imigração internacionais*, 53–66.

Buijs, Gina. 1993. *Migrant Women*. Oxford, England: Berg.

Burt, Ronald S. 1992. *Structural Holes*. Cambridge: Harvard University Press.

Butler, John S., and Patricia G. Greene. 1997. "Ethnic Entrepreneurship: The Continuous Rebirth of American Enterprise." In *Entrepreneurship 2000*, ed. D. L. Sexton and R. W. Smilor, 267–289. Chicago: Upstart.

Caccamali, Maria Cristina. 1997. "Notas sobre o processo de informalização no mercado de trabalho no contexto da globalização" [Notes on the process of informalization in the labor market in the context of globalization]. Paper presented at the workshop O Setor Informal Revisitado: Novas Evidências e Perspectivas de Políticas Públicas [The informal sector revisited: New evidence and public policy perspectives]. Instituto de Pesquisa Econômica Aplicada (IPEA), Brasília, July.

Caldwell, Kia Lilly. 2007. *Negras in Brazil.* Piscataway, N.J.: Rutgers University Press.

Camargo, C.P.A.F., A. F. Pierucci, F. Procópio, and M. S. Beatriz. 1980. "Comunidades eclesiais de base." In *São Paulo: O povo em movimento*, ed. Paul Singer, 59–81. São Paulo: Vozes/CEBRAP.

Candland, C. 2000. "Faith as Social Capital: Religion and Community Development in Southern Asia." *Policy Sciences* 33, no. 3/4: 355–374.

Capuano, Adriana. 2002. "Brasileiros em Miami" [Brazilians in Miami]. Research report for Ph.D. diss., Departamento de Ciências Sociais, Universidade Estadual de Campinas.

Cardoso, Fernando Henrique. 1993. "Livros que inventaram o Brasil" [Books that invented Brazil]. *Novos Estudos* (Centro Brasileiro de Análise e Planejamento, CEBRAP), no. 37 (November).

Cardoso, Fernando Henrique, and Otávio Ianni. 1959. *Cor e mobilidade social e Florianópolis* [Color and social mobility and Florianópolis]. São Paulo: Companhia Editora Nacional.

Cardoso, Ruth. 1978. "Sociedade e poder: As representações dos favelados em São Paulo" [Society and power: The representations of São Paulo slumdwellers]. *Ensaios de Opinião* 6: 38–44.

Cardoso de Oliveira, Luís Roberto. 1996. "Entre o justo e o solidário: Os dilemas dos direitos de cidadania no Brasil e nos EUA" [Between fairness and solidarity: The dilemmas of the rights of citizenship in Brazil and in the USA]. *Revista Brasileira de Ciências Sociais* (ANPOCS) 11, no. 31: 67–81.

———. 2001a. "Direitos republicanos, identidades coletivas e esfera pública no Brasil e no Quebec" [Republican rights, collective identities and the public sphere in Brazil]. Série Antropologia, no. 304, Universidade de Brasília, Departamento de Antropologia.

———. 2001b. *Individualismo, identidades coletivas e cidadania: Os Estados Unidos e o Quebec vistos do Brasil* [Individualism, collective identities and citizenship: The United States and Quebec seen from Brazil]. Série Antropologia, no. 299, Departamento de Antropologia, Universidade de Brasília.

Carlini-Cotrim, Beatriz. 1995. "Percepções sobre o papel da família na determinação do comportamento de usar drogas: Um estudo exploratório entre imigrantes brasileiros vivendo em Boston, MA" [Perceptions on the role of the family in the determination of drug use behavior: An exploratory study of Brazilian immigrant families living in Boston, Mass.]. Mimeograph. Boston.

Carvalho, José Alberto Magno. 1995. *Um novo padrão demográfico brasileiro* [A new Brazilian demographic pattern]. Brasília: Demográfica.

Carvalho, José Murilo. 2002. *Cidadania no Brasil* [Citizenship in Brazil]. Rio de Janeiro: Civilização Brasileira.

Cashmore, Ellis. 1996. *Dictionary of Race and Ethnic Relations.* London: Routledge.

Castro, G. P. 1987. *As comunidades de dom: Um estudo de CEBs no Recife* [Gifted communities: A study of CEBs in Recife]. Recife, Brazil: Massangana Editora.

Castro, Mary Garcia. 1982. "Mary and Eve's Social Reproduction in the Big Apple: Colombian Voices." Occasional Papers, no. 35; presented at the conference Colombians and Dominicans in New York: Life Strategies in the Household and at Work, New York, June 4.

———, ed. 1989. "Mulheres latino americanas e caribenhas na migração: Bibliográfica comentada" [Latin American and Caribbean women in migration: Annotated bibliography]. Salvador, Brazil: Centro de Recursos Humanos/Universidade Federal da Bahia.

———. 1995. "Latinos nos Estados Unidos: Unindo Américas, fazendo a América de lá ou perdendo a nossa América?" [Latinos in the United States: Uniting Americas, making the America of over there, or losing our America?]. In *A sociologia entre a modernidade e a contemporaneidade* [Sociology between modernity and contemporaneity], ed. Sérgio Adorno. Porto Alegre, Brazil: Editora UFRGS.

———, ed. 2001. *Migrações Internacionais: Contribuições para políticas.* Brasília, Brazil: Comissão Nacional de População e Desenvolvimento (CNPD).

Centro de Estatísticas Religiosas e Investigações Sociais (CERIS). 2004. http://www.ceris.org.br, accessed September 14, 2009.

Centro do Imigrante Brasileiro (CIB). 2009. http:www.braziliancenter.org/site, accessed March 3, 2009.

César, Waldo. 1974. "Urbanização e religiosidade popular" [Urbanization and popular religiosity]. *Revista de Cultura Vozes* 68, no.7. pp.19–28. (September).

Chavez, Leo R. 1998. *Shadowed Lives: Undocumented Immigrants in American Society.* 2d edition. Fort Worth: Harcourt Brace College.

Chen, Carolyn. 2006a. "Evangelical Christianity Reconstructing Taiwanese Immigrant Families in the United States." *International Migration Review* (Center for Migration Studies, New York) 40, no. 3: 573–602.

———. 2006b. "From Filial Piety to Religious Piety: Christianity, Social Change, and Globalization in the City of Somerville." *International Migration Review* 40, no. 3: 573–602.

Christian, Shirley. 1998. "Hispanic Workers Revitalize a Town." *New York Times*, January 29.

Colen, Shlee. 1989. "Just a Little Respect: West Indian Domestic Workers in New York City." In *Muchachas no more: Household workers in Latin America and the Caribbean*, eds. Elsa Chaney and Mary Garcia Castro. Philadelphia: Temple University Press.

Coleman, James. 1990. *Foundations of Social Theory.* Cambridge: Harvard University Press.

Cornelius, Wayne. 1982. "Interviewing Undocumented Immigrants: Methodological Reflections-Based Fieldwork in Mexico and the U.S." *International Migration Review* 16, no. 2: 378–411.

Cornelius, Wayne, and Jorge Bustamante. 1989. *Mexican Migration to the United States: Origins, Consequences, and Policy Options.* San Diego, California: Center for U.S.-Mexican Studies, University of California.

Costa, Heloisa. 1995. "Vale do Aço: Da produção da cidade moderna sob a grande indústria à diversificação do meio ambiente urbano" [Steel valley: From the production of the modern city under big industry to the diversification of the urban environment]. Research report for Ph.D. diss., Centro de Desenvolvimento e Planejamento Regional, Faculdade de Ciências Econômicas, Universidade Federal de Minas Gerais, Belo Horizonte.

Cox, Harvey. 1995. *Fire from Heaven: The Rise of Pentecostal Spirituality and the Reshaping of Religion in the 21st Century*. Reading, Massachusetts: Addison-Wesley.

Cunha, Manuela Carneiro. 1985. *Negros estrangeiros* [Foreign blacks]. São Paulo: Brasiliense.

da Matta, Roberto. 1983. *Carnaval malandros e heróis: Para uma sociologia do dilema brasileiro* [Carnaval, rogues, and heroes: Toward a sociology of the Brazilian dilemma]. Rio de Janeiro: Editora Guanabara.

———. 2000. Interview in *Quatro autores em busca do Brasil* [Four authors in search of Brazil], ed. Leny Cordeiro and Jose Geraldo Couto. Rio de Janeiro: Rocco.

Da Vanzo, Julie. 1981. *Review of Migration and Economic Growth in the United States: National, Regional, and Metropolitan Perspectives*. Santa Monica, Calif.: Rand Corp.

Davis, Kingsley. 1989. "Social Science Approaches to International Migration." In *Population and Resources in Western Intellectual Traditions*, ed. Michael S. Teitelbaum and Jay M. Winter, 245–261. New York: Cambridge University Press.

De Biaggi, Sylvia. 1992. "From Minas to Mass: A Qualitative Study of Five Brazilian Families in Boston." Master's thesis, Department of Psychology, Boston University.

———. 2002. *Changing Gender Roles: Brazilian Immigrant Families in the U.S.* New York: LFB Scholarly Publishing.

de Freitas, Gregory. 1991. *Inequality at Work—Hispanics in the U.S. Labor Force*. New York: Oxford University Press.

DHS. See U.S. Department of Homeland Security.

Dillon, Sam. 1997. "Job Search Lures Mexicans to Far Corners of U.S." *New York Times*, February 4.

Dunning, John H., and Khalil A. Hamdani. 1997. *The New Globalism and Developing Countries*. New York: United Nations University Press.

Durkheim, Émile. 1984. *The Division of Labor in Society*. New York: Free Press.

Dzidzienyo, Anani, and Suzanne Oboler, eds. 2005. *Neither Enemies nor Friends: Latinos, Blacks, Afro-Latinos*. New York: Palgrave Macmillan.

Ebaugh, H. R. 2003. "Religion and the new immigrants." In *Handbook for the sociology of religion*, ed. M. Dillon, 225–240. New York: Cambridge University Press, 2003.

Ebaugh, H. R., and Janet S. Chafetz. 2000. *Religion and the New Immigrants: Continuities and Adaptations in Immigrant Congregations*. Walnut Creek, Calif.: Altamira Press.

Ehrenreich, Barbara, and Arlie Russell Hochschild. 2002. *Global Woman: Nannies, Maids, and Sex Workers in the New Economy*. London: Granta Books.

Emmanuel Gospel Center. *The Boston Church Directory*. Boston: Emmanuel Gospel Center. http://www.egc.org/churches, accessed June 22, 2009.

Eriksen, Thomas. 1991. "The Cultural Contexts of Ethnic Differences." *Man: The Journal of the Royal Anthropological Institute* 26, no. 1: 127–144.

Fazito, Dimitri. 2008. "Reflexões sobre os sistemas de migração internacional: Proposta para uma análise estrutural dos mecanismos intermediários" [Reflections on the systems of international migration: proposal for a structural analysis of the intermediary mechanisms]. Research report for Ph.D. diss., Centro de Desenvolvimento e Planejamento Regional, Universidade Federal de Minas Gerais, Belo Horizonte, Brazil.

Fazito, Dimitri, and Ana Cristina Braga Martes. 2004. "Novas tramas, novos dramas: O emigrante brasileiro negro nos Estados Unidos" [New tales, new dramas: The black Brazilian immigrant in the United States]. Paper presented at the 28th annual meeting of the Associação Nacional de Pós-Graduação em Ciências Sociais, October 27–29, Caxambu, Brazil.

Feldman-Bianco, Bela, and Graça Capinha, eds. 2000. *Identidades: Estudo de cultura e poder* [Identities: A study of culture and power]. São Paulo: Editora Hucitec.

Feldman-Bianco, Bela, and Donna Huse. 1995. "Entre a saudade da terra e a América: Memória cultural, trajetórias de vida e (re)construção de identidade feminina na interseção de culturas" [Between missing the homeland and América: Cultural memory, trajectories of life, and (re)construction of feminine identity in the intersection of cultures]. *Ler História* (Lisbon) 27/28: 45–73.

Fernandes, Florestan. 1965. *A integração do negro na sociedade de classes* [The integration of blacks into class society]. São Paulo: Companhia Editora Nacional.

Fernandes, L. B. A. 1985. "The Contribution of Basic Ecclesial Communities to an Education for Social Transformation in Brazil." Ph.D. diss., Graduate School of Education, Harvard University.

Fernandes, Ruben César, coord. 1996. *Novo nascimento: Os evangélicos em casa, na igreja e na política* [New birth: Evangelicals at home, in church, and in politics]. Research report. Rio de Janeiro: Instituto de Estudos da Religião (ISER).

Ferro, José Roberto. 1988. "Strangers and Clandestines in America: Brazilian Immigrants in the Boston Area." Mimeograph. Cambridge: MIT.

Fleischer, Soraya. 2002. *Passando a América a limpo: O trabalho de housecleaners brasileiras em Boston, Massachusetts* [Cleaning America: The work of Brazilian women housecleaners in Boston, Massachusetts]. São Paulo: Annablume.

Fligstein, Neil. 2001. *The Architecture of Markets*. Princeton, N.J.: Princeton University Press.

Flores, Juan. 1993. *Divided Borders: Essays on Puerto Rican Identity*. Houston: Arte Público Press.

Foner, Nancy, ed. 1987. *New Immigrants in New York*. New York: Columbia University Press.

Forjás, Maria Cecília S. 1993. "Os exilados da década de 80: Imigrantes brasileiros nos Estados Unidos" [Exiles of the 1980s: Brazilian immigrants in the United States]. *Revista de Administração de Empresas* 33, no. 1 (January–February): 66–83.

Fortuna, Juan, and Suzana Prates. 1989. "Informal Sector Versus Informalized Labor Relations in Uruguay." In Portes, Castells, and Benton, *Informal Economy*.

Freire, Paulo. 1979. *A pedagogia do oprimido* [Pedagogy of the oppressed]. São Paulo: Brasiliense.

Freitas, P. S., and P. Montagner. 1997. "Evolução das inserções ocupacionais na região metropolitana de São Paulo" [Evolution of Ocupational insertions in São Paulo's metropolitan region]. Paper presented at the workshop O Setor Informal Revisitado:

Novas Evidências e Perspectivas de Políticas Públicas [The informal sector revisited: New evidence and public policy perspectives]. Instituto de Pesquisa Econômica Aplicada (IPEA), Brasília, July 9–10.

Freyre, Gilberto. 2003. *Casa grande e senzala: Formação da família brasileira sob regime de economia patriarcal* [The masters and the slaves: The formation of the Brazilian family under the regime of the patriarchial economy]. Rio de Janeiro: Maia e Shmidt.

Fry, Peter, and G. Howe. 1975. "Duas respostas à aflição: Umbanda e pentecostalismo" [Two answers to affliction: Umbanda and Pentacostalism]. *Debate e Crítica*, no. 6: 75–94.

Fukuyama, F. 1995. *Trust: Social Virtues and the Creation of Prosperity*. New York: Free Press.

Fusco, Wilson. 2001. "Redes sociais na migração internacional: O caso de Governador Valadares" [Social networks in international migration: The case of Governador Valadares]. Campinas, Brazil: Universidade Estadual de Campinas (Unicamp), Núcleo de Estudos de População (NEPO) 40.

———. 2005. "Capital cordial: A reciprocidade entre os imigrantes brasileiros nos Estados Unidos" [Cordial capital: Reciprocity among the Brazilian immigrants in the United States]. Research report for Ph.D. diss., Departamento de Demografia do Instituto de Filosofia e Ciências Humanas, Universidade Estadual de Campinas, Brazil.

Galetti, R. 1995. "Migrantes estrangeiros no centro de São Paulo: Coreanos e bolivianos" [Foreign migrants in downtown São Paulo: Koreans and Bolivians]. In Patarra, *Emigração e imigração internacionais*, 133–143.

Gans, Herbert. 1979. "Symbolic Ethnicity: The Future of Ethnic Groups and Cultures in América." *Ethnic and Racial Studies* 2, no. 1 (January): 1–20.

Geertz, Clifford. 1962. "The Rotating Credit Association: A 'Middle Rung' in Development." *Economic Development and Cultural Change* 10, no. 3 (April): 241–263.

———. 1983. *Local Knowledge: Further Essays in Interpretative Anthropology*. New York: Basic Books.

George, A., and T. Achilles. 1969. *Modern Dictionary of Sociology*. New York: Thomas Crowell.

Giannini, Deborah, and Rachel Guedes. 2005. "Terra estrangeira" [Foreign land]. *Revista Folha* (São Paulo), March.

Giannocaro, Daniela. 2006. "Empreendedorismo étnico e políticas públicas" [Ethnic entrepreneurialism and public policies]. Final report to the Programa Institucional de Bolsas de Iniciação Científica (PIBIC). São Paulo: Fundação Getulio Vargas.

Glazer, Nathan, and Daniel P. Moynihan. 1970. *Beyond the Melting Pot: The Negroes, Puerto Ricans, Jews, Italians, and Irish of New York City*. Cambridge: MIT Press.

———, eds. 1975. *Ethnicity: Theory and Experience*. Cambridge: Harvard University Press.

Goldstein, Donna. 2003. *Laughter out of Place: Race, Class, Violence, and Sexuality in a Rio Shantytown*. Berkeley: University of California Press.

Goza, Franklin. 1992. "A imigração brasileira na América do Norte" [Brazilian Immigration in North America]. *Revista Brasileira de Estudos de População* 9, no. 1: 65–81.

———. 1994. "Brazilian Immigrants to North America." *International Migration Review* 28, no. 1: 136–152.

———. 2003. "Redes sociais e integração dos brasileiros nos Estados Unidos e no Canadá" [Social networks and the integration of Brazilians in the United States and Canada]. In Martes and Fleischer, *Fronteiras cruzadas*, 263–288.

———. 2004. "An Overview of Brazilian Life as Portrayed by the 2000 U.S. Census." Paper presented at the 14th Encontro Nacional de Estudos Populacionais, Associação Brasileira de Estudos Populacionais (ABEP), Caxambu, Brazil, September 20–24.

Granovetter, Mark. 1973. "The Strength of Weak Ties." *American Journal of Sociology* 78, no. 6: 1360–1380.

———. 1985. "Economic Action and Social Structure: The problem of embeddedness." *American Journal of Sociology* 91, no. 3: 481–510.

———. 1995. *Getting a Job: A Study of Contacts and Careers*. 2d edition. Chicago: University of Chicago Press.

Greear, Priscilla. 2005. "Brazilian Catholics Celebrate Foothold at St. Jude's." *Georgia Bulletin*. http://www.georgiabulletin.org/local/2005/09/01/brazilian/, accessed July 2009.

Greeley, Andrew M. 1997. *Religious Change in America*. Cambridge: Harvard University Press.

Gremaud, Amaury P., Marco Antônio Vasconcelos, and Rudinei Toneto Junior. 2002. *Economia brasileira contemporânea* [Contemporary Brazilian economy]. São Paulo: Atlas.

Grün, Roberto. 1992. "Sindicalismo e anti-sindicalismo e a gênese das novas classes médias brasileiras" [Unionization and anti-unionization, and the genesis of new Brazilian middle classes]. *Dados: Revista de Ciências Sociais* 35, no. 3: 435–471.

Guimarães, Antônio Sérgio. 1999. *Racismo e anti-racismo no Brasil* [Racism and antiracism in Brazil]. São Paulo: Editora 34.

Gans, Herbert. 1979. "Symbolic Ethnicity: The Future of Ethnic Groups and Cultures in America." *Ethnic and Racial Studies*, no. 2 (January): 1–20.

Gutierrez, Gustavo. 1973. *A Theology of Liberation*. New York: Orbis Books.

Habermas, Jürgen. 1995. "O estado-nação europeu frente aos desafios da globalização" [The European nation-state in the face of the challenges of globalization]. *Novos Estudos* (Centro Brasileiro de Análise e Planejamento, CEBRAP), no. 43: 87–101.

Hagan, Jacqueline, and Helen Rose Ebaugh. 2003. "Calling upon the Sacred: The Use of Religion in the Process of Migration." *International Migration Review* 37, no. 4 (Winter): 1145–1162.

Hall, Stuart. 2001. *A identidade cultural na pós-modernidade* [Cultural identity in postmodernity]. Rio de Janeiro: DP&A.

Halter, Marilyn, ed. 1995. *New Migrants in the Marketplace: Boston's Ethnic Entrepreneurs*. Cambridge: University of Massachusetts Press.

Hanchard, Michael, ed. 1999. *Racial Politics in Contemporary Brazil*. Durhan, NC: Duke University Press.

Handlin, Oscar. 1973. *The Uprooted: The Epic Story of the Great Migrations That Made the American People*. 2d edition. Boston: Little Brown. Originally published 1951.

Hardy-Fanta, Carol. 1993. *Latina Politics, Latino Politics*. Philadelphia: Temple University Press.

Harris, J., and M. Todaro. 1970. *Migration, Unemployment, and Development: A Two-Sector Analysis*. New York: American Economic Review.

Harvey, David. 1992. *The Condition of Postmodernity*. Cambridge: Blackwell.

Hasenbalg, Carlos. 2005. *Discriminação e desigualdade raciais no Brasil* [Racial discrimination and inequality in Brazil]. Belo Horizonte: Editora UFMG; Rio de Janeiro: Editora UFRJ.

Hayek, Friedrich. 1985. *Direito, legislação e liberdade: Uma nova formulação dos princípios liberais de justiça e economia política* [Law, legislation, and liberty: A new formulation of the liberal principals of justice and political economy]. 3 volumes. São Paulo: Visão.

Heisler, Michele. 1997. "Brazilians in East Boston: A Demographic Description and Assessment of Health Status, Services Utilization, and Barriers to Access to Health Care." *East Boston Neighborhood Health Center* (January).

Hellwig, David, ed. 1992. *African-American Reflections on Brazil's Racial Paradise*. Philadelphia: Temple University Press.

Herberg, W. 1960. *Protestant-Catholic-Jew: An Essay in American Religious Sociology*. Garden City, N.Y.: Doubleday.

Hero, Rodney, 1992. *Latinos and the U.S. Political System*. Philadelphia: Temple University Press.

Hirschman, Charles. 2004. "The Role of Religion in the Origins and Adaptation of Immigrant Groups in the United States." *International Migration Review* 38, no. 3: 1206–1233.

Holanda, Aurélio Buarque. 1985. *Dicionário Aurélio*. Rio de Janeiro: Editora Nova Fronteira.

Holanda, Sergio Buarque. 1973. *Raízes do Brasil* [The roots of Brazil]. Rio de Janeiro: José Olympio Editora.

Hollinger, David. 2000. *Postethnic America*. New York: Basic.

Hondagneu-Sotelo, Pierrette. 2001. *Doméstica: Immigrant Cleaning and Caring in the Shadows of Affluence*. Berkeley: University of California Press.

Instituto Brasileiro de Geografia e Estadística (IBGE). 2000. Censo 2000. http://www.ibge.gov.br/home/estatistica/populacao/censo2000/default.shtm, accessed April 12, 2006 and March 19, 2010.

———. 2004. "Pesquisa nacional por amostra de domicílios (PNAD), 2004" [National research through domicile sampling]. http://www.ibge.gov.br, accessed April 12, 2006.

International Labor Organization (ILO). 2006. *Trabajo Decente en las Américas: Una agenda hemisférica, 2006–2015* [Decent work in the Americas: A hemispheric agenda, 2006–2015]. http://www.ilo.org/public/spanish/standards/relm/rgmeet/16amr/dwork.pdf accessed in December 12, 2009.

Isto É. 1995. "Muito além do diploma" [Far beyond the diploma]. November 15.

Iyer, G. R. 2004. "Ethnic Business Families." In Stiles and Galbraith, *Ethnic Entrepreneurship*.

Iyer, G. R., and J. M. Shapiro. 1999. "Ethnic Entrepreneurship and Marketing Systems: Implications for the Global Economy." *Journal of International Marketing* 7, no. 4: 83–110.

Janowitz, Morris. 1966. *On Social Organization and Social Control.* Chicago: University of Chicago.

Jarim, Denise Fagundes. 2006. "Os imigrantes palestinos na América Latina" [Palestinian immigrants in Latin America]. *Estudos Avançados* 20, no. 57 (May/August): 171–181.

Jones, Gareth. 1983. "Life History Methodology." In Morgan, *Beyond Method*, 147–159.

Jones-Correa, Michael. 1998. *Between Two Nations: The Political Predicament of Latinos in New York City.* New York: Cornell University Press.

Jordan, Miriam. 2002. "With Millions on the Move, This Guide Maps the Routes to Prosperity." *Wall Street Journal*, December 27.

Jorge, Angela. 1997. "Pesquisa de economia informal urbana" [A study of the informal urban economy]. Paper presented at the workshop O Setor Informal Revisitado: Novas Evidências e Perspectivas de Políticas Públicas [The informal sector revisited: New evidence and public policy perspectives]. Instituto de Pesquisa Econômica Aplicada (IPEA), Brasília, July.

Josselson, Rutlellen, and Amia Liblich, eds. 1995. *Interpreting Experience: The Narrative Study of Lives.* Vol. 3. London: Sage.

Jouët-Pastré, Clémence, and Leticia J. Braga, eds. 2008. *Becoming Brazuca: Brazilian Immigration to the United States.* Cambridge: Harvard University Press.

Kawamura, Lili. 1999. *Para onde vão os brasileiros?* [Where are the Brazilians going?]. Campinas, Brazil: Editora Unicamp.

Kelly, Patricia Fernandez. 1995. "Social and Cultural Capital in the Urban Ghetto: Implications for the Economic Sociology of Immigration." In Portes, *Economic Sociology of Immigration.*

———. 1998. "From Estrangement to Affinity: Dilemma of Identity among Hispanic Children." In Bonilla et al., *Borderless Borders.*

Kim, Illsoo. 1987. *The New Urban Immigrants: The Korean Community in New York.* Princeton, N.J.: Princeton University Press.

King, Gary, Robert Keohane, and Sidney Verba. 1994. *Designing Social Inquiry.* Princeton, N.J.: Princeton University Press.

Klor de Alva, Jorge. 1988. "Telling Hispanics Apart: Latino Sociocultural Diversity." In *The Hispanic Experience in the United States*, Edna Acosta-Belén and Barbara R. Sjostrom. New York: Praeger.

Kritz, Mary, Charles Keely, and Silvano Tomasi, eds. 1981. *Global Trends in Migration: Theory and Research on International Population Movements.* Staten Island, NY: Center for Migration Studies.

Lado, Karen. 1994. "Immigrant Workers in the Cleaning Industry: The Central American Experience in Boston." Master's thesis, Department of Urban Studies and Planning, MIT.

Lapham, Susan. 1990. "The Foreign Born Population in the United States: 1990." Washington, D.C.: U.S. Bureau of the Census, Population Division, Ethnic and Hispanic Branch.

Lawrence-Lightfoot, Sara. 2000. *Respect: An Exploration*. Reading, MA: Perceus.

Levenson, Michael, and Yuxing Zeng. 2006. "Immigrant Numbers up 15% in State since 2000—Biggest Hike Comes from Latin America." *Boston Globe*. http://www.boston.com/news/local /articles/2006/08/16/immigrant_numbers_up_15_in_state_since_2000/, accessed August 16, 2006.

Levitt, Peggy. 1995. "A Todos los Llamo Primo: The Social Basis for Latino Small Businesses." In Halter, *New Migrants in the Marketplace*.

———. 1996. "Assimilation, Pluralism, or Transnationalism?: Migration's Transformation of Religious Life in Boston and the Dominican Republic." Paper presented at the American Sociological Association meetings, New York, August.

———. 2000. *The Urban Villagers*. Berkeley: University of California Press.

———. *2003*. "You Know, Abraham Was Really the First Immigrant: Religion and Transnational Migration." *International Migration Review* 37, no. 3: 847–873.

Light, Ivan Hubert. 2004. "The Ethnic Ownership Economy." In Stiles and Galbraith, *Entrepreneurship: Structure and Process*.

Light, Ivan Hubert, and E. *Bonacich*. 1988. *Immigrant Entrepreneurs*. Berkeley: University of California Press.

Light, Ivan Hubert, and Steven J. Gold. 2000. *Ethnic Economies*. San Diego, Calif.: Academic Press.

Light, Ivan Hubert, and Carolyn Nancy Rosenstein. 1995. *Race, Ethnicity, and Entrepreneurship in Urban America*. New York: A. de Gruyter.

Light, Ivan, Georges Sabagh, Mehdi Bozorgmehr, and Claudia Der-Martirosian. 1995. "Ethnic Economy or Ethnic Enclave Economy?" In Halter, *New Migrants in the Marketplace*, 23–42.

Light, Ivan, Richard Bernard, and Rebecca Kim. 1999. "Immigrant Incorporation in the Garment Industry of Los Angeles." *International Migration Review* 33, no. 1 (Spring): 5–25.

Machado, Maria das Dores Campos. 1996. Carismáticos e pentecostais: Adesão religiosa na esfera familiar [Charismatics and pentecostals: Religious adherence in the family sphere]. Campinas: Editora Autores Associados/ANPOCS.

Machado, Maria das Dores, and Cecília Mariz. 1997. "Mulheres e prática religiosa nas classes populares" [Women and religious practice in the working classes]. *Revista Brasileira de Ciências Sociais* 12, no. 34: 71–87.

Maclaughlin, Virginia. 1990. *Immigration Reconsidered*. Oxford, England: Oxford University Press.

Mahler, Sarah. 1995. *American dreaming: Immigrant life on the margins*. Princeton, N.J.: Princeton University Press.

Mainwaring, S. 1986. *The Catholic Church and Politics in Brazil: 1916–1985*. Stanford, Calif.: Stanford University Press.

Maldonado, Carlos. 1997. "Setor informal: Legalização ou laissez-faire?" [The informal sector: Legalization or laissez-faire?]. Paper presented at the workshop O Setor Informal Revisitado: Novas Evidências e Perspectivas de Políticas Públicas [The informal sector revisited: New evidence and public policy perspectives]. Instituto de Pesquisa Econômica Aplicada (IPEA), Brasília, July.

Marcuse, Peter. 1997. "The Informal Sector as a Structure of Relationship among Groups." Paper presented at the workshop O Setor Informal Revisitado: Novas Evidências e Perspectivas de Políticas Públicas [The informal sector revisited: New evidence and public policy perspectives]. Instituto de Pesquisa Econômica Aplicada (IPEA), Brasília, July.

Margolis, Maxine L. 1992. "Women in International Migration: The Case of Brazilians." Conference paper no. 66, Columbia University–New York University Consortium for Latin American and Caribbean Studies.

———. 1994. *Little Brazil.* Princeton, N.J.: Princeton University Press.

———. 2002. "Becoming Brazukas." Paper presented at the conference What about Other Latinos?, Harvard University, Cambridge, April 5.

———. 2005. "At the Turn of the Millennium: Brazilian Emigration to the Contemporary United States." *Human Organization* (October).

———. 2008a. "Brazilian Immigration to the U.S.: Future Research and Issues for the New Millennium." In Jouët-Pastré and Braga, *Becoming Brazuca.*

———. 2008b. "September 11th and Transnationalism: The Case of Brazilian Immigrants in the United States." *Human Organization* 67, no. 1: 1–11.

———. 2009. *An Invisible Minority: Brazilians in New York City.* Boston: Allyn and Bacon.

Mariano, Ricardo. 2004. "Expansão pentecostal no Brasil: O caso da Igreja Universal" [Pentecostal expansion in Brazil: the case of the Universal Church]. *Estudos Avançados* 18, no. 52 (September/December): 121–132.

Mariz, Cecília. 1994. *Coping with Poverty: Pentecostals and Christian Base Communities in Brazil.* Philadelphia: Temple University Press.

Marrow, Helen B. 2003. "To Be or Not to Be (Hispanic or Latino): Brazilian racial and ethnic identity in the United States." *Ethnicities* 3, no. 4: 427–464.

———. 2004. "Coming to Grips with Race: Second-Generation Brazilians in the United States." Paper presented at Brazilian Studies Association (BRASA) Congresso Internacional 7, Pontifícia Universidade Católica do Rio de Janeiro (PUC-RJ), Rio de Janeiro, June 9–12.

Martes, A. C. B. 1996a. "Access to the Labor Market and Job Selling among Brazilian Immigrants." Paper presented at American Anthropological Association Conference, November 20th 1996 San Francisco, Calif.

———. 1996b. "Solidarity and Competition: Access to the Labor Market and the Role of Churches Among Brazilian Immigrants." Paper presented at New England Sociological Association Annual Meeting, April Fall River, Mass.

———. 1998a. "Brasileños em Massachusetts" [Brazilians in Massachusetts]. *Estudios Migratorios Latinoamericanos* (Buenos Aires) 39 (Agosto): 257–288.

———. 1998b. "Cidadania e solidariedade entre imigrantes brasileiros nos EUA" [Citizenship and solidarity among Brazilian immigrants in the United States]. Paper presented at the International Congress of the Latin American Studies Association (LASA), Chicago, September 24–26.

———. 2000a. *Brasileiros nos Estados Unidos: Um estudo sobre imigrantes em Massachusetts* [Brazilians in the United States: A study of immigrants in Massachusetts]. São Paulo: Paz e Terra.
———. 2000b. "Brazilian Immigrants in the United States: An Overview." Paper presented at the Internacional Congress of the Latin American Studies Association (LASA), Miami, Fla., March 16–18.
———. 2000/2001. *Empresários brasileiros em Boston* [Brazilian entrepreneurs in Boston]. Relatório de Pesquisa no. 45. São Paulo: Fundação Getúlio Vargas.
———. 2001a. "Brazilian Entrepreneurs in Boston: Trust and Solidarity." Paper presented at the 23rd Internacional Congress of the Latin American Studies Association, Washington, DC. Latin American Studies Association (LASA), September 6–8,
———. 2001b. "A emigração brasileira e os pequenos empresários." In Mary Garcia Castro, ed. *Migrações internacionais: Contribuições para políticas* [International migrations: Contributions to politics]. Brasília, Brazil: Comissão Nacional de População e Desenvolvimento (CNPD).
———. 2001c. "Empresários brasileiros em Boston" [Brazilian businesspeople in Boston]. Research report no. 45/2001. Núcleo de Pesquisas e Publicações, Escola de Administração de Empresas, Fundação Getúlio Vargas.
———. 2001/2003. *Empresários brasileiros em Cambridge e East Boston* [Brazilian businesspeople in Cambridge and East Boston]. Research report no. 20/2004. São Paulo, Brazil: Núcleo de Pesquisas e Publicações, Escola de Administração de Empresas, Fundação Getulio Vargas
———. 2002a. "Neither Hispanic nor Black: We Are Brazilians." Paper presented at the conference What about Other Latinos?, Harvard University, David Rockefeller Center (DRC), April 7.
———. 2002b. "A Safe Place for Sociability: Brazilians and Church Affiliation in Massachusetts." *Migration World* 29: 28–33.
———. 2003a. "Brazilians in the United States: A Study of Immigrants in Massachusetts." Paper presented at the workshop New Immigrants in Urban New England, Providence, R.I., April 25.
———. 2003b. "Raça e etnicidade: Opções e constrangimentos" [Race and ethnicity: Options and limitations]. In Martes and Fleischer, *Fronteiras cruzadas.*
———. 2004a. "Brazilian Immigration: Historical Perspective and Identity." In *Giving voice to a nascent community: Exploring Brazilian immigration to the U.S. through research and practice*, ed. Clémence Jouët-Pastré, Megwen Loveless, and Leticia Braga, 38–41. Working paper no. 04/05–2. Cambridge, Mass.: David Rockefeller Center for Latin American Studies.
———. 2004b. "Nos EUA, o que somos nós? Latinos, hispanics, brancos ou others?" [In the USA, what are we? Latino, Hispanic, white, or other?]. In *Psicologia, e/imigração e cultura* [Psychology, e/immigration, and culture], ed. Sylvia Dantas DeBiaggi and Geraldo José da Paiva. São Paulo: Casa do Psicólogo Livraria e Editora.
———. 2005a. "Afiliação religiosa e empreendedorismo étnico: O caso dos brasileiros nos Estados Unidos" [Religious affiliation and ethnic entrepreneurialism: The case of Brazilians in the United States]. In *Empreendedorismo além do plano de negócio*

[Entrepreneurialism beyond the business plan], ed. Eda Castro Lucas de Souza and Tomás de Aquino Guimarães. 1 São Paulo: Editora Atlas.
———. 2005b. *Lições fora de casa: Imigração como forma de aprendizado* [Lessons away from home: Immigration as a type of apprenticeship]. Research report no. 05/2009. São Paulo, Brazil: Núcleo de Pesquisas e Publicações, Escola de Administração de Empresas, Fundação Getulio Vargas
———. 2005c. "Verbete Brazilians." In *The Encyclopedia of New England*, ed. Burt Feintuch and David H. Watters. London: Yale University Press.
———. 2006a. "The Commitment of Return: Remittances of Brazilian Émigrés." Paper presented at the 16th ISA World Congress of Sociology, Durban, South Africa, July. In *Anais do XVI International Sociological Association (ISA) World Congress of Sociology*.
———. 2006b. "De volta aos clássicos" [Return to the classics]. Paper presented at Encontro Nacional da Associação Nacional de Pesquisa em Administração (EnANPAD), Salvador, Brazil, October.
———. 2006c. "Dissimulation and (In)adequate Place. Black Brazilians in Boston." Paper presented at the international colloquium Actualité d'Abdelmalek Sayad, Association des Amis d'Abdelmalek Sayad, Paris, June 15–16.
———. 2007. "Neither Hispanic nor Black: We're Brazilian." In *The Other Latinos: Central and South Americans in the United States*, ed. José Luis Falconi and José Antonio Mazzotti. Cambridge: David Rockefeller Center (DRC), Harvard University Press.
———. 2008a. "The Commitment of Return: Remittances of Brazilian Émigrés." In Jouët-Pastré and Braga, *Becoming Brazuca*. Cambridge: David Rockefeller Centre/ Harvard University Press.
———. 2008b. "L'Engagement en retour: Le transfert d'argent des émigrés brésiliens" [The commitment of return: Remittances of Brazilian immigrants]. *Hommes et Migrations*, no. 1272, (March-April): 110–125.
Martes, Ana Cristina Braga, and Soraya Fleischer, eds. 2003. *Fronteiras cruzadas: Etnicidade, gênero e redes sociais* [Crossed borders: Ethnicity, gender, and social networks]. São Paulo: Paz e Terra.
Martes, Ana Cristina Braga, and Carlos L. Rodriguez. 2004. "Church Membership, Social Capital, and Entrepreneurship in Brazil Communities in Brazilian Communities in the U.S." In Stiles and Galbraith, *Ethnic Entrepreneurship*.
Martes, Ana Cristina Braga, and Weber Soares. 2004. "Remessas de recursos dos imigrantes" [Immigrants' remittances of resources]. *Estudos Avançados* (São Paulo) 20, no. 57 (May/August): 41–54
Martin, David. 1990. *Tongues of Fire: The explosion of Protestantism in Latin America*. Oxford, England: Blackwell.
Martine, George. 2005. "A globalização inacabada: migrações internacionais e a pobreza no século 21" [Unfinished globalization: International migrations and poverty in the 21st century]. *São Paulo Perspectiva* 19, no. 3: 3–22.
Massey, Douglas S. 1990. "The Social and Economic Origins of Migration." In *Annals of the American Academy of Political and Social Science (AAPSS)* 510 (*World Population: Approaching the Year 2000*): 60–72.

Massey, Douglas S., Rafael Alarcón, Jorge Durand, and Humberto Gonzáles. 1987. *Return to Aztlán*. Los Angeles: University of California Press.

Menezes, Gustavo. 2002. "Filhos da imigração: Sobre a segunda geração de imigrantes brasileiros nos EUA" [Children of immigration: About the second generation of Brazilian immigrants in the USA]. Master's thesis, Programa de Pós-Graguação em Antropologia Social, Universidade de Brasília.

———. 2003. "Filhos da imigração: A segunda geração de brasileiros em Connecticut" [Children of immigration: The second generation of Brazilians in Connecticut]. In Martes and Fleischer, *Fronteiras cruzadas*.

Menjivar, Cecilia. 2000. *Fragmented Ties: Salvadorian Immigrant Networks in America*. Los Angeles: University of California Press.

———. 2003. "Religion and Immigration in Comparative Perspective: Catholic and Evangelical Salvadorans in San Francisco, Washington, D.C., and Phoenix." *Sociology of Religion* 64, no. 1 (Spring): 21–45.

Meriz, Gisele, and Natália Cristina Ihá. 2006. "A segunda geração de emigrantes brasileiros: Problemas e perspectivas" [The second generation of Brazilian immigrants: Problems and perspectives]. Paper presented at Encontro Regional de História, Associação Nacional de História (ANPUH), Niterói, Brazil, August 14–18.

Merton, Robert K. 1968. *Social Theory and Social Structure*. New York: Free Press.

Millman, Joel. 1997. *The Other Americans*. New York: Viking Press.

Min, Pyong Gap. 1992. "The structure and social functions of Korean immigrant churches in the United States." *International Migration Review* 26, no. 4 (Winter): 1370–1394.

Ministério Internacional Restaurando Vidas. 2009. http://www.mirv.org.br/principal/player.htm, accessed November 11, 2009.

Model, Suzanne. 1993. "The Ethnic Niche and the Structure of Opportunity: Immigrants and Minorities in New York City." In *The Underclass Debate: Views from History*, ed. Michael Katz. Princeton, N.J.: Princeton University Press.

Montero, Paula. 1997. "Globalização, identidade e diferença" [Globalization, identity and difference]. *Novos Estudos* (CEBRAP), no. 49 (November): 47–69.

Morgan, Gareth, ed. 1983. *Beyond Method: Strategies for Social Research*. Thousand Oaks, Calif.: Sage.

Mota, Kátia Santos. 2004. "Aulas de português fora da escola: Famílias imigrantes brasileiras, esforços de preservação da língua materna" [Extracurricular Portuguese classes: Brazilian immigrant families, efforts to preserve the mother tongue]. *Cadernos CEDES* (Campinas, Brazil) 24, no. 63 (May/August): 149–163.

Movimento de Cursilhos de Cristandade do Brasil. 2010. Estatuto. http://www.cursilho.org.br/interna.php?pag=estatuto&PHPSESSID=e03ff5df26ea6623a98014323aa1718, accessed March 10, 2010.

Moya, José C. 1998. *Cousins and Strangers: Spanish Immigrants in Buenos Aires, 1850–1930*. Berkeley: University of California Press.

Myers, Scott M. 2000. "The Impact of Religious Involvement on Migration." *Social Forces* 79, no. 2 (December): 755–783.

Myrdal, Gunnar. 1962. *An American Dilemma*. New York: Pantheon Books.

Nahapiet, J., and S. Ghoshal. 1998. *Social Capital, Intellectual Capital, and the Organizational Advantage*. New York: Academy of Management Review.

Nee, Victor, and B. Nee. 1986. *Longtime Californ': A Study of an American Chinatown*. Stanford, Calif.: Stanford University Press.

Nee, Victor, Jimy M. Sanders, and Scott Sernau. 2002. "Asian Immigrants' Reliance on Social Ties in a Multiethnic Labor Market." *Social Forces* 81, no. 1 (September): 281–314.

Nelli, Humbert S. 1980. *From Immigrants to Ethnics: The Italian Americans*. New York: Oxford University Press.

Nobles, Melissa. 2000. *Shades of Citizenship: Race and Census in Modern Politics*. Stanford, Calif.: Stanford University Press.

Nogueira, Oracy. 2007. "Preconceito racial de marca e preconceito racial de origem: Sugestão de um quadro de referência para a interpretação do material sobre relações raciais no Brasil" [Racial appearance prejudice and racial origin prejudice: A suggested frame of reference for the interpretation of the material about race relations in Brazil]. *Tempo Social 19*, no. 1: 287–308.

North American Society. 1995. *Americas*. New Brunswick, N.J.: Rutgers University Press.

Oboler, Suzanne. 1995. *Ethnic Labels, Latino Lives*. Minneapolis: University of Minnesota Press.

O'Donnel, Guillermo, and Fábio Reis. 1986. *A democracia no Brasil: Dilemas e perspectivas* [Democracy in Brazil: dilemmas and perspectives]. São Paulo: Vertice.

O'Hare, William P. 1992. "America's Minorities: The Demographics of Diversity." *Population Bulletin of the Population Reference Bureau* 47, no. 4.

Ocké-Reis, Carlos Octávio. 2006a. "O público e o privado na saúde" [Public and private in health care]. *Cadernos de Saúde Pública* 22, no. 12: 2722–2727.

———. 2006b. "Sistemas de saúde comparados: Gasto, acesso e desempenho" [Health care systems compared: Spending, access, and performance]. Rio de Janeiro: IPEA. http://www.ipea.gov.br/sites/000/2/destaque/seminario0237.pdf, accessed November 12, 2006.

Office of Immigration Statistics. See U.S. Department of Homeland Security (DHS).

Oliveira, Carlos A., and Álvaro Augusto Comin, eds. 1994. *O mundo do trabalho: Crise e mudança no final do século* [The world of work: Crisis and change at the end of the century]. Campinas, Brazil: Editora Página Aberta, Scritta.

Oliveira, Márcia Maria. 2006. "A mobilidade humana na tríplice fronteira: Peru, Brasil e Colômbia" [Human mobility on the triple border: Peru, Brazil, and Colombia]. *Estudos Avançados* 20, no. 57 (May/August): 183–196.

Oliveira, Roberto Cardoso. 1976. *Identidade, etnia e estrutura social* [Identity, ethnicity, and social structure]. São Paulo: Livraria Editora Pioneira.

Osterman, Paul. 1989. *In the Midst of Plenty: A Profile of Boston and Its Poor*. Boston: Boston Foundation.

Padilha, F. 1985. *Latino Ethnic Consciousness: The Case of Mexican Americans and Puerto Ricans in Chicago*. South Bend, Ind.: University of Notre Dame Press.

Palau, Tomás. 2001. "Brasiguaios." In *Migrações internacionais: Contribuições para a política*, ed. Mary Garcia Castro. Brasília: CNPD.

Pap, Leo. 1981. *The Portuguese in the United States: A Bibliography*. New York: Center for Migration Studies.

Parreñas, Rhacel Salazar. 2001. *Servants of Globalization: Women Migration and Domestic Work*. Stanford, Calif.: Stanford University Press.

Pastore, José. 1979. *Desigualdade e mobilidade social no Brasil* [Inequality and social mobility in Brazil]. São Paulo: EDUSP.

———. 1990. "Desigualdade e mobilidade social: Dez anos depois" [Inequality and social mobility: Ten years later]. In *A transição incompleta* [The incomplete transition], ed. E. Bacha and H. Klein. São Paulo: Paz e Terra.

Patarra, Neide, ed. 1995. *Emigração e imigração internacionais no Brasil contemporâneo* [International emigration and immigration in contemporary Brazil].Campinas: Programa Interinstitucional de Avaliação e Acompanhamento das Migrações Internacionais no Brasil, Fundo das Nações Unidas para a População.

Patarra, Neide, and R. Baeninger. 1995. *Migración y integración: Nuevas formas de mobilidad de la población. Migrações internacionais recentes: O caso do brasil: Considerações preliminares* [Migration and integration: New forms of population mobility. Recent international migrations: The case of Brazil: Preliminary considerations]. Montevideo, Uruguay: Ediciones Trilce.

Penha, Marcelo. 2001. "Two Cases of Brasilidade in New York City." In *Raízes e rumos* [Roots and routes], ed. Sonia Torres. Rio de Janeiro: Editora Sete Letras.

Personal Narratives Group. 1989. *Interpreting Women's Lives: Feminist Theory and Personal Narratives*. Bloomington: Indiana University Press.

Peterson, Anna L. and Philip J. Williams, eds. 2001. *Christianity, Social Change, and Globalization in the Americas*. New Brunswick, N.J.: Rutgers University Press.

Pessar, Patricia. 1995. "The Elusive Enclave: Ethnicity, Class, and Nationality among Latino Entrepreneurs in the Greater Washington, D.C." *Human Organization* 54, no. 4: 383–392.

———. 1999. "The Role of Gender, Households, and Social Networks in the Migration Process: A Review and Appraisal." In *The Handbook of International Migration: The American Experience*, ed. Charles Hirschman, Philip Kasinitz, Josh DeWind. New York: Russell Sage Foundation.

Pickel, Andréas. 2000. *The Problem of Order in the Global Age: Systems and Mechanisms*. New York: Palgrave.

Pierucci, Antônio Flávio, and Reginaldo Prandi. 1983. "Comunidades eclesiais de base." In *São Paulo: O povo em movimento* [São Paulo: The people in movement], ed. Paul Singer and Binícius Brant. Petrópolis, Brazil: Editora Vozes.

———. 1987. "Assim como não era no princípio: Religião e ruptura na obra de Procópio Ferreira de Camargo" [As it was not in the beginning: Religion and rupture in the work of Procópio Ferreira de Camargo]. *Novos Estudos* (CEBRAP) 17 (May): 29–35.

———. 1995. "Religiões e voto no Brasil: A eleição presidencial de 1994" [Religions and the vote: The 1994 presidential election]. *Opinião Pública* (Unicamp, Centro de Estudos de Opinião Pública) 3, no. 1 (May): 20–44.

Piore, Michael. 1979. *Birds of Passage: Migrant Labor and Industrial Societies*. New York: Cambridge University Press.

Piore, Michael, and Suzanne Berger. 1980. *Dualism and Discontinuity in Industrial Societies*. Cambridge, England: Cambridge University Press.

Piore, Michael, and Charles Sabel. 1984. *The Second Industrial Divide*. New York: Basic Books.

Polanyi, Karl. 1944. *The Great Transformation: The Political and Economic Origins of Our Time*. Boston: Beacon Press.

Portes, Alejandro, ed. 1995. *The Economic Sociology of Immigration*. New York: Russell Sage Foundation.

Portes, Alejandro, and Robert Bach. 1985. *Latin Journey: Cuban and Mexican Immigrants in the United States*. Berkeley: University of California Press.

Portes, Alejandro, Manuel Castells, and L. Benton, eds. 1989. *The Informal Economy: Studies in Advanced and Less Developed Countries*. Baltimore, Md.: Johns Hopkins University Press.

Portes, Alejandro, and Rubén Rumbaut. 1990. *Immigrant in America: A Portrait*. Los Angeles: University of California Press.

Portes, Alejandro, and Julia Sensenbrenner. 1993. "Embeddedness and Immigration: Notes on the Social Determinants of Economic Action." *The American Journal of Sociology* 98, no. 6: 1320–1350.

Prandi, Reginaldo. 1992. "Perto da magia, longe da política" [Close to magic, far from politics]. *Novos Estudos*, no. 34 (November): 81–91.

Prandi, Reginaldo, and Antônio Flávio Pierucci. 1996. *A realidade social das religiões no Brasil* [The social reality of religions in Brazil]. São Paulo: Hucitec.

Putnam, Robert. 1996. *Comunidade e democracia: A experiência da Itália moderna* [Community and democracy: The experience of modern Italy]. São Paulo: Fundação Getúlio Vargas

Reichert, J. S. 1979. "The Migrant Syndrome: An Analysis of U.S. Migration and Its Impact on a Rural Mexican Town." Ph.D. diss., Department of Anthropology, Princeton University.

Reis, Rossana, and Teresa Sales. 1999. *Cenas do Brasil migrante* [Scenes of migrant Brazil]. São Paulo: Boitempo.

Resende, Rosana. 2002. "Tropical Brazucas: A Preliminary Study of Brazilians in South Florida." Paper presented at Brazilians outside Brazil: Brasileiros fora do Brasil Conference, April 8, University of Miami, Coral Gables, Fla.

———. 2003. "Brasileiros no sul da Flórida: Relatos de uma pesquisa em andamento" [Brazilians in South Florida: Tales from a study in progress]. In Martes and Fleischer, *Fronteiras cruzadas*.

Ribeiro, Darcy. 1995. *O povo brasileiro: A formação e o sentido do Brasil* [The Brazilian people: The formation and the meaning of Brazil]. São Paulo: Companhia das Letras.

Ribeiro, Gustavo. 1998a. *Goiânia, Califórnia. Vulnerabilidade, ambigüidade e cidadania transnacional* [Goiânia, California. Vulnerability, ambiguity, and transnational citizenship]. Série Antropologia, Departamento de Antropologia, Universidade de Brasília.

———. 1998b. *Identidade brasileira no espelho interétnico. Essencialismos e hibridismos em São Francisco* [Brazilian identity in the interethnic mirror. Essencialisms and hybridisms in San Francisco]. Série Antropologia, Departamento de Antropologia, Universidade de Brasília.

———. 2002. *Argentinos e brasileiros: Encontros, imagens e estereótipos* [Argentines and Brazilians: Encounters, images, and stereotypes]. Rio de Janeiro: Editora Vozes.

Romualdo, Antonio Donizeti. 2004. "Seja a Bíblia verdadeira e o TEI mentiroso" [That the Bible is true and the TEI deceitful]. http://www.jesussite.com.br/acervo.asp?id=905, accessed March 10, 2010.

Sales, Teresa. 1992. "Imigrantes estrangeiros, imigrantes brasileiros: Uma revisão bibliográfica e algumas anotações para pesquisa" [Foreign immigrants, Brazilian immigrants: A review of the literature and some notes for research]. *Revista Brasileira de Estudos de População* 9 (January/July): 50–64.

———. 1993. "Novos fluxos migratórios da população brasileira." *Revista Brasileira de Estudos da População* 8, nos. 1/2: 21–32.

———. 1994. "O trabalhador brasileiro no contexto das novas migrações internacionais" [The Brazilian worker in the context of the new international migrations]. In Patarra, *Emigração e imigração internacionais.*

———. 1999. *Brasileiros longe de casa* [Brazilians far from home]. São Paulo: Editora Cortes.

———. 2006. "ONGs brasileiras em Boston" [Brazililan NGOs in Boston]. *Estudos Avançados* 20, no. 57 (*Dossiê Migrações*): 75–91.

Sales, Teresa, and Márcia Loureiro. 2004. "Imigrantes brasileiros adolescentes e de segunda geração em Massachusetts, EUA" [Adolescent and second-generation Brazilian immigrants in Massachusetts, USA]. *Revista Brasileira de Estudos de População* 21, no. 2 (July/December): 217–239.

Sanjejek, R., and S. Colen, eds. 1990. *At Work in Homes: Household Workers in World Perspective.* Washington, D.C.: American Anthropological Association

Santos, Boaventura. 1994. "Modernidade, identidade e cultura de fronteira" [Modernity, identity, and border culture]. *Tempo Social* (São Paulo) 5, nos. 1–2 (November): 31–52.

———. 1997a. "Informalization as a Systemic Trend in Advanced Market Economies." Paper presented at the workshop O Setor Informal Revisitado: Novas Evidências e Perspectivas de Políticas Públicas [The informal sector revisited: New evidence and public policy perspectives]. Instituto de Pesquisa Econômica Aplicada (IPEA), Brasília, July.

———. 1997b. *Pela mão de Alice* [By Alice's hand]. São Paulo: Cortez Editora.

Sanyal, Bishwapriya. 1988. "The Urban Informal Sector Revisited." *Third World Planning Review* 10, no. 1: 65–83.

———. 1991. "Organising the Self-Employed: The Politics of the Urban Informal Sector." *International Labour Review* (Geneva) 130, no. 1: 39–56.

Sasaki, Elisa Massae. 1999. "Movimento dekassegui: A experiência migratória identitária dos brasileiros descendentes de japoneses no Japão" [The dekassegui movement: The migratory identity experience of Brazilians of Japanese descent in Japan]. In Reis and Sales, *Cenas do Brasil migrante.*

Sassen, Saskia. 1988. *The Mobility of Labor and Capital.* New York: Cambridge University Press.

———. 1995. "Immigration and Local Labor Markets." In *The Economic Sociology of Immigration: Essays on Networks, Ethnicity, and Entrepreneurship*, ed. Alejandro Portes, 87–127. New York: Russell Sage Foundation.

Sassen-Koob, Saskia. 1981. "Exporting Capital and Importing Labor: the Role of Women." In *Female Immigrants to the United States: Caribbean, Latin American, and African Experiences*, eds. Delores M. Mortimer and Roy S. Bryce-Laporte. Washington, D.C.: Research Institute on Immigrant and Ethnic Studies

———. 1985. "Changing Composition and Labor Market Location of Spanish Immigrants in New York City, 1960–1980." In Borjas and Tienda, *Hispanics in the U.S. Economy.*

Sayad, Abdelmalek. 1998. *A imigração: Ou os paradoxos da alteridade* [Immigration: Or the paradoxes of otherness]. São Paulo: EDUSP.

Sayad, Abdelmalek, and Pierre Bourdieu. 1991. *L'Immigration: Ou les paradoxes de l'altérité* [Immigration: Or the paradoxes of otherness]. Paris: Editions Universitaires Bruxelles, De Beck Université.

Schiller, Nina Glick, Linda Basch, and Cristina Blanc-Szanton, eds. 1992. "Towards a Transnational Perspective on Migration." *Annals of the New York Academy of Sciences* 645: 1–24.

Schiller, Nina, and Georges Fouron. 2000. *"Laços de sangue: Os fundamentos raciais do estado-nação transnacional"* [Blood ties: The racial bases of the transnational nation-state]. Brasília: CNPD.

Schumpeter, Joseph A. 1934. *The Theory of Economic Development.* Cambridge: Harvard University Press.

Sennett, Richard. 2004. *Respeito: A formação do caráter num mundo desigual* [Respect: Character formation in an unequal world]. Rio de Janeiro: Record.

Sequeira, Jennifer, and Abdul M. Rasheed. 2004. "The Role of Social and Human Capital in the Start-Up and Growth of Immigrant Businesses." In Stiles and Galbraith, *Ethnic Entrepreneurship.*

Shelley, Toby. 2007. *Exploited: Migrants Labour in the New Global Economy.* London: Zed Books.

Silva, Sidney. 1995. "A presença da igreja entre os imigrantes latino-americanos em São Paulo" [The presence of the church among Latin American immigrants in São Paulo]. In Patarra, *Emigração e imigração internacionais.*

———. 2006. "Bolivianos em São Paulo: Entre o sonho e a realidade" [Bolivians in São Paulo: Between dream and reality]. *Estudos Avançados* 20, no. 57 (May/August): 157–170.

Silver, Hilary. 2001. "Dominicans in Providence: Transnational Intermediaries and Community Institutional Building." *Focal European Journal of Anthropology* (Prague), no. 38.

Silvera Beraldo, Lea. 2000."Imigrantes italianos" [Italian immigrants]. http://www.imigrantesitalianos.com.br, accessed July 2009.

Siqueira, Eduardo, and Cileine Lourenço. 2007. "Brazilians in Massachusetts: Migration, Identity, and Work." In *Latinos in New England*, ed. Andres Torres. Philadelphia: Temple University Press.

Smelser, Neil J., and Talcott Parsons. 1984. *Economy and Society*. New York: Routledge.

Smelser, Neil J., and Richard Swedberg. 1994. "The Sociological Perspective on the Economy." In *The Handbook of Economic Sociology*, ed. Neil J. Smelser and Richard Swedberg. New York: Russell Sage Foundation; Princeton, N.J.: Princeton University Press.

Soares, Weber. 1995. "Imigrantes e investidores: Redefinindo a dinâmica imobiliária na economia valadarense" [Immigrants and investors: Redefining the real estate dynamic in the economy of Governador Valadares]. Master's thesis, Instituto de Pesquisa e Planejamento Urbano e Regional (IPPUR), Universidade Federal de Rio de Janeiro.

———. 2002. "Da metáfora à substância: Redes sociais, redes migratórias e migração nacional e internacional em Valadares e Ipatinga" [From metaphor to substance: Social networks, migratory networks, and national and international migration in Valadares and Ipatinga]. Research report for Ph.D. diss., Centro de Desenvolvimento e Planejamento Regional (CEDEPLAR), Universidade Federal de Minas Gerais, Belo Horizonte.

Somerville, MA, City of. 1992. "A Community Health Agenda of Agencies." Report. Somerville Hospital.

Souza, André Portela Fernandes de. 2005. "The Impact of Cash Transfer Programs on School Attendance and School Progression in Brazil." Paper presented at the Research for Results in Education: Global Conference on Education Research in Developing and Transition Countries. Prague, March 31–April 2.

Soysal, Yasemin. 1994. *Limits of Citizenship: Migrants and Post-National Membership in Europe*. Chicago: University of Chicago Press.

Stavrianos, L. S. 1968. "The Global Redistribution of Man." In *World Migration in Modern Times*, ed. F. D. Scott. Englewood Cliffs, N.J.: Prentice Hall.

Steinberg, Stephen. 1989. *The Ethnic Myth: Race, Ethnicity, and Class in America*. Boston: Beacon Press.

Steiner, Philippe. 1999. *La Sociologie économique* [Economic sociology]. Paris: La Découverte, Syros, Collection Repères.

Stiles, Curt H., and Craig S. Galbraith, eds. 2004. *Ethnic Entrepreneurship: Structure and Process*. Vol. 4 of *International Research in the Business Disciplines*. Bingley, England: Emerald Group.

———. 2006. *Developmental Entrepreneurship: Adversity, Risk, and Isolation*. Amsterdam: Elsevier.

Stoll, David. 1990. *Is Latin America Turning Protestant?* Berkeley: University of California Press.

Suárez-Orozco, Carola. 1995. "Migration: Generational Discontinuities and the Making of Latino Identities." In *Ethnic Identity: Creation, Conflict, and Accommodation*, ed. Lola Romanucci-Ross and George De Vos. Walnut Creek, Calif.: Altamira Press.

Suárez-Orozco, Carola, and Marcelo Suárez-Orozco. 2001. *Children of Immigration*. Cambridge: Harvard University Press.

Suárez-Orozco, Marcelo. 2000. "Everything You Ever Wanted to Know about Assimilation but Were Afraid to Ask." *Daedelus* 129, no. 4 (Fall): 1–30.

Swedberg, Richard. 1992. *Economics and Sociology*. Princeton, N.J.: Princeton University Press.

Taguieff, Pierre-André. 1987. "*La Force du préjugé: Essai sur le racisme et ses doubles*" [The power of prejudice: An essay about racism and its doubles]. Paris: Gallimard.

Thomas, Brinley. 1973. *Migration and Economic Growth*. 2d edition. Cambridge, England: Cambridge University Press.

Tienda, Marta, and Rebeca Raijman. 2000a. "Immigrants' Income Packaging and Invisible Labor Force Activity." *Social Science Quarterly* 81, no. 1: 291–310.

———. 2000b. "Pathways to Business Ownership among Immigrants to Chicago: A Comparative Ethnic Perspective." *International Migration Review* 34, no. 3: 681–705.

Tilly, Charles. 1990. "Transplanted Networks." In *Immigration Reconsidered: History, Sociology and Politics*, ed. Virginia Yans-McLaughlin. New York: Oxford University Press.

Torres, Sonia, ed. 2001. *Raízes e rumos: Perspectivas interdisciplinares em estudos americanos*. Rio de Janeiro, Brazil: Sete Letras.

Torres-Saillant, Silvio, and Ramona Hernández. 1998. *The Dominican Americans*. Westport, CT: Greenwood Press.

Tota, Antonio. 2000. *O imperialismo sedutor: A americanização no Brasil na época da Segunda Guerra* [Seductive imperialism: The Americanization of Brazil in the time of the Second World War]. São Paulo: Companhia das Letras.

Truzzi, Oswaldo M. S. 2001. "Etnias em convívio: O bairro do Bom Retiro em São Paulo" [Ethnicities in harmony: The Bom Retiro neighborhood in São Paulo]. *Estudos Históricos* (Rio de Janeiro) 27: 143–166.

———. 2008. "Redes em processos migratórios" [Networks in migratory processes]. *Revista Tempo Social* (São Paulo) 20, no. 1: 199–218.

United Nations Population Fund (UNPF). 2006. "*A Passage to Hope: Women and International Migration.*" In *State of the Population Fund 2006*. New York: United Nations Population Fund (*UNFPA)*.

U.S. Department of Homeland Security (DHS), Office of Immigration Statistics. 2006a. *2004 Yearbook of Immigration Statistics*. Washington, D.C. http://www.dhs.gov/xlibrary/assets/statistics/yearbook/2004/Yearbook2004.pdf, accessed May 14, 2006.

———. 2006b. *Yearbook of Immigration Statistics*, 2001 to 2005. Washington, DC: *U.S. Department of Homeland Security, Office of Immigration Statistics*. www.uscis.gov, accessed May 14, 2006.

U.S. Department of State, Bureau of Consular Affairs. 2010. Nonimmigrants Visa Statistics. http://travel.state.gov/visa/frvi/statistics/statistics_4582.html, accessed March 10, 2010.

Veja. 1990. May 30, 13–15.

Waldinger, R., H. Aldrich, and R. Ward. 2000. "Ethnic Entrepreneur." In *Entrepreneur-*

ship: The Social Science View, ed. Richard Swedberg. Oxford, England: Oxford University Press.

Warner, Stephen R. 1998. "Immigration and Religious Communities in the United States." In *Gatherings in Diaspora: Religious Communities and the New Immigration*, ed. Stephen R. Warner and Judith G. Wittner. Philadelphia: Temple University Press.

Warner, Stephan R., and Judith G. Wittner, eds. 1998. *Gatherings in Diaspora: Religious Communities and the New Immigration*. Philadelphia: Temple University Press, 1998.

Waters, Mary. 1990. *Ethnic Options*. Los Angeles: University of California Press.

Weber, Max. 1968. *Economy and Society*. Ed. Guenther Roth and Claus Wittich. New York: Bedminister Press.

———. 1982. *A ética protestante e o espírito do capitalismo* [The protestant ethic and the spirit of capitalism]. Rio de Janeiro: Zahar.

Wilson, Kenneth L., and Alejandro Portes. 1980. "Immigrant Enclaves: An Analysis of the Labor Market Experiences of Cubans in Miami." *American Journal of Sociology* 86, no. 2: 295–319.

World Bank. 2006. World Development Indicators Online. http://web.worldbank.org/WBSITE/EXTERNAL/DATASTATISTICS/0,,contentMDK:20398986~menuPK:64133163~pagePK:64133150~piPK:64133175~theSitePK:239419,00.html, accessed November 20, 2009.

World Christian Database. 2004. "Center for the Study of Global Christianity, Gordon-Conwell Theological Seminary." http://www.worldchristiandatabase.org/wcd, accessed June 21, 2009.

World Health Organization (WHO). 2006. *World Health Statistics*. Geneva: WHO.

Zaluar, Alba. 1985. *A máquina e a revolta* [Machine and revolt]. São Paulo: Brasiliense.

Zimmer, Catherine, and Howard E. Aldrich. 1987. "Entrepreneurship through Social Networks." In *The Art and Science of Entrepreneurship*, ed. Donald Sexton and Raymond Smilor. New York: Ballinger.

Index

Ana Cristina Braga Martes is a professor of sociology at the Escola de Administração de Negocios [MBA School] of the Fundação Getúlio Vargas in São Paulo, Brazil. She is the author of the chapter "The Commitment of Return: Remittances of Brazilian Émigrés" in *Becoming Brazuca: Brazilian Immigration to the United States* (Harvard University Press, 2008) and of numerous articles and books in Portuguese on Brazilian immigration to the United States, including the book *Brasileiros nos Estados Unidos: Um estudo sobre imigrantes Brasileiros em Massachusetts* [Brazilians in the United States: A study of Brazilian immigrants in Massachusetts] (Paz e Terra Press, São Paulo, 2003). She is the editor of the book *Redes e sociologia econômica* [Networks and economic sociology] (Universidade Federal de São Carlos Press, 2009).

New World Diasporas
Edited by Kevin A. Yelvington

This series seeks to stimulate critical perspectives on diaspora processes in the New World. Representations of race and ethnicity, the origins and consequences of nationalism, migratory streams and the advent of transnationalism, the dialectics of homelands and diasporas, trade networks, gender relations in immigrant communities, the politics of displacement and exile, and the utilization of the past to serve the present are among the phenomena addressed by original, provocative research in disciplines such as anthropology, history, political science, and sociology.

More Than Black: Afro-Cubans in Tampa, by Susan D. Greenbaum (2002)
Carnival and the Formation of a Caribbean Transnation, by Philip W. Scher (2003)
Dominican Migration: Transnational Perspectives, edited by Ernesto Sagás and Sintia Molina (2004)
Salvadoran Migration to Southern California: Redefining El Hermano Lejano, by Beth Baker-Cristales (2004)
The Chrysanthemum and the Song: Music, Memory, and Identity in the South American Japanese Diaspora, by Dale A. Olsen (2004)
Andean Diaspora: The Tiwanaku Colonies and the Origins of South American Empire, by Paul S. Goldstein (2005)
Migration and Vodou, by Karen E. Richman (2005)
True-Born Maroons, by Kenneth M. Bilby (2005)
The Tears of Hispaniola: Haitian and Dominican Diaspora Memory, by Lucía M. Suárez (2006)
Dominican-Americans and the Politics of Empowerment, by Ana Aparicio (2006)
Nuer-American Passages: Global Migration in the Twentieth Century, by Dianna J. Shandy (2006)
Religion and the Politics of Ethnic Identity in Bahia, Brazil, by Stephen Selka (2007)
Reconstructing Racial Identity and the African Past in the Dominican Republic, by Kimberly Eison Simmons (2009)
Haiti and the Haitian Diaspora in the Wider Caribbean, edited by Philippe Zacaïr (2010)
From Douglass to Duvalier: U.S. African Americans, Haiti, and Pan Americanism, 1870–1964, by Millery Polyné (2010)
New Immigrants, New Land: A Study of Brazilians in Massachusetts, by Ana Cristina Braga Martes (2011)